Literature, Politics and Intellectual Crisis in Britain Today

Also by Clive Bloom

CULT FICTION: Popular Reading and Pulp Theory

READING POE, READING FREUD: The Romantic Imagination in Crisis

GOTHIC HORROR: A Reader's Guide from Poe to Stephen King (*editor*)

AMERICAN DRAMA (*editor*)

SPY THRILLERS: From Buchan to le Carré (*editor*)

TWENTIETH-CENTURY SUSPENSE: The Thriller Comes of Age (*editor*)

JACOBEAN POETRY AND PROSE (*editor*)

AMERICAN POETRY: The Modernist Ideal (*co-editor with Brian Docherty*)

PERSPECTIVES ON PORNOGRAPHY: Sexuality in Film and Literature (*co-editor with Gary Day*)

Literature, Politics and Intellectual Crisis in Britain Today

Clive Bloom
Professor of English and American Studies
Middlesex University
London

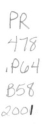

First published 2001 by
PALGRAVE
Houndmills, Basingstoke, Hampshire RG21 6XS and
175 Fifth Avenue, New York, N. Y. 10010
Companies and representatives throughout the world

PALGRAVE is the new global academic imprint of
St. Martin's Press LLC Scholarly and Reference Division and
Palgrave Publishers Ltd (formerly Macmillan Press Ltd).

ISBN 0–333–77832–4 hardback
ISBN 0–333–77833–2 paperback

This book is printed on paper suitable for recycling and
made from fully managed and sustained forest sources.

A catalogue record for this book is available
from the British Library.

Library of Congress Cataloging-in-Publication Data
Bloom, Clive.
    Literature, politics, and intellectual crisis in Britain today / Clive Bloom.
        p. cm.
    Includes bibliographical references (p.) and index.
    ISBN 0–333–77832–4 (cloth)
    1. English literature—20th century—History and criticism. 2. Politics
    and literature—Great Britain—History—20th century. 3. Popular
    culture—Great Britain—History—20th century. 4. Great Britain—Politics
    and government—20th century. 5. Great Britain—Intellectual life—20th
    century. I. Title.
    PR478.P64 B58 2000
    941.082—dc21
                                                            00–064033

10   9   8   7   6   5   4   3   2   1
10   09 08 07 06 05 04 03 02 01

Printed and bound in Great Britain by
Antony Rowe Ltd, Chippenham, Wiltshire

For Charmian and Tim

In the Moon is a certain Island near by a mighty continent, which small island seems to have some affinity to England, &, what is more extraordinary, the people are so much alike, & their language so much the same, that you would think you were among your friends. In this island dwells three Philosophers – Suction the Epicurean, Quid the Cynic, & Sipsop the Pythagorean. I call them by the names of those sects, tho' the sects are not ever mention'd there, as being quite out of date; however, the things still remain, and the vanities are the same. The three Philosophers sat together thinking of nothing. In comes Etruscan Column the Antiquarian, & after an abundance of Enquiries to no purpose, sat himself down & described something that nobody listen'd to.

William Blake, *An Island in the Moon* (1784–5)

Contents

Acknowledgements   viii

Part I   Something in the Air: Culture and Politics Now

1   Introduction: Resistible Culture   3

2   Just the Way it is   42

Part II   And our Friends are all Aboard: Literary Culture

3   1910 was a Good Year: Connoisseurs and Book Lists   73

4   Eyes on the Prize: Booker and the Orange People;
    Joan Collins in Court   90

Part III   Under Dreaming Spires: The Academic World

5   The Nature of the University at the Present Time   123

Part IV   Canned Heat: Resistance

6   The Sixties in your Head: An Aborted Experiment?   147

7   The Role of the Intellectual at the Turn of the Century   165

8   The Abyss of History and the Nature of the Fantastic   181

9   Children of Albion: Dr Leavis amongst the Dongas Tribe   192

Notes   210

Works Cited   217

Index   224

Acknowledgements

Thanks are due to the following people for their help and encouragement over the years with this and other projects: Vivien Miller; Gary Day; Brian Docherty; Michael Woolf; Paul Bradshaw; Kay Henderson; Sandra Berry; Hugh Wilford; Val Weinstein; Rachel Morgan; Ben Scott; Gabrielle Parker. Special thanks go to John Simons; Hans Bertens and Peter Brooker; Lesley and James Bloom. A number of people gave time to be interviewed, including Martyn Goff; Christine Shaw; Jeremy Treglown; Ion Trewin; Julian Birkett; Peter Kemp; Penny Perrick; Greg Woods; Lynne Truss; Faith Brooker; Lola Bubbosh; Jenny Turner; Alan Jenkins; Gerald Jacobs.

Finally, I am especially grateful to Helena Blakemore for her interviews and research, for her collaboration on Chapter 3 and for her patience with this project.

Part I

Something in the Air: Culture and Politics Now

1
Introduction: Resistible Culture

I won't go into details and ask, for instance, whether the storming of a cold buffet is likely to call the attention of the masses to the concentration of power under late capitalism.

> Günter Grass, 'Literature and Revolution or the Rhapsodist's Snorting Hobbyhorse' (address delivered at the Belgrade Writers' Conference, 17–21 October 1969)

I

In 1997, thirty years after the demise of swinging London, Britain again seemed to be the centre of the cultural universe, with a thriving arts scene, a new Labour government and a young and enterprising prime minister. London was again swinging with both a resurgent music scene and a hip new style. Indeed, the sixties (refracted through the rediscovery of the 1970s) seemed as if it might reach its apotheosis in the nineties – a *fin de siècle* decade played out over thirty years too early. Not only did high street fashion and pop reflect the 'retro' mood, but advertising too put it into words and pictures. The sixties seemed the perfect subject for an ironic seance played out in videos, retrospective conferences, and pop posturing. John Lennon was even electronically revivified to help the Beatles become the bestselling group of 1996 in the United States, and in 1999 Ken Kesey and the Magic Bus came to England in search of Merlin![1] Yet the mood was short lived and 'Cool Britannia' proved just a slogan.

Reaction was, as ever, swift. The rock opera *Tommy* (although revived at the Shaftesbury Theatre) closed during 1997 after a short run, journalist Tony Parsons was soon gleefully dismissing J. R. R. Tolkien's *Lord of the Rings* (recently voted in a booksellers' poll the greatest book of all

3

time!) as simple 'hippy garbage', whilst the anniversary rock festival 'Woodstock 99' ended in riots.[2]

Nineties style seemed vibrant and optimistic. The Royal Academy was host to Damien Hirst and his colleagues in an exhibition celebrating the new British artistic vanguard and appropriately entitled 'Sensation'; the Booker Prize, most prestigious of all British literary prizes, was awarded to a young Anglo-Indian woman for her first novel. And yet on the day the Royal Academy show opened, an irate 'artist' threw ink and eggs at one of the more controversial paintings (of child-killer Myra Hindley), whilst former Virago publisher Carmen Callil called Arundhati Roy's book *The God of Small Things* 'execrable' just moments after the author was awarded her prize. Both 'Sensation' and the Booker Prize focused the smouldering hatreds and evident fractures of the British cultural scene and established values. There was nothing new in all this, for the debates of the last century form an integral part of the artistic life and the literary culture of these islands.

In 1998 the Booker Prize went to Ian McEwan's *Amsterdam*, a book considered of such inferior quality by some commentators that it led Will Self to denounce the 'secret' machinations of the cabal-like selection committee.[3] The most prestigious art prize in Britain, the Turner, currently sponsored by Channel Four to the tune of £20,000, has an equally contentious history. The 1998 prize went to Chris Ofili, a painter who is most famous for the incorporation of elephant dung into his psychedelic work, including the black 'superstar' series *Captain Shithead*. Ofili has described his work as 'rap' and Sam Taylor Wood, a photographer who was also a finalist, made quite clear that there was a relationship between contemporary British art, pop music and youth. Yet in 1999, the Brit Awards for pop music achievement were themselves accused of being 'rigged' by a leading producer. Britain's biggest pop music export of the year, The Spice Girls, failed not only to get an award but also to get a mention. Even in the world of pop culture there is snobbery and violence.

As always, the Turner (like the Booker) was a media event, televised at peak viewing time. Thus, interposed with the 'hip' grandeur of the Tate Gallery and the sage (if shrill) pronouncements of veteran feminist Germaine Greer, were commercials selling the latest home computer packages and a CD compilation called *Music of the Night* featuring Sir Cliff Richard, Sir Elton John and Michael Bolton. This juxtaposition highlighted only too well the complicity between art and commercialism, kitsch and aesthetic endeavour, highbrow and lowbrow culture. Across all was stamped unconsciously the need to be *popular* and to be liked: the *Music of the Night* or a visit to the Tate Gallery or both, in the same breath.

When Chris Ofili was awarded the prize, judges were delighted that a painter (and a black artist, to boot), after over a decade, had again been awarded the highest British artistic accolade. The traditional (painting) and the popular ('proper' art) had finally been vindicated against a background of champagne corks and Andrew Lloyd Webber show tunes.

II

It is often said by people who show a conspicuous lack of it that taste is a personal thing. For those whose interests are professional the concept of taste seems to have no place in the scientific analysis of texts. For this latter group, the nature of discrimination and judgement has long been a problem more often than not attributed to the ideological pomposities of rivals or the incompetence of an older generation of critics. Where questions of current fashion and sensibility are supposedly relegated to the vagaries of journalism, academic critics have substituted an analytics of form and function (social, historical, linguistic, etc.). The fact that much objective analysis is framed by questions neither objective nor analytic but rather moral and ethical is often quietly forgotten. What remain unsaid, despite the vast output of professional academic criticism, are the forgotten polemical currents which form opinion in the first place and then allow opinion to disengage itself from those very same currents.

Academic contempt for journalist critics and reviewers has left the problem of judgement fractured and the critical judgement of professionals terminally schizophrenic. When academics do become reviewers (except in professional or university 'trade' journals) their work is seen as, at best, a concession to 'swimming with the tide', at worst the suicide of critical integrity. The emergence of prestigious prizes and their panels of mixed academics and reviewers has further blurred the line of demarcation and obscured the nature of critical activity. Critics who have tried to combine academic life with 'higher' journalism (such as F. R. Leavis) found their enterprises confined to a dubious cottage industry produced on kitchen tables (literally so in the case of *Scrutiny*).

The history of these fluctuations and fragmentations is no less than the history of the critical enterprise this century: the emergence of both 'disinterested' and 'engaged' criticism and their dubious relationship with the long-abused concept of the connoisseur. Yet, it is also much more than this for it takes us to the heart of cultural sensibility in the fading light of the twentieth century, itself subject to those selfsame fragmentations and fluctuations that produced not only the taste of that century but the belief systems from which that taste emerged.

Whilst it can be argued with some authority that British social, communal and economic life show considerable continuity, with gradual accretions and accommodation being the normal pattern, this cannot be argued for the history of British perceptions. Although social history has, in the main, been set by tradition, perceptual history has measured this tradition against the crises of continuous change. Popular moral panics have consistently posited a traditional way of life threatened by alien forces that bring chaos and disruption. Cultural critics have been the victims of moral panics to an even greater extent than the general population, this itself conditioned by their greater 'sensitivity'. Loss of certainty and fear of discontinuity have plagued both the general populous and British intellectuals for the whole of the twentieth century.

The language of conservatively minded, politically left- or right-wing British cultural critics is often even more extreme than that of either the population at large or even the tabloid media. For most cultural critics, from Matthew Arnold to F. R. Leavis, from George Orwell to Richard Hoggart and from Robert Hewison to Tony Parsons, cultural life in Britain is in a continuous state of apocalyptic breakdown. It is always in the process of imminent collapse because it is too philistine, boorish or bourgeois and therefore being bored to death or too liberal is always over-stimulated to the point of death.

Distaste for technology, mass consumption, popular culture, the masses and suburban life styles (bourgeois concerns) has led critics on both sides of the Atlantic to see the twentieth century as an age of unprecedented decline in cultural standards. By the 1980s this had become a critical industry in the United States with books by Paul Fussell, Allan Bloom, Robert Hughes, Robert Bly and many others – the difference in Britain being that throughout the century 'Americanisation' has long been added to the list of degenerative factors. This latter determinant has also figured in the Marxist work of the Frankfurt School, the humanism of the New Critics and the reactionary conservatism of high modernism, and has a history of being a staple of much of what the British establishment measures itself against:

> The most familiar feature of the Penguin look is, of course, the avoidance of pictorial covers. In America the lurid cover is considered essential for securing mass sales of paper-backed books; and in this

country also, most of the cheap reprints are presented in picture covers. It has often been urged that Penguins might do better business if it conformed to this general practice; but whatever truth there may be in that supposition, the decision has been made, as a matter of taste, to reject the American kind of cover.

(Allen Lane, quoted in Williams, *The Penguin Story*)

It can be rightly claimed that for cultural observers the twentieth century took on a tradition of apocalyptic and doom-laden criticism: a literature of continuous and degenerative processes without an absolute end. This is either celebrated or denigrated according to whether the 'traditional' community is one you wish to preserve or destroy. In either case the traditional community is the focus of contention: an ideal or utopian site always posited 'elsewhere' to be protected or attacked.

The perceived unpleasantness of British modern culture lent urgency to the critical desire to hierarchise both the products of culture and the specifics of taste. At the same time, criticism itself attempted to become both more professional and scientifically more objective, paradoxically defending the traditional organic community by the use of rhetoric borrowed from the technician, manager and engineer. Literary language, the world of books and literature symbolised not only the significance but also the objects of critical attention. It was literature that offered the best defence for and the most evident representation of individualism *within* the community (a tradition of critical thought which united George Orwell, F. R. Leavis, Raymond Williams and Richard Hoggart).

It would be literature that would be defined and redefined in order to stabilise both itself and the ethical prerequisites of the critic in defence of society and 'values'.

Over the past few decades, in the blink of the eye of history, our culture has begun to go through what promises to be a total metamorphosis. The influx of electronic communications and information processing technologies, abetted by the steady improvement of the microprocessor, has rapidly brought on a condition of critical mass. Suddenly it feels like everything is poised for change; the slower world that many of us grew up with dwindles in the rear-view mirror. The stable hierarchies of the printed page – one of the defining norms of that world – are being superseded by the rush of impulses through freshly minted circuits. The displacement of the page by the screen is not yet total (as evidenced by the book you are holding) – it may never be total – but the large-scale tendency in that direction has to be obvious to anyone who looks. The shift is, of course, only part of a larger transformation that embraces whole economies and affects people at every level. But, living as we do in the midst of innumerable affiliated webs, we can say that changes in the immediate sphere of print refer outward to the totality; they map on a smaller scale the riot of societal forces. . . . – all of the old assumptions are under siege. . . .

(Sven Birkerts, *The Gutenberg Elegies*)

To many critics the equation is all too simple: print culture is good; electronic culture is bad. Despite every historical indication, print was believed to represent fixity and permanence; it was linear and therefore taxonomic; its linearity organised and clarified; it was based on grammar and therefore logic; it was also holistic, though sequential; filled with value, memory, history, the eternal. It stood for a more deliberate culture, a serious non-commercial culture of enlightened individuals in the slow spaces of private meditation. On the other, hand electronic media were virtual; ephemeral; non-linear, non-hierarchic; confused and confusing; relativistic and anarchic; non-sequential and therefore fragmented, and as fragmented a valueless and abysmal fall from grace without memory or history. Thus it was also commercial; propagandistic; parasitic; mass 'kulcher', false and manipulative.

Ironically, it was the very stability of print (and its dependent culture) that seemed most to threaten change. Intellectuals from the late 1950s to the 1990s became increasingly convinced that textual stability was a corollary of political stability and the hierarchies of taste were an exact corollary of the political culture of the establishment (the state, the bourgeoisie, etc.). John Calder's 'Death of the Word' conferences and John Latham's Skoob Towers were just two manifestations of intellectual distrust in the stability of literature. By an ironic twist 'destructivism' was meant to be a positive unmasking of liberalism's fascistic reality.

Such thinking left writers (especially of novels) in a dilemma. If the older tradition of the novel appeared to be moral, realistic and bourgeois, encapsulated in plot, character, setting, theme, denouement, then the 'new' novel was to be mythic, symbolic and semiotic, incorporating abstraction, angle of vision, point of view, discovery, polyphony, self-exploration and the questioning of conscious agency. The novel would no longer be instruction with entertainment but a mode of discovery, iconoclasm and alienation: a 'provisional form', as Malcolm Bradbury called it.

The new novel writer (the disestablishment of whose chosen artistic form was the goad to both artistic as well as political radicalism) was

now caught in a fix. This could lead to a rebelliousness which apotheos-
ised adolescent subjectivity as a higher virtue than mature reflection.
Hence, Doris Lessing's reply to an imagined student enquirer:

> These requests I answer as follows: 'Dear Student, You are mad. Why
> spend months and years writing thousands of words about one book,
> or even one writer, when there are hundreds of books waiting to be
> read. You don't see that you are the victim of a pernicious system.
> And if you have yourself chosen my work as your subject, and if you
> do have to write a thesis – and believe me I am very grateful that
> what I've written is being found useful by you – then why don't you
> read what I have written and make up your own mind about what
> you think, testing it against your own life, your own experience.
> Never mind about Professors White and Black'.
>
> 'Dear Writer' – they reply. 'But I have to know what the authorities
> say, because if I don't quote them, my professor won't give me any
> marks.'
>
> This is an international system, absolutely identical from the Urals
> to Yugoslavia, from Minnesota to Manchester.
>
> (Preface to *The Golden Notebook*)

For Lessing, the central concern was not 'women's liberation' (which
she felt would be 'small and quaint' in a few years – she was writing in
1971) but 'relevance'.

Rebelliousness could also lead to a simple relativism renamed 'a
respect for the contingent'. For Iris Murdoch, a call 'for a new vocabulary of attention' had nevertheless to be set against her fear that 'a
Welfare State will weaken the incentives to investigate the bases of a
Liberal democratic society' ('Against Dryness').

But it was precisely liberal ideals that could not be abandoned in
favour of a socialist solution.

> It is here, however much one may criticize the emptiness of the Liberal
> idea of freedom, however much one may talk in terms of restoring a
> lost unity, that one is forever at odds with Marxism. Reality is not a
> given whole. An understanding of this, a respect for the contingent,
> is essential to imagination as opposed to fantasy.
>
> (Murdoch, 'Against Dryness')

Murdoch could claim that her 'moral' stance was in recognising the
contingent and that 'reality is not a given whole', but what remained

was little other than micro histories – the type of recuperation that becomes familiar in Jean-François Lyotard's work. Murdoch's contradictory stance was actually on behalf of the traditions (liberal democracy and the novel) she tried to liberate herself from. In 'demolishing' the shibboleth of the traditional novel (at best and most exemplified by D. H. Lawrence) Murdoch recalled the novel to its baggy anarchic history. Micro history too often provides less a history of community than a tittle-tattle tale told at a village pump.

The gleeful and naïve gloating of media advocates, the cool cats of cyberspace and virtual anything are themselves no less pitiable than the Arnoldian/Leavisite remnant that think the age of literature is over. The apparently anti-literary aspects of cyberspace have failed to open up discourse to anything like a democratic or anarchic plurality, instead the malleability of 'virtual' language has done nothing to disestablish or destabilise old hegemonies. English remains the overwhelming language of internet traffic, controlled almost exclusively by the United States and Britain, in discourse now being labelled imperialist and Anglo-Saxon and accused of *restabilising* and re-establishing 'English' cultural hegemony. English-speaking users now account for between 56.5 per cent and 52 per cent of online use (or 160 million owners/users), so substantially ahead of all other nations that by the first decade of the new millennium over 80 per cent of the Net could be English-language controlled. English is the consultation language of 55 per cent of European users compared with 16 per cent in German or 24 per cent in French. Even if English is overwhelmed as the language of the Net, it is still the language (between 70 per cent and 90 per cent) of information being provided and in certain circumstances may be ten times more used than other languages.

At present (although maybe not for long) this key technology favours English and, whilst Europeans and others may dislike this, they use it as a *necessary* means of international communication. It is also the case that most popular consumer culture is embedded in English. Cyber-English may very well mutate linguistically but it poses no essential threat to literary English nor to the values *embedded* in Anglo-American culture. Rather, the adulation accorded cyber-culture *masks* the ideological structure in which it is embedded. Cyber-culture is pure market-force capitalism. The ability to 'deconstruct' texts or hide people's identity, so lauded by cybernauts, is nothing other than an immense repetitive system of substitutions of exactly similar value.

What McLuhan's babes tend to forget is that the global village, in 'bypassing' the hierarchies of print, actually creates the very *organic community* dreamed of by such as F. R. Leavis, a community in which textuality is directly embedded in social activity and is inscribed as social expression and in which the community's desires are expressed, stabilised and regulated in 'literature'.

> It confronts us all. For it is true that culture in the past has borne a close relation to the 'methods of production'. A culture expressing itself in a tradition of literature and art...can be in a healthy state only if this tradition is in living relation with a real culture, shared by the people at large. The point might be enforced by saying...that Shakespeare did not invent the language he used. And when England had a popular culture, the structure, the framework, of it was a stylization,...of economic necessities...the 'methods of production', was an art of living, involving codes, developed in ages of continuous experience of relations between man and man, and man and the environment....This culture the progress of the nineteenth century destroyed, in country and in town; it destroyed...the organic community.
>
> (F. R. Leavis, *Scrutiny*, vol. 1, 1932)

In the light of Leavis and read correctly, the irony of the cyber-babe position cannot be any clearer: cyber-celebration is nothing less than historical revisionism, in other words, the obsession with cyber communities is *not* progressive but retrogressive – an attempt to return to a *pre-technological* organic popular culture! Cyber-praise is the new pastoral poetry! What survives of 'the organic community', Levis tells us, survives despite 'the means of production' as 'cultural tradition'. Virtual reality is the site for a *recuperation within* capital without the disturbance of market forces. Indeed, it is the guarantor of the success of Internet *laissez-faire*.

Belief that the Internet is ideologically neutral because technically uncontrollable, and is therefore the first fully participative and democratic medium, is not confined to overawed or naïve observers but can be found at the pinnacle of network research. Bill Gates, in a chapter indicatively entitled 'Friction-Free Capitalism' (in his book *The Road Ahead*) seems actually to believe that Adam Smith's vision of the fully informed market had to wait for the Internet. Hence,

> A few markets are already working fairly close to [Adam] Smith's ideal....The Internet will extend the electronic marketplace and become the ultimate go-between, the universal middleman. Often the only humans involved in a transaction will be the actual buyer and

> seller, all the goods for sale in the world will be available for you to examine, compare, and often customise. When you want to buy something, you'll be able to tell your computer to . . . 'haggle' with the computers of various sellers. . . . We'll find ourselves in a new world of low-friction, low-overhead capitalism . . . it will be a shopper's heaven.

Laissez-faire Internet marketeering returns capital to micro-scale bazaar 'haggling', returning to consumers their sovereign control of choice (or in other words their absolute subjecthood as consumers). So bizarrely naïve is this view of markets unconnected to production, controlling interests and debt that one wonders if what is at work here is a hardly repressed *nostalgia* for the heroic age of entrepreneurial capital (represented by Adam Smith) to which the fully functioning Internet will allow us all access.

In such a vision, the Internet becomes a mechanism for nostalgia, a means to return us (now in the future) to a pre-corporate economy: communal, responsive and determined by fully informed participants. The Internet becomes nothing less than the rumbustious, free-for-all of the eighteenth century with its merchants, artisans and adventurers. Moreover, this vision of the eighteenth century will be nothing less than an Anglo (American) revolution – the triumph of the English-speaking peoples.

> Most sites on the World Wide Web are in English, so far, which confers economic and entertainment benefits on people around the world who speak English. English-speaking people will enjoy this advantage until a great deal more content is posted in a variety of languages.
>
> (Gates, *The Road Ahead*)

The novel has always had an ambiguous relationship with the culture which it represents and from which it emerges. If this relationship is always expressed as contradiction, it is nevertheless also true that this position can only occur because the novel is an inherently *oppositional form*. Framed against a background of industrialisation, bureaucratisation and consumer conformity, the novel stands, above all, for the moral transcendence of the individual. If the myth of the individual is a 'capitalist' myth, the novel is one way in which such a myth is able to slip its capitalist origins and return as a challenge (if a recuperable one). The 'serious' novel (however defined – by intention or reception) has the individual as the central pivot of its themes (this includes the doubt over individuality as well). Such novels stand in contrast to conformism,

the market and the popular (as conformism); they are not mere entertainment nor fantasy, but representations of the 'real' (as it is). Even
popular fiction, excepting some forms of pulp (the apparent polar
opposite of the serious novel), participates in the same structural and
contextual conditions. It too relies on a reader sequestered in privacy
and silence: insubordinate and antisocial. But the serious novel also
aspires to be a public statement and make a communal claim.

Yet it is here that it meets its most serious challenge in the resistance
of the popular culture of insubordination. Whilst the serious novel
makes a claim for the sorority and fraternity of an international community of like-minded individuals, nevertheless, at home, it is challenged
by the popular as a communal expression of refusal (best summed up in
Britain by the group insubordination of those national icons, the *Carry
On* films and the Bash Street Kids!)[4]

The innate individualism of the novel confuses its 'moral' position
with regard to the communal. A community of internationally like-
minded souls is not the same as a group whose identity comes from
close and prolonged contact. In this sense, the novel cannot represent
the community but must in some *fundamental* way oppose it. The
novel's individualism reflects that of authorship itself (despite Barthes):
as it is individualistic and a child of capital it is also therefore entrepreneurial and competitive. The novel resists co-optive rewards and is therefore more greatly rewarded: corporate culture's nostalgia for its origins
is reflected in its prizes to those who supposedly oppose it. The novel is
not a reflection of capital but its *enactment* in art. (The novelists who
have suffered under totalitarian regimes either stand for the tenets of
Western democratic liberalism or stand for a spectrum of right-wing
views often trailing into fascism or nationalistic xenophobia.) Novelists
have a more than grudging relationship to prize giving and competition
because their work presupposes these things as an (unconscious)
prerequisite of the art itself. The dilemma of the novelist is to *oppose* as
one represents.

When *technical* change threatened literature and literary culture then
it also threatened a critical culture tied to the literary and therefore
engaged willy-nilly and almost always in a reactionary manner. Beginning in the late nineteenth century, technical changes have included
the rise of 'yellow' journalism and mass publishing, the appearance of
radio, cinema and *commercial* television; the rise of paperbacks; the
appearance of videos, personal stereos, computer games, the Internet,
and satellite and cable television. Each change has brought a wave of
cultural concern not only because of the problem of availability and

control but also because each brings its own conditions to the form and content of aesthetic experience. Across all are posed questions of education and its purpose, the role of the citizen and the responsibility of the individual.

In his 1995 book *The Way We Live Now*, Richard Hoggart described the 1980s and 1990s as a cultural wasteland no longer representable by reference to communities, common speech patterns and class identity. Rather it was an age of reduced quality, concentration of power, demagogic populism and instrumentalism. Hoggart, an advocate of the notion that reading is connected to moral health and wholeness, was only too aware that faith in literature was all that was left and defending such literature were a few remaining *disinterested* intellectuals. Hoggart's book could have been written in the 1880s or 1930s or any time during the twentieth century. He finds himself adrift in an unrepresentable landscape of cultural malaise (where even pop music has declined), no longer able to hear the nuances of communal speech, drowned out in MTV and cable.

It was not necessary to be a septuagenarian to find oneself adrift amidst the perceived cultural decay of the late twentieth century and the detritus of a defunct welfare state. For Patrick Wright, culture consultant and fierce critic of Thatcherism, the heritage culture of the 1980s was neither heritage nor culture, but a brutalistic dance in the wasteland of a lost community. Picking his way through one of the poorest parts of London, he saw little more than ruins, lost opportunities and personal corruption (we had yet to be reassured about ourselves by Bill Bryson). Even so, Wright cannot restrain himself from a swipe at the welfare state's democratisation of higher education (the polytechnic system). His own experience, paid for by Conservative money, was nothing less than a salutary lesson from which he recoiled in horror, his distaste for his hosts and the system in general nothing less than a residual connoisseurship (displaced from the Athenaeum and Joint University Club onto the streets of Dalston) reeling from its tainted contact with mass education.

> At the end of the [1980s] I had another brief encounter with the polytechnic world, and it really was just like staggering from the demolished station at Dalston Junction to the derelict hulk of St Bartholomew's up at Lebon's corner. . . . [I]t was a polytechnic . . . that asked me to become a 'visiting fellow' . . . in a newly established 'Centre for Applied Historical Research'. . . . [F]unded as it was through the Training Agency, [it] was to engage in 'applied' activities that would find new sources of income for the polytechnic's beleaguered

demoralized historians. Knowing better than to look even a modest gift horse in the mouth, I accepted the offer. . . . One evening I went to . . . a seminar and found that nearly all the students had backed off. . . . Of the four who did turn up one sat there reading a book on an entirely unrelated subject. Eventually I confronted the fellow and he explained, with a certain amount of indignation in his voice, that he wasn't even enrolled on the course: indeed, I should get on with it, since he was just waiting to go for a drink with his friend as soon as the seminar was over. I also spoke at a day-long conference, finding that most of the delegates (assorted antiquarians and museum administrators from within the polytechnic's catchment area) had been begged to attend without charge and, in a good number of cases, with the promise of a free lunch thrown in. It was at this event that a long-serving lecturer, whose confusions were doubtless aggravated by the fact that he had recently been converted into an 'enterprise officer', told me that 'everything is discourse' and then moved on to suggest that I spoke with the voice of an 'ideological State apparatus'.

(Patrick Wright, A Journey through Ruins)

Wright's experience stands for nothing less than the disillusionment of the liberal intellectual. Everything ends in disgust, even more so in relation to those things one holds dearest. Wright's final remark about the confused lecturer is both snide and snobby. There is no sympathy here, only contempt.

In 1998, a well-known professor of English literature at the University of Kent broke off from a public lecture in order to give an off-the-cuff diatribe against the new universities (recently converted polytechnics) and their destruction of standards. Until rebuked by an academic who worked at a new university, his audience heard the professor with approval. In his defence of the ideal university (Cardinal Newman's ideal, that is) he conveniently forgot that his own university was not itself created until the 1960s and that it was itself regarded with contempt by the academic old guard.

And so the contempt piles up in the rubble of lost hope, in personal regret and political impotence and in the decrepitude of a neglected welfare state brought to senility by those it served best. The very success of the young welfare state is the embarrassment of its old age.

The conspicuous failure of the Attlee administration to bring about a lasting redistribution of wealth or a significant irruption of existing social arrangements has been well documented by historians. . . . What might, in the hands of the genuine ideologues, have become the seed-bed of socialist revolution perished in sleepy inertia. The period 1945–51 brought no significant institutional reform either of local government, industrial relations or the civil service.

Far from introducing a social revolution, the Labour victory of 1945 resulted in what Anthony Howard has called 'the greatest restoration of traditional values since 1660'.[5]

If the welfare state was not a mere deception then it certainly soon came to represent for many intellectuals the culmination of a process of 'dumbing down', brought about by a neglect of theory in favour of an over-concern for empiricism. Thus for Iris Murdoch, in 1961,

> The Welfare State has come about as a result, largely, of socialist thinking and socialist endeavour. It has seemed to bring a certain struggle to an end; and with that ending has come a lassitude about fundamentals. . . . We no longer see man against a background of values, of realities, which transcend him.
>
> (Murdoch, 'Against Dryness')

This was also true for Robert Hewison, whose historical account of avant-garde culture in Britain since 1940, entitled *Culture and Consensus*, was quite unable to do anything except provide a weak narrative of institutional patronage and change without once really tackling the contemporary problems of either culture or consensus, something Hewison had been quite able to do in books on the 1950s and 1960s. Hewison's conclusions were grim indeed:

> The question was whether Major could restore the consensus that the Thatcherite machine had smashed so determinedly that even those who had set it in motion no longer had it under control. . . . By the end of the 1980s the Thatcherite juggernaut had run out of control, bringing down the symbols of national identity: the cultural consensus, the Church, the Monarchy, and eventually the Conservative party itself. The Arts were brushed aside in the crush. John Major was unable to pick up the pieces.

Elsewhere (in Kavanagh and Seldon), Hewison has documented the confusion and misdirection of governmental involvement with the arts during the Thatcher and Major years.

The newly created Department of National Heritage (later renamed the Ministry of Culture, Media and Sport) was soon nicknamed the ridiculous 'Ministry of Fun' under its minister David Mellor, which said all there was to say about this sad exercise, Mellor himself soon leaving after a sex scandal only to be resurrected as a radio football commentator.[6] The term heritage sat uneasily between its old meaning of a shared traditional culture and its post-Thatcherite meaning of a 'tradition' of individual enterprise and entrepreneurial activity (with the Victorian industrial revolution as its terminus). Heritage was both the marker of opera and high art and of football and local radio, of real historical sites, which needed preservation, and of heritage sites which turned history into entertainment. The business of heritage in which the past had to pay its way or vanish could not easily be disentangled from what needed preserving as national heritage. The grants from the National Lottery (which was meant to pay for the Department of National Heritage) seemed to institutionalise a direct relationship between gambling, greed and the arts, but the conversion of self-interest into altruism seemed to vindicate the processes as the Arts Council of Great Britain (facing eventual disestablishment) and other bodies lost direction or control. By a quirk of fate the Lottery gave back to the State its role as chief patron of the arts (via a semi-autonomous private company) and (in direct opposition to this principle of State directions) made the arts into a competitive market following the pure principles of nineteenth-century economic liberalism and *laissez-faire*.

III

The cultural uncertainties of the twentieth century gave simultaneous impetus to cultural criticism and the importance of cultural critics. It was not long before critics could be grouped together according to the characteristics they shared.

- *The Connoisseur–Scholar.* Urbane and perhaps aloof, embracing neither theory nor technique, the connoisseur–scholar is, in essence, a highly sensitive and informed amateur whose innate good taste comes from breeding and manners and whose sense of moral integrity comes from a commitment to national tradition and classical order. The independent connoisseur will bear his (sometimes her) learning as lightly as possible, cultivating a provisional, apolitical and 'jovial' attitude which nevertheless sees art as the culmination of civilised behaviour, and beauty as a matter of intense seriousness.

Conservative (with a small 'c'), the connoisseur is often (and not unjustly) associated with the outmoded nature of the gentleman's club, class privilege, social exclusivity and patronage and may very well enjoy *in person* the privileges of rank or money.

- *The Trained Professional.* A salaried, academic bureaucrat at worst, a committed educator at best, the trained professional critic is the direct product of changes in university organisation and expectation. Using learned rules and objective, 'scientific' standards, the professional is concerned with *systemic* integration and theoretical and paradigmatic approaches to cultural products. Conducting technical debates amongst a like-minded and exclusive group, the professional sees his or her work as final (non-provisional), determining, disinterested and deadly serious (they are, after all, on a salary!). Professional verdicts are final and exclusive even as the professional is personally excluded from the society of the connoisseur. Unlike the connoisseur, the professional may have little education in the classics, have no commitment to European culture or humanist tradition; unlike the connoisseur the focus will be contemporary and structural, not attributive and historical.

- *The Evangelical Professional.* Such critics combine many of the features of the two previous groups. Passionately committed to a literary culture under siege from commercialism, consumerism and managerialism, they are concerned to redevelop a direct moral link between the community and literature. Their watchwords are organicism and tradition and their prejudices are always towards the primacy of literature in the hierarchy of culture. Technically trained, nevertheless they believe education only makes clear 'what is there' whose obviousness can be expressed as a dialogue of acquiescence: 'it is so – isn't it'. In this way technical training is a means to bypass theory (it is anti-intellectual) in order to study (to intuit) particularity. Especially important is the connection these critics make between the structural integrity of works of literature and the moral integrity of authors (or characters). Exclusivity and canonicity are important to these critics and value judgements are of primary concern in their work. As such, tradition and communal coherence and the humanistic values expressed in literature which tradition and communalism give rise to form the basis for work by these critics. The proselytising sense of these critics lends itself to serious journalism and the attempt to defend (or even resurrect) a lost holistic (organic) communal way of life. This type of critical approach is both prescriptive (what is good and popular), descriptive (why it is good) and proscriptive (what should not be read and why). It is inherently both modern and reactionary, believing modernity to be decadent but using modernity's idea of *structure* as a guide to traditional values (which modernity is believed to have disrupted).

For I. A. Richards, the ethical justification for literary criticism, was its (unexpectedly) instrumentalist possibilities, now put to the service of a culture too sick to serve itself without professional help but not yet aware of the need for help at all. What was at stake was the psychic well-being of a whole civilised way of life based upon a communal and traditional order.

> With the increase of population the problem presented by the gulf between what is preferred by the majority and what is accepted as excellent by the most qualified opinion has become infinitely more serious and appears likely to become threatening in the near future. For many reasons standards are much more in need of defence than they used to be. It is perhaps premature to envisage a collapse of values, a transvaluation by which popular taste replaces trained discrimination. Yet commercialism has done stranger things: we have not yet fathomed the more sinister potentialities of the cinema and the loud-speaker, and there is some evidence, . . . that such things as 'best-sellers' . . . are decreasing in merit.
>
> (Richards, *Principles of Literary Criticism*)

To defeat this national malaise only the 'most qualified' are eligible.

> What is needed is a defensible position for those who believe that the arts of are value. Only a general theory of value which will show the place and function of the arts in the whole system of values will provide such a stronghold. At the same time we need weapons with which to repel . . . misconceptions.
>
> (Richards, ibid.)

And this is because 'The critic is as closely occupied with the health of the mind as the doctor with the health of the body'. The critic and the doctor, the critic *as* doctor and as health visitor to the unwary reader makes explicit the moral relationship between reading 'good' literature and healthy bodily functions. This relationship is never just merely metaphorical, but is a viral condition which lies dormant inside every critic until activated by debates about 'value' and literary 'worth'. It is one step away from debates about a healthy diet and the bodily functions of the nation. Such considerations were central to the original ethos of literary studies at Cambridge. Sir Arthur Quiller-Couch reminisced to students in 1917:

> I had a friend once who, being in doubt with what picture to decorate the chimney-piece in his library ... put up ... ΨΥΧΗΕ ΙΑΤΡΕΙΟΝ; ... the hospital – the healing place – of the soul.
>
> (*On the Art of Reading*)

Even those critics whose entire careers have been dedicated to opposing Cambridge humanism are prone to this attitude. Terry Eagleton, Thomas Wharton Professor of English at Oxford and Britain's leading Marxist critic, finally succumbed as the millennium approached. A perfect (and very late) example of the combination of the connoisseur, professionalism and evangelism can be found in an article ostensibly on the subject of the metaphoric relationship between food and Irish writing. Eagleton cannot resist (despite some knowing comments that he is lapsing into platitude) a direct comparison between healthy eating and healthy reading, a comparison which soon loses any *metaphoric* awareness and which rapidly declines into the proscription of debased (and Americanised) popular culture and the elevation of a 'serious' culture in which health is the key. 'Digestion' is now the key to the post-structuralist feast, in which words are never just reducible to their meanings (Richards's position) but are always carriers of that something extra (which returns), in which interpretation becomes the equivalent of eating. But the invocation of post-structuralism is a façade, which hides Eagleton's latent conservatism and less than residual élitism. Without irony, Eagleton writes,

> Nobody will perish without Mars bars, just as nobody ever died of not reading *Paradise Lost*, but food and language of some sort are essential to our survival. Fast Food is like cliché or computerese, an emotionless exchange or purely instrumental form of discourse. Genuine eating combines pleasure, utility and sociality, and so differs from a take-away in much the same way that Proust differs from a bus ticket. Snatching meals alone bears the same relation to eating in company as talking to yourself does to conversation. It is hardly surprising that a civilisation for which a dialogue of the mind with itself has provided a paradigm of human language should reach its apotheosis in the Big Mac.
>
> (*Times Higher Education Supplement*, 25 October 1997)

The quest for 'genuine eating' is the exact equivalent (in fact actually is) the quest for genuine reading. No humanist ever knew how to read or how to eat and only post-structuralists can ever know the full range of experiences in both reading and eating that humanists have impoverished. The protection of civilisation is the demented project of humanist and (post-structural) Marxists alike, a slow, painful and embarrassing death by cultural proscription and prescription, both the product of the secular monastery and the aristocratic palazzo of modern academic life. Eagleton's entire diatribe is blatantly anti-popular, latently anti-America and amusingly Leavisite.

The more Eagleton attempts (very belatedly) to deny the accusation that post-structuralism impoverishes reading, the more he is embroiled in yet another debate over the port and cheese about the merits of one culture over another, the more he finds the health metaphor to be one too many – an indigestible bone of contention. So much so that, finally defeated, Eagleton can do little more than invoke a metaphoric description of the feast that is both food and language and *language as psychic food*. In a book review from the late 1990s, Eagleton quotes with approval the following passage.

> [Food's] disintegration in the stomach, its assimilation in the blood, its diaphoresis in the epidermis, its metempsychosis in the large intestine; its viscosity in okra, gumbo, oysters; its elasticity in jellies; its deliquescence in blancmanges; its tumescence in the throats of serpents, its slow erosion in the bellies of sharks; its odysseys through pastures, orchards, wheat fields, stock-yards, supermarkets, kitchens, pig troughs, rubbish dumps, disposals; the industries of sowing, hunting, cooking, milling, processing, and canning it; the wizardry of its mutations, ballooning in bread, subsiding in soufflés; raw and cooked, solid and melting, vegetable and mineral, fish, flesh and fowl, encompassing the whole compendium of living substance food is the symbol of the passage, the totem of sociality, the epitome of all creative and structured labour.
>
> (Maud Ellmann, quoted by Eagleton, op. cit.)

He concludes on this evidence that,

> [Maud Ellmann's *The Hunger Artists*] quite properly makes a meal of it. Her paragraph coils like an intestine, the sense slipping from clause to clause like a morsel down the oesophagus. As these lines track the processing of food, so they in turn process that subject

matter, by the cuisinary transformations of style, into a delectable feast.

(Eagleton, op. cit.)

Whatever 'cuisinary transformations of style' are, the simile is itself a hopeless attempt at joining two distinctly different forms of experience: eating and reading. No more obvious sign of this is that Eagleton seems so in love with the simile that he never notices that the function of taste is entirely absent from the oesophagus and its proper function or that an intestine is merely an agent of digestion without any subjectivity or self-awareness either *post* or *proctor hoc* to be worked upon. Returning to his Stilton, Eagleton joins the chattering classes and abandons criticism; one whose guiding principle is a way of life available to those who finally free themselves from the tyranny of Big Macs, popular culture and MTV.

That Eagleton has always been a cultural moralist is clear from his other explicitly Marxist writings. At the end of *Criticism and Ideology* (1975) Eagleton postpones the moral question until a 'science' of critical discourse can properly liberate it.

It is necessary, then, to refuse a 'moralism' of literary value: to reunite the question of a work's quality with the question of its conditions of possibility. Men do not live by culture alone: far from it. But the claim of historical materialism is that, in effect, they will. Once emancipated from material scarcity, liberated from labour, they will live in the play of their mutual significations, move in the ceaseless 'excess' of freedom. In that process, the signs of sense and value by which previous societies have lived their life-conditions will still, no doubt, be relevant. Yet if Marxism has maintained a certain silence about aesthetic value, it may well be because the material conditions which would make such discourse fully possible do not as yet exist. The same holds for 'morality': if Marxism has had little to say directly about the 'moral', one reason for this obliquity is that one does not engaged in moral debate with those for whom morality can only mean moralism. It is not a question of injecting a different content into these categories, but of transvaluating the categories themselves; and that cannot be done by a simple act of will. The 'aesthetic' is too valuable to be surrendered without a struggle to the bourgeois aestheticians, and too contaminated by that ideology to be appropriated as it is. It is, perhaps, in the provisional strategic silence of those who refuse to speak 'morally' and 'aesthetically' that something of the true meaning of both terms is articulated.

In *The Function of Criticism* (1984) Eagleton again postpones the moment of moral judgement, but now he makes explicit the ethical nature of criticism.

> The role of the contemporary critic, then, is a *traditional* one. The point . . . is to recall criticism to its traditional role. . . . 'English litera-ture' is now an inherited label for a field within which many diverse preoccupations congregate. . . . These pursuits have no obvious unity beyond the concern with the symbolic of social life, and the social production of forms of subjectivity. . . . [F]or it is surely becoming apparent that without a more profound understanding of such symbolic processes, through which political power is deployed, rein-forced, resisted, at times subverted, we shall be incapable of unlocking the most lethal power-struggles now confronting us. Modern criti-cism was born of a struggle against the absolutist state; unless its future is now defined as a struggle against the bourgeois state, it might have no future at all.

Criticism is and always has been a *medicinal* process determined to 'cure' authoritarianism in the name of health (utopian or post-revolution, post-capitalist *pure* culture) and the nature of this ethical struggle is not historical but *traditional* (Eagleton's emphasis) at war with the 'ersatz' of modern social life ('modern' being a movable term across cultures and back and forth across history). The golden age, both lost and about to be, is the age of purity (puritanical health) and indulgence (the connois-seur's pure culture). A case of having your cake and eating it:

> if a food critic were presented with a plate of greasy fish and chips, reviewed it unfavorably, and was then handed another identical plate of fish and chips to review, she/he would soon become weary and disillusioned. ('Doctor, this analogy has just died on the operating table.')
>
> (*Tripwire*, September 1997)

Maud Ellmann, in the quoted passage with which Eagleton concluded his newspaper review, comes dangerously close to assimilating labour to biological processes. Biology is *not* the epitome of anything, especially not the forces and processes of labour and capital. This is the collapse of everything into a first term which signifies for all else. The idea that 'labour' underlies biological process makes little if any sense – the terms are *not* therefore reciprocal. In collapsing labour and biology the critic can fatten morality whilst eviscerating logic.

Hardly surprisingly, the metaphoric comparison of food with literature has a venerable past and is certainly as old as modern English criticism (and indeed as old as modern English literature itself). Its first use in English Studies (at Cambridge University) can be dated to the comments by Sir Arthur Quiller-Couch in the series of lectures that he delivered between 1916 and 1917. In one lecture (II, 15 November 1916), he reminded his listeners of the food/literature metaphor, whilst in another (VI, 17 October 1917) he administered a culinary admonition to those who had participated in the growing professionalisation of academic English:

> And the next news is that these cooks...have formed themselves into professional associations to protect 'the study of English Literature'....To write English, so as to make Literature may be *hard*. But English Literature is *not* a mystery, *not* a Professor's Kitchen.
>
> (Quiller-Couch, *On the Art of Reading*)

The food metaphor, it seems, goes to the heart of English literary studies.

IV

The last thirty years of the twentieth century have therefore witnessed unprecedented levels of debate over the nature of cultural change. Central to much of this debate has been the role and significance of literature. As literature (and the 'serious' novel in particular) has been alternately buffeted by popular entertainment (non-printed media and popular fiction) and supported and promoted by popular entertainment (literary prizes, increased bookshop sales), so too an almost obsessive level of critical analysis (post-structuralism, cultural studies, feminism, etc.) has grown up to consider the decline of humanist culture and its embodiment in the printed word.

The cultural debates of the last three decades have focused attention on the necessary value systems that sustain communities, ranging across political, moral and aesthetic questions, which focus on the disintegration of older literary taxonomies and categories of taste. Consideration of the canon and its place in Western civilisation is almost the least of the worries confronting those who are attempting to disentangle the meaning of representation and the relationship of language to reality. This itself is crossed by ethnic, gender and anti-humanist inquisition and the new disciplines of cultural and media studies. Those analytic debates are themselves predicated on the importance of technological changes, which have suggested the decline of the printed word in the face of electronic media.

This book presents chapters which concentrate on the political preju-dices, cultural debates, commercial interests and shifting tastes and values of those concerned with the arbitration of academic and public literary taste and the interaction of popular consumer desires with the conditions which decide literary representation and the moral imper-atives of the novel. Political and cultural relativism has apparently now replaced the pluralism which appeared to uphold humanist debate, consensus and older tastes (moral and aesthetic), now fractured by the impossibility of reconciling these versions of democratic participation. In addressing these *fin de siècle* issues the chapters in this volume range across highbrow, middlebrow and lowbrow cultural debates, and the relationships and networks, both intellectual and commercial, that unite and (often) divide them.

V

Almost seventy years ago the study of English Literature occupied the same position that Cultural Studies and Communication Studies do today. Here was a radical attempt to seize the high ground of contemporary cultural debate: modern artistic and perceptual space were the goals to be won. And in the study of literature's formal properties was to be found the social values required of a complex new phenomenon: mass industrial society. Thus, literary studies joined psychology, anthropology, archae-ology and sociology as the latest subject area in the Human Sciences.

The study of literature in any modern sense fits into a period which saw the opening of opportunities for Nonconformists, women, Jews and Catholics. The enfranchisement of young middle-class and later working-class men and women was related to the central role that the study of science and technology had for the newly 'educated' masses of Britain, Europe and the United States. What occupied the scientific departments also directed the interests of progressive English professors. The central problem for these academics was not one of meaning but one of *organisation*.

I. A. Richards hoped, indeed, that one day he would prove English literary studies part of the wider scientific pursuit of behavioural psychology, with its chemical and neural impulses. Richards's philosophy was part of modernism and it was the functionalist morality of modernism that informed the origins of literary studies. Indeed, aesthetic value was considered in direct proportion to the formal properties of complex structures. In a word, the organisation of a work was aesthetically pleasing (of value) if it showed a perfect fit between function and material – language and meaning. Perfect organisation was therefore the equivalent of perfect moral order and mental health; popular art was considered to be poorly organised and therefore 'unhealthy' or 'immoral'.

These definitions were evolving even as they were created. In fact, in 1926 a young F. R. Leavis attempted to introduce a banned pornographic book into the syllabus. That book was James Joyce's *Ulysses*, which was first taught to mixed-sex classes in 1928: its location not Cambridge, but Eastbourne.

So English Studies began by being progressive and modern: organisational study was its *raison d'être* and its goal was enlightened pluralism. The general forms of approach to English Literary Studies were driven by a need not only to discover a subject matter but also to confirm a recognised method of study. This, in itself, was the neurosis of literary analysis – the quest for legitimation.

Media and Cultural Studies now stand in relation to mass culture as 'Eng Lit' once stood in relation to High Literature. They now feature as the central academic arbiters of mass late twentieth-century industrial culture in the First World. High culture is now dead. It is dead, not because it cannot still fulfil or enlighten its recipient, nor because it died of neglect amid the philistinism of the masses. It is dead because it no longer has the right environmental conditions to sustain its creation.

Cultural Studies belongs to the age of chemistry and electronics. To Cultural Studies belongs the analysis of the relationship between text and electronic provision, video, film, television and radio, computers, audio tape and computer disk. Its 'other' is actually management and commerce which produce the material that it takes as its area of study. Contemporary novels, poetry and drama, under the pressures of technology, have adapted and flourished. The narrative, linear taxonomies of the classic novel have been refashioned in the postmodern age.

It was not only technology's relentless pursuit of subject-matter that killed high culture. This just made it easily available. Yet, in so doing it gave high culture technology's shape and made it conform to techno-logy's rules. Technology de-emphasised the notion of creation and replaced it with the conditions of consumption. What ended the age of high culture was the loss of a foundation. Its own material circum-stances changed and so did the make-up of its recipients. The autonom-ous, bourgeois, enlightened individual of the classic novel ceased to exist as a valid intellectual concept or even as a contemporary human type.

Ironically in the 1990s, popular art was becoming more self-referential and in so doing was effectively effacing itself as 'popular' as it appropri-ated high literary style. The central position of opera, of Shakespeare and Jane Austen in the commercial and popular market place clearly indicated a collapse of category boundaries. English Literature was *again* popular literature.

English Literary Studies began as the study of the organisation of great literature. Through an evolution in the term 'text' and changes wrought by technology on art's reception, cultural studies and media and communication studies also gained a legitimate place through studying the material conditions of contemporary perceptual organisation. This organisation was created in the first place by managerial decisions and commercial activities which are themselves communal activities and social relationships. The aesthetic, the organisational and the financial now showed their relationship with knowledge. Cultural Studies is also, however, a university programme.

The modern university has developed as a large commercial enterprise. It shares many, if not all, of the conditions which govern the structure and bureaucracy of any large company and is managed and organised to maintain its solvency. All large companies manage solvency before profits, that is, if they are to create the conditions for sustained exist-ence, adaption and growth. Any modern university is in the knowledge industry. In such a world, where a university *competes* with others in information, media and knowledge production, information acts like finance and it fulfils the rules of finance. The economics of information are those of financial transferable capital. Thus occurs an important qualitative change in the notion of knowledge on a 'global' level. Furthermore, the university is now directly competing with other knowledge industries for funds and customers.

Significantly, on the local level of the school or department, it is knowledge (linear, teleological and hierarchical) that holds sway. At the level of the university this intriguingly mutates into capital and acts as such (non-hierarchical, functional, non-directed and circulatory).

The intellectual ideal of address and reception is replaced by circulation and return. It will be part of the tasks and responsibilities of the next decade that we find ways to redefine and reconstitute the relationship between individuals, knowledge and corporate control and in so doing ensure the vitality of a common culture.

VI

This book, like others of its kind, bears a health warning from no less a critic than George Steiner. Writing in 1979, he warned that

> To adduce the patent relativity and instability of 'taste', to cite the historicity of every aesthetic ranking – is a boringly self-evident move. What needs to be understood is the rationale, the integral structure of the arbitrariness of all acts of criticism.
>
> (Steiner, quoted in Philip Davis [1997])

Need it be said? Of course taste is relative and unstable, but surely not 'boringly self-evident'?

The 'decline' of English culture, variously attributed to the growth of philistinism (Matthew Arnold), effeminacy due to attendance at football terraces (Baden-Powell), tinned food (George Orwell), regional accents (Beryl Bainbridge), seems both never-ending and arbitrarily determined, little more than a pastime for snobs and fools. Yet such people are not only the arbiters of taste but also the pillars of the institutions of culture. In their very pronouncements of inadequacy they form a powerful lobby that makes the rules, and, often as not, *all* the rules by which the game of taste is played out.

It is the contention in these pages that no act of criticism nor any act of aesthetic creativity can escape its history and that it is history which allows us to explore a world of taste in which nothing is 'self-evident'. Indeed, to avoid so doing tempts us back into the trap of criticism which leads nowhere except to essence, description, praise and condemnation. Only when materially placed within a context both social and conceptual can critical ideas be understood not as 'arbitrary' but as meaningful. The act of criticism is worthless without this, an act motivated not by profound consideration but merely the 'derivative, parasitic "job of work"' that Steiner would reduce it to.

Perhaps, in the end, this book does need a health warning. It is neither an historical survey of British cultural taste nor merely an attempt to lay out the grounds upon which good taste might be formed. It is not intended to be fair nor well balanced. Instead, it offers a *polemical* history of cultural consensus and cultural disarray in an attempt to resituate the idea of the *historical* and of the *political* within culture (the specific culture of value and authority) and thereby reawaken certain ideas dismissed as apparently no longer relevant. The heart of this book can be located in parts III and IV which deal with the university and its relationship to knowledge and the role of the avant-garde and the intellectual. I do not attempt to give a balanced view but a *committed* and political view which seeks to open up a disjunction in the consensus and conformity that has taken such a hold of cultural, social and political theory.

VII

The contest between traditional cultural criticism and contemporary literary theory has, in one sense, been disastrous for politicised criticism. This is especially true when a critique of representation (subjectivity) is mistaken for a critique of agency (personhood). What is substituted is a critique of symbolisation *as if* it were action. Hence, one example of such substitution is an inability to distinguish real bodies from metaphysical concepts.

> Physicality – body colour, shape, size; facial structure, noses, eyes, hair; sexual body parts, penis, breasts, vaginas, clitoris – is symbolized as the body.... There is no body, as fact, without interpretation.... The body is then many things simultaneously: 'It is a thing and a sign, an inside and an outside, a boundary constantly crossing itself.' Bodies absorb meaning and elicit meaning. Politics processes the definitions.
>
> (Zillah Eisenstein, *Hatreds*)

The symbolic body and the existent body may interact at certain levels but the physical presence of the body is neither the only site for polit-ical exchange nor the final site of politicised discourse. Here the body, subjecthood, agency and individualism are all hopelessly conflated in a rhetoric of action. The nature of the individual and the body as that individual's presence in space and time is not the same as a diffusion of body parts 'symbolised as the body'. The body is *not* 'many things simultaneously' but *this* body, here and now in all its factuality. It can be many things only *in a context* and thus allows 'politics [to] process the definitions' only if it is *placed*.

If, as Germaine Greer argues in *The Whole Woman* (1999), 'the personal is still the political' exerted through 'intimate relationships', the political decision and the personal experience of that decision still remain separate processes – the former acting upon and through the latter as its agent. The politicised body is not *itself* a site for struggle but the *agent* of struggle in the political realm. Greer's long-held belief that female identity disfunction is political simply reduces all political oppression to patriarchal oppression, itself a metaphysical concept. Government agency and capitalist activity are not merely reducible to the actual, conspiratorial, but hidden politics of patriarchal order. Such conflation robs Greer of anything other than mere outrage and disbelief.

The political realm may be in some instances the mere analogue of the representation of the body (as may be a legal entity like a corporation) but to understand them we must understand government and law, not aesthetics and metaphor. It is not possible to simply short-circuit debates in culture with a debate that makes anything culture and therefore under the sway of representation (now substituted for 'the world').

The 'political' juncture I wish to bring to the fore (in terms of cultural critique) is that of the supposedly discredited egalitarian and liberation movements of the 1960s (in which Germaine Greer was such a key figure) and their significance and impact on millennial aesthetics and politics. The appeal at the heart of this book (Chapters 5 to 9) is to the debates of the sixties which were prematurely cut off through economic pressure, consensual pressure and 'right-wing' political pressure; they were discredited *tout court* by politicians and cultural thinkers whose platform *required* the *denial* of sixties radicalism. This is precisely what Margaret Thatcher meant when she declared the end of society (that is, the social realm as a realm of action). The curtailed experiment was represented everywhere as an aberration and a defeat: a moment of madness. The radical paths which were opened up fell prey to absorption into non-radical jockeying which *posed* as a radical realignment on behalf of consensus. One cannot revisit the past and there is no attempt to do so in this book nor to idealise its, now old, notions. The point at stake is that the notions which came to a head in 1968 are not yet played out, have not yet succumbed to an indifferent post-modernity. The heart of this book is concerned with what the sixties means, not merely as a historical period but also as an ontological and epistemological position *now* at the turn of the millennium.

It is not a coincidence that the 1990s chose the 1960s as its mask. 'Cool Britannia' heralded political and social attitudes that borrowed from the sixties but emptied that decade of its edge and turned it into mere chic. There is also no coincidence here, at the edge of the millennium. The sixties stood for a future, *the* future. For Ken Kesey the sixties was about going 'further' (as was the name of his original bus) exploring both outer space and inner space, for which Cape Kennedy and psyche-delia were the symbols.[7] In 1999, the thirtieth anniversary of the first moon walk in 1969 was cause only for mass nostalgia. Thirty years later that future is thirty years old and still to come.

This problematic is nowhere more clearly and acutely felt than at the juncture of culture and politics. The discourse of revolution and libera-tion which emerged in the 1960s was a *mélange* of critical positions only partially informed by Marxist or 'classical' theorisation. The necessary liberationist message required both a personal realm of freedom as well as a social realm of freedom – both inner and outer liberation. The means to achieve these ends would be both cultural (i.e. aesthetic–subjective) and social (that is, institutional–economic).

The left decisively won the cultural battle and decisively lost the political. Political aspirations then filtered back into the realm of culture *as if* it was the political, as if decisive and dynamic change could be generated from there. From the sixties to the mid-seventies culture ceased to mean the established culture of the ruling élite but instead became a word available only in the plural, defining a multiplicity of practices, attitudes, aesthetic forms: from this emerged a rich, and hith-erto poorly documented series of areas vying for attention, in which classes, groups and communities previously ignored were allowed a voice, whilst élite group expression was criticised and disabused of its confident sense of superiority.

The pluralisation of terminology (the proliferation of analytic nouns) has resulted in words with relatively vague but consensual meanings degenerating into 'scientific' terms of micro discourse without any general applicability beyond the local (at best) or rhetorical (at worst). Such a movement in language is clearly demonstrated in Stuart Hall's concept of 'identity through difference' which implies multiplicity of selfhood through multiple distancing effects (difference), both 'identity' and 'difference' being, in effect, 'plural' in order to avoid accusations of essentialism. This leads to a call for a 'cultural politics which engages rather than suppresses *difference*' (Stuart Hall, 'New Ethnicities', quoted in Mercer). The confusion inherent in the phrase 'cultural politics' suggests pluralism is an end in itself, containing both resolution on the level of the political and that of self-identity. It is clear that nothing of the sort happens when these terms are conflated. Such solutions fall back into rhetorics which are *disengaged* because lacking sites for engagement except at the level of specific agency. The conflation only gives rise to wishful thinking.

> I think for black people who live in Britain this question of finding some way in which the white British can learn to live with us and the rest of the world is almost as important as discovering our own identity. I think they are in more trouble than we are. So we ... have to rescue them from themselves – from their own past. We have to allow them to see that England is a quite interesting place with quite an interesting history that has bossed us around for 300 years [but] that is finished. Who are they now?
>
> (Stuart Hall, BBC Radio 4 broadcast, quoted in Solomos and Black)

Hall's rhetorical flourish conflates 'who are they' with where are they? The answer is simple – they (the generalised 'white' community) are still the vast majority and still in charge. Even hybrid cultures are still consensual cultures in their relations with the larger community and it is this area *alone* from which new and vital public forms arise. In this context deconstruction is not dissent but a mobilization of public consensual culture *on its own behalf* to defend, by diffusion, its inherent interests. Hybridity in its belief in vital change within conformity does not redraw the boundaries of the philosophy of identity *per se* but merely points out that identity is always changing *in history* and in *social contexts*. It does not alter those factors because it is essentially *descriptive* not dynamic. It cannot fully address dissent as dissent which is essentially *no longer a negotiation on accepted terms*.

Can one seriously accept, in an era dominated by the image of displaced peoples, refugees, émigrés and exiles, the *positive* aspect of existing *between* borders or of exemplifying that state? Liminality, a term used by Homi Bhabha to describe the condition of existing between borders (Bhabha's 'in-between'), is nothing less than the abject condition of the refugee caught in transit in the no man's land between custom posts. In order to dissent it is necessary to have a consensual order to dissent *from*: a public realm. If the public realm (i.e. the state establishment) embraces 'polyphony' then that is reason enough to suspect the terms given![8]

VIII

The challenge of pluralism was, at least initially, a political challenge which saw public culture as monolithic and oppressive, working through institutions whose rhetorics were authoritarian and exclusive. The emergence of pluralist culture would be the decisive blow to discussions of acceptance and quietism, having exposed the unspoken 'power' at the heart of discourse (i.e. *historicised* language) itself. During the 1970s, 1980s and 1990s the struggle for political gains took on, for the academic left, an *aesthetic* which the politically empowered right simply chose to ignore. The liberation discourse of Thatcherism only occurred when the control of the state became more and more centralised. The left/radical rhetoric of plurality could not cope theoretically with this contradiction. If Margaret Thatcher and Francis Fukuyama had declared the end of the ideological (i.e. the end of the social realm) then left-radical critics had declared both the end of the autonomous individual (the agent of change) and the veracity of history (the stage for the agency of change – Marx's 'real'). In their place, however, emerged not a liberated multiculturalism but a new *authoritarian pluralist consensus* which could not be challenged from the left because it was the product of anti-establishment thinking itself.

The through critique of public culture and its institutions carried out by the radical left was an ironic analogue of that carried on by the right for other reasons. The split between the cultural and political libertarian movements of the sixties, and the defeat of the political challenge, meant that the fight for control of public culture could not be waged against an ever hardening right-liberal consensus. Governmental politics fell into the hands of the right whilst the cultural became 'politicised' by the left. The politicisation of representation and the demand for plurality in culture meant that the public realm (both cultural and political) seemed to become a meaningless term – no longer a place to fight the new battles for liberty. Yet without a public sphere – a consensual and established realm of debate *and* power, as well as aesthetic expression – what was left was mere parochial gossip: something always and only (because *unverifiable*) personal – bereft of objectivity, connectedness and justice.

The victory of pluralism, because won only in the realm of the cultural, left the political untouched. In dismantling 'culture', the radical thinkers of the 1960s and 1970s performed an incalculable service, but the democratisation of social expression carried a difficulty which could not have been foreseen – that lay at the frontier between pluralism and relativism. At that boundary precisely the radical left could not decide on what, if anything, could be accorded priority in a structure of expressiveness unbounded because unverifiable, unverifiable because all the tests (linguistic and institutional) were suspect. Having robbed itself of the tools by which an assault on consensus could take place, the left quietly disbanded and voted for Euro-Christian socialism.

It is no coincidence that 'New Labour's' dedication to Scottish and Welsh devolution, as well as to the disestablishment of the Lords, is not a pledge to pluralist democracy but an attempt to create benevolent authoritarian Christian socialist hegemony in Great Britain whose powers, ironically, will become more centralised and in fewer hands. There can be no more urgent task than the creation of a twenty-first century radical intelligentsia whose task would be the redefinition of a *public* cultural realm which could be repoliticised in order to find an 'aesthetic' in the political realm which cannot simply perpetuate itself in the self-sustaining rhetorics of an increasingly authoritarian consensus. Indeed, this authoritarian consensus creates instrumentalist educational policies which serve only to diminish, year by year, the possibility of an educated radical challenge.

The gimlet-eyed critic will no doubt notice all manner of errors and inconsistencies in my arguments, my selection of material and even my style. The subject is a difficult and complex one: the interrelationship between literary culture, political enquiry and intellectual endeavour. I can do little by way of apology except to say that my first aim was not consistency but a radical scepticism of all positions – showing, to continue a certain culinary metaphor, what is on the end of the fork.

I do not advocate that the intellectual avant-grade of the twenty-first century go back to the 1960s even if nostalgia and compulsion drive them there. There is no longer a clear radical catechism, but if there were it would have to include the decision to distrust all forms of liberation *approved* by the state; the decision to always take the money and spend it (on yourself); the refusal to offer coherent arguments that can be debated away (with patronising looks of pity); the determination to be *useless* and therefore pointless to co-opt; the need to be invisible: never to appear on television, radio or any form of the media; to debate only in order to disengage (step away) and disengage in order to become invisible. Remember that the invisible agent is always visible *somewhere else*, therefore always be a double agent: work for both sides and suit yourself.

IX

The Millennium Dome stands on reclaimed wasteland, purified of its pollution; the Millennium Dome stands adjacent to the centre of terrestrial time. Subject to controversy and disquiet on its being built (at a cost of £449 million), both the form of its construction and the dubious nature of its content were symbolic of the doubt and disease that greets a new century and a third millennial era (subsidised at a cost of £89 million to date). And yet it was hardly about such apocalyptic matters. Rather it marked the end of the *future* that crashed in 1968 and the beginning of a future that was born in the disillusion of the 1970s – its vision epitomised by a prime minister and advisers who inherited both the Millennium Project and their views from those others who had created the decade in which they came to their adulthood.

It was an age which appeared to one contemporary commentator 'to have come to a dead end, to have turned back on itself', an age in which 'the corrupt welfare state [had] passed beyond its ability to order itself, to posit values worthy of itself' (Digby Anderson, *This Will Hurt*). Such feelings settled deep in the psyche of young socialists and slowly matured through the filtration of Margaret Thatcher's neo-liberal anti-'conservatism', finding expression in the Millennium Project. Young Socialism's heady grammar school flirtation with the liberationist, communalist politics of the 1960s – politics of self-awareness, struggle, emancipation, tolerance, played out against the dowdiness and security of a benevolent welfare state – was always bound to crash in the cynicism of those who wanted to join in but were too young to join the party. Instead they joined *a* party. The founding principles (if not the actual practice) of the welfare state were those on which a decent, caring, fair-minded, communal, law-abiding, united and indeed respectable society might be fairly based. They were essentially British pragmatic ideals and they carried the less-than-exciting necessary concept of *decency* (and tolerance) deep within them.[9] The benevolent authoritarian character of the provision of welfare and its burdensome and problematic bureaucratic layers tarnished one of the greatest social achievements of twentieth-century liberal democracy. Under the onslaught of ideological and economic change the shadow of welfare was increasingly mistaken for its substance.

New Conservatism (neo-liberalism) taught New Labour (neo-liberalism) the necessary lessons that must be learnt by all parricides. The welfare state, within whose rickety but benevolent authority new socialists were allowed the liberty of their uncertain views, crashed under the authoritarian managerialism of those who only learnt to understand the shadow of social civility but despised the substance of its organisation. As we moved into 2000 the political landscape folded not around the future and its possibilities and hopes but around a never-ceasing and never-ending *present* which needed to be *managed*. The vision of the future was, finally, not that of George Orwell's *1984*, but Aldous Huxley's *Brave New World*. The Great Exhibition of 1851 celebrated Britain's sense of its place in contemporaneity and thus its assurance about the future, its sense of *progress*: the Festival of Britain in 1951 rallied Britain to the cause of the future; both astonished by their use of new technology (the new and glass Crystal Palace and the Skylon). The Millennium Dome continues the tradition of drawing parallels between technology and progress (technology *as* progress the embodiment of it) but it lacks the grand vision required of a future that must be emancipatory, liberating and *tolerant*.

Nowhere is tolerance and respect more urgently needed at the millennium than in 'race' relations, especially following the furore which followed the murder of Stephen Lawrence, in 1993, the 'deliberately' bungled investigation by the police and the subsequent inquiry which published its findings (also bungled) in early 1999 after six years of media attention. In the end no prosecutions were brought and the Metropolitan Police Force, though castigated for being 'institutionally racist', required no officers to resign nor brought any officers to book. Sir Paul Condon's utter failure to reform the 'Met', the very platform upon which he had taken office, though discredited, did not bring his resignation. The men suspected of Stephen Lawrence's murder themselves remained immune from prosecution. Highlighted, too, were other cases involving Black-British and Asian-British citizens where the possibility of murder had been ignored in favour of a verdict of 'suicide', and whose cases were opened only after prolonged campaigning by bereaved families.[10]

Ethnic relations and multicultural Britishness are two aspects of a debate about civilised behaviour which will increasingly affect all aspects of British life and identity in the next century as the children of immigrants and their children are pulled between tradition and assimilation and are forced to reconcile the two. In the same way the arts of many minority cultures are now penetrating a number of aspects of British culture, from eating habits, to pop music, film making and literature. Linguistic usage may also increasingly penetrate mainstream culture.

Like other immigrant and second-generation settlers before them, the black and Asian British communities have developed a dual identity which has both a public and a private face. It is the interpretation of these two sides that has provided the dynamic for a cultural exchange generated into mainstream Britishness from its minority groups. This 'third' way could 'dilute' both cultures but this is very unlikely. Indeed Britain has never had a *single* culture but rather a diversity of cultures (Celtic, Anglo Saxon, etc.) which are multiplied by region and which have themselves reblended ethnic identity for those whose British family roots go back two or three generations. The challenge is to harness this in a British form between federalism (Europe) and nationalism (Scottish independence) and where older, festering racial attitudes are still deeply entrenched within all sectors of the 'white' populations, including, and perhaps especially, the growing number of disempowered white working class (a new underclass).

For at least two hundred years there have been visible communities of Caribbean, Chinese and Asian people living in Britain (as many as 10,000 in the late eighteenth century). These groups were often isolated or transient and usually remained invisible to the (non-metropolitan) general population (and to historians). The large-scale immigration which followed the Second World War established new communities, much larger than before and, moreover, much more visible. Agitation and political concern began to restrict the numbers of immigrants entering the United Kingdom through a series of parliamentary acts (1962, 1968, 1971, 1981, 1987) and the fear of foreign 'invasion' has been used as a rallying cry for 'Englishness' by right-wing politicians from Enoch Powell to Peter Lilley (at the 1993 Conservative Party Conference). Both Conservative and Labour governments have passed immigration acts. Nevertheless, as early as 1967, Roy Jenkins made it clear that Labour did not 'seek a flattening process of uniformity, but cultural diversity, coupled with equal opportunity in an atmosphere of mutual tolerance' (quoted in Zig Layton-Henry, *The Politics of Race*). Despite this, some of the most restrictive immigration legislation and enforcement occurred under Labour.

West Indian and black Caribbean immigration, which had dominated immigrant numbers and rose steadily throughout the 1950s and very early 1960s, was superseded by Asian immigration from Uganda, India, Pakistan and Bangladesh. These new communities were themselves divided on regional, religious, gender and class lines and settled in communities in different, usually urban and suburban, areas. With legislative changes and economic stability these communities have stabilised into permanent settlement, born, marrying, and dying as UK citizens. By 1985 the whole 'non-white' community was estimated at

3.4 per cent of the total population and of this non-white community almost 50 per cent were born in Britain.

In 1991, the census recorded 5.5 per cent of the population as from an 'ethnic' group: 2.7 per cent from South Asia, 1.5 Indian; 0.9 Pakistani; 0.3 Bangladeshi; 1.6 per cent called themselves black, divided between Black Caribbean at 0.9 per cent and Black African at 0.4 per cent.

If the black Caribbean community was most visible in the 1950s and 1960s and the Ugandan Asians in the 1970s, by the 1980s and 1990s it was the Muslim community that had attracted attention. Both the 'Honeyford Affair' (in which a Bradford headteacher challenged multi-culturalism in the name of social integration) and the Rushdie Affair (in which Salman Rushdie's *Satanic Verses* was publicly destroyed in Bradford and his effigy burnt) suggested a sinister 'third force' had also arrived with these new and usually poorer migrants. This was exacerbated by the creation of a Muslim Parliament which seemed to challenge the role of democratic debate. The peaceful coexistence of three-quarters of a million Muslims with the wider population suggested these 'crises' were more the invention of the media or demagogues than the greater public.

In 1991 there were 477,000 Pakistanis, 163,000 Bangladeshis and 134,000 Indian Muslims living in Britain, of whom 47 per cent were born in the UK. Almost all this population remains urban (mostly in Bradford, Birmingham or concentrated in London's poorest boroughs). They all now have thriving religious, educational and cultural centres. Such centres are actively modelling responses to situations that are new and unexpected, confronting issues (especially around 'youth' culture) that were not evident until now and rethinking religious and other experience in the light of new limitations or re-evaluations.

Whilst communities in Britain coexist with a high level of tolerance it would be untrue to say that prejudice does not continue to dog relations. Stereotyping and hysteria have led to the extremes of riot and murder but Britain has never had a *state* or quasi-state policy of racial discrimination such as had occurred in Tzarist Russia, the United States, Germany, South Africa, etc. Nevertheless, the British government has hardly been free from prejudice, especially as it has radiated from the Foreign and Home Office bureaucracy, yet governmental policy since the creation of the Commonwealth has, on the whole, been responsive rather than pre-emptive, haphazard, pragmatic and unconceptualised, which is not to deny that its application has almost always been racially biased and exclusive; a situation noted again and again by those black and Asian interrogatees suspected of entering illegally or of bringing in relatives, wives or children illegally. Such pressure rarely applies to white immigrants.

Prejudice within the wider community has, more often than not, when it exists, been passive rather than actively aggressive and has never been formulated into a mass political movement. That prejudice exists and occurs at all levels is, however, clear and has been exacerbated by *economic* inequality rather than cultural division. In one sense *prejudice can only be defined by its victims* and therefore the hope of a prejudice-free country is unlikely.[11]

Passive prejudice in the wider population may take the form of disguised messages about Englishness or the 'British way' or it may take a verbal, literary or media form. Jewish immigrants at the turn of the century were considered to be verminous, plague-bringing and swarthy (i.e. *non* European) and much literature was expended upon the 'problem' of the non-assimilable Jews and on the *more* dangerous *assimilated* Jews! Even today, such prejudice is part of Conservative backstairs debate.[12]

There was much debate and disquiet about 'Black Sections' in the Labour Party and even here candidates have been denied party selection for fear of losing local elections. In the education system disguised prejudice may be behind recent debates (in December 1998) surrounding extended school 'holidays' undermining the curriculum. Muslim schools still do not get state funding as do Christian and Jewish Schools. The new 'borderless' Europe has also brought 'verminous' eastern and central European 'scroungers' to the south coast (the local media being reprimanded for its demagogic stance on the issue) whilst in 1999 Nazi bombs exploded in Brixton, Brick Lane and Soho.

There are also worrying signs that in some areas minority communities are themselves perpetuating or generating new forms of prejudice. There has certainly been trouble between Hindu and Muslim youths in various cities and anti-Semitic attitudes have been recorded amongst Muslim schoolchildren in areas where there is also a large Jewish population. These are small but worrying developments in children and teenagers whose first language is English and who count Britain as home, and it may give rise to new permutations of racial division under local economic, social and cultural pressure, not least between the young of differing cultures, but also between the young and parents which may be exaggerated by political change towards both federalism (Europe) and nationalism (Scotland) in the UK. One worrying trend is the division on racial lines of secondary education.[13] This follows the Conservative reforms of the 1980s which were originally intended to offer parents greater choice and secure higher educational standards. Such reforms have been reinforced by Tony Blair's Labour government and at least one Labour minister (Harriet Harman) took advantage of them by moving her children from an educationally low-achieving but high-immigrant area. Segregation on racial lines in very mixed areas has had the effect of creating local *social* and communal ghettoisation *through* educational choice (a symptom itself of economic pressures to succeed in a competitive world) and this may store up problems for the future.

What must emerge is not the demonic face of multiculturalism (the type conjured up by scaremongers) – one in which the majority population is somehow swamped to leave merely a race of hybrids – but a form of cultural interaction in which *public* tolerance and decency towards different groups is grounded in mutual respect for each other's *private* life. A sense of 'at homeness' in a country can never fully occur for any minority ethnic group however long they have lived in peace alongside their majority neighbours. What can be worked towards is a private confidence in one's culture which is taken out into the public sphere without threatening others and which produces a *new public sphere* – the very sphere long neglected by government and long eroded by political ill will or disinterest. It is only in this sphere that a new multicultural Britain will emerge, in dynamic relations with private experience. At such a point the term multicultural will be made redundant. It is no coincidence that in a benevolent authoritarian state it is reform of the agencies of law and order from which this new public sphere must emerge, *not* from changes in tastes in food, fashion, music or literature.

Tolerance is a silent virtue with no appropriate civic symbol (it is quite the opposite of relativism which is always strident). Benevolent authoritarianism (with its increasing battery of surveillance, control of access and movement and restriction of liberty and knowledge generally) is always intolerant of tolerance. It always prefers relativism because, at heart, relativism, despite its claims, does not challenge or change the *political* system and its control. Hence, personal, social and cultural relativism is positively encouraged because it provides, in an apparently democratic liberal manner a filtering downwards of political democratic values. It does little of the sort. Such relativism serves to remove apparent personal stigma ('victim' culture) at the expense of actual political challenge. Those obsessed with such activities divert attention from the politics of governmental control (civil order and obedience) and mask them with a personal politics of identity.

All benevolent authoritarian governments (as Aldous Huxley pointed out in 1932 in *Brave New World*) are happy to encourage and accede to such local demands because the political base is left unchallenged. Furthermore, such personal, cultural and artistic relativism allows disadvantaged groups into government and apparently liberal activity but actually hides the needs of such governments to both widen their power base and do so only with those from disadvantaged groups who are willing to 'play the game' at the level of governmental control. Relativisim is tolerance without principle. Thus everything changes in order to reconstitute the ruling group's power.

Walter Bagehot pointed out in the nineteenth century that the key to British political life was the 'secret' of cabinet decision; New Labour learnt the lesson that the ideological secret is the use of toleration for intolerant ends (control, submissiveness, cynicism) – a lesson learned in the 1970s and 1980s and brought into practice in the 1990s as an 'antidote' to Thatcherite excess. Whatever the prospects, it will be almost a decade before we get another chance.

2
Just the Way it is

Any discussion of the past is fraught with danger, for evidence may be scant or contradictory; any discussion of the present will inevitably tend towards opinion as conditions rapidly alter; how much more difficult a discussion of the future where events have not yet occurred and where only the past is a guide.

Sam Goldwyn once remarked, 'Never prophesy, especially about the future', and one cannot help but notice the path of history littered with rash comments about our fate. One comment will stand for all. Thus Dr Richard van der Riet's classic 'Space travel is utter bilge' must act as a cautionary signpost for all futurologists (quoted in Arthur C. Clarke, *Profiles of the Future*). Yet predicting future patterns is not merely a matter of punditry or pollsterism or reading Nostradamus. Disregarding the more extreme advocates of technological or ecological change and discounting the unpredictable terrors of war, famine and pestilence, a number of writers have attempted a futurological study of the United Kingdom based upon patterns of industrial growth and cultural change.

Arthur C. Clarke pointed out that there are two types of change. The first is a consequence of known and understandable factors; for the population of 1900 this would have included the possibilities of flight, the inevitable rise of the United States, the importance of the Labour Party, trouble in Ireland and the Empire and even a large continental war. Many technological changes could also be predicted. The second type of change requires a qualitative leap. Here prediction finds itself adrift. The population of 1900 would have been far less equipped to predict television, computer technology, miniaturisation, a second continental war, the loss of the Empire and rapid changes in British ethnic mix since the 1950s. These would have been impossible to predict. With these caveats in mind we can look at some leading futurologists, especially as they considered cultural changes predicted for the next century. Indeed, by the 1980s futurology was almost a new literary genre.

The influential political and cultural theorist Alvin Toffler saw the 1980s and 1990s as a period of immense and cataclysmic change. For Toffler, as for those who lived through the first quarter of this century, the age was and remains one of crisis.

> Today we are living through one of those exclamation points in history when the entire structure of human knowledge is once again trembling with change...[W]e are totally reorganising the production and distribution of knowledge and the symbols used to communicate it.
>
> (Alvin Toffler, *Power Shift*)

Indeed, this crisis was so profound it was creating a new world order, sweeping aside not only the central tenets of socialist states but also the antiquated notions of a managerially hidebound capitalism. In short, the appearance of a new system for creating wealth had begun to undermine every pillar of the old power system, ultimately transforming family life, business, politics, the nation-state, and the structure of global power itself. Such profound changes were also predicted by James Robertson in his book *Future Work*. For Robertson 'a [profound] change in worldviews and values is taking place today' as a consequence of 'coming to the end of the period of history which we call the industrial age.'

Kenichi Ohmae viewed such change as wholly beneficial, regulated not by officials and bureaucrats, but by the demands of market forces, led by the self-regulation of the customer and their values which, he believed, were infinitely more subtle than usually imagined. 'By [commercial] "strategy" I mean creating sustaining values for the customer', he argued. 'It therefore means invention and the commercialisation of invention . . . all this has made the key objective a company's ability to *create new value*' (Kenichi Ohmae, *The Borderless World*). Such changes in value, sustained by entrepreneurial zeal and inventive genius, unfettered by interest rate controls or other 'artificial' means of reining in an economy, were, Ohmae argued, the only true means of sustaining economic growth and the limitless creation of wealth. Ohmae's uncompromising stand was consistent with what became known in the 1980s as Reaganomics and Thatcherite monetarism.

For advocates of this policy such deregulation by the state and its servants during the 1980s put power into the pockets of the individual, who as a consumer could *restate* lost rights of choice, freedom of action and self-determination. Such philosophy harked back to the earlier heroic age of Adam Smith and, indeed, one vociferous voice for such policies (which also opposed closer European links) was the right-wing Adam Smith Institute.

Unlike Ohmae, and opposed to his whole philosophy, were those who viewed such change in 'values' as detrimental to human happiness and who looked to a new age of regulation by consent: a world beyond the age of crude market forces and geared towards a planetary altruism. For many such changes in value were part of a crisis in consciousness itself: a crisis almost of personal identity in which the era of the history of growth and progress has ended in profound failure, as Christopher Lasch concluded in his book *The True and Only Heaven*:

> The premise underlying [his] investigation – [was] that old political ideologies [were] exhausted . . . our society has taken a wrong turn . . . [suffering] erosion of its psychological, cultural, and spiritual foundations from within [with] authority in serious decline.

Critics of progressive ideology have become more vocal since the 1970s when Charles A. Reich produced *The Greening of America* with its hopes of a youth revolution based on love. Indeed European 'green' politics are a part of Western culture with ideas that have become some of the main pillars of many 'responsible' lobby groups.

The ecology movement as it became embraced more than just a naïve love of nature. It covered a whole spectrum of political and personal issues. For Robert J. Lifton, this was the 'beginnings of species politics and species ethics'.

> Species awareness inevitably extends to the habitat of all species, to the earth and its ecosystem. Our awareness of our relationship to the sun, to the oceans, to the earth's resources of food, energy, and materials of every kind, to all animals and plants – becomes intensified as both we and that ecosystem are simultaneously threatened. We experience a deepened respect for all animals that inhabit the greater ecosystem with us, and we question assumptions of human entitlement that permit us to abuse these fellow inhabitants of ours. Yet whatever our efforts at greater empathy for other species, we remain aware that the problems we confront are those of the *human* imagination.
>
> (Robert J. Lifton and Eric Markusen, *The Genocidal Mentality*)

The problem for such ecologists was not merely the physical health of the ecosystem (its 'balance'), but the very nature of humankind; the human species dangerously out of control and on a destructive and *self*-destructive binge. The enemy was not industrial pollution but a mind set (both capitalist and patriarchal) which did not recognise anything except exploitation. Such an extreme view was held by Anthony Wilden in his work during the 1970s but it re-emerged during the 1980s and 1990s in Gaia philosophy. For Norman Myers, it was modern life which 'pollute[d]' consciousness and debilitated the self:

> We endure a daily barrage of advertising, muzak, and mass media, among many other forms of cultural noise . . . we thus suffer . . . which leaves us with less psychic energy to exercise value judgements about the quality of input.
>
> > (*The Gaia Atlas of Future Worlds*)

Anthony Wilden found pollution in the very processes which produced knowledge. Indeed, the problem as he saw it in the 1970s and 1980s was that capitalist-debased knowledge (knowledge as consumer-orientated product) *was* pollution, hence,

> In retrospect, it seems clear that the so-called 'knowledge explosion' of the past thirty years or so has little to do with knowledge as such. It has primarily to do with knowledge as a commodity produced by the 'knowledge industry' . . . and like every other form of industrial production, . . . its most significant side-effect is pollution.
>
> > (*System and Structure*)

Raymond Williams in his speculation about the future found debasement (i.e. pollution) even in the act of speculation itself.

> For it is this style of the whole culture, initially promoted by the techniques and relationships of modern corporate selling, which has reduced the only widely available form of positive thinking about the future . . . to a discredited game.
>
> > (*Towards 2000*)

Radical feminism also challenged the 'exploitative' nature of capital as an incarnation of patriarchy (or rather capitalism as one form of patriarchal organisation). For such feminists the species question is a *gender* question. Mary Daly, an outspoken lesbian-feminist theologian, restated in her 1991 introduction to *Gyn/Ecology* her hatred of male forms and her 'theology' of earthlove: 'our sister earth is in mortal danger'. That which is male, including the printed word, was seen by Daly as a polluting threat to Gaia-consciousness: '"texts" are the kingdom of males; they are the realm of the reified word.' This outspoken hatred of 'male' systems found its apotheosis in the Greenham Common Women who equated American cruise missiles (based in Britain) with patriarchal capitalist aggression against a 'female' planet. So it was that ecological politics reinforced gender politics: the definition and survival of self.

In its most naïve incarnation this rejection of industrial capitalism can be seen as a call to a 'return' to an inner wildness. 'The true wild is becoming something few of us will truly know... with it goes our inner "wildness", our capacity to enjoy the untravelled spaces of the mind', Norman Myers lamented in 1990 (in *The Gaia Atlas of Future Worlds*).

And it was this condition that Robert Bly saw as the essential element lost by men through the rise of the women's movement and the increased pressure on masculinity by feminists. A 'true' masculinity for Bly was represented by the quest for the 'hairy man' inside: a Jungian archetype of a strong manliness, finally repressed in the feminist 1960s. Moreover, 'the grief in men has been increasing steadily since the start of the Industrial Revolution'. Worse still, the problem lay deep within the visual and symbolic storehouse of capitalism itself: 'the images of adult manhood given by the popular culture are worn out' (*Iron John*).

In this scenario capitalism, and more especially industrialisation and feminist power, have emasculated the energetic, self-dependent male. Bly lamented,

> But many of these men are not happy. You quickly notice the lack of energy in them. They are life-preserving but not exactly life-giving. Ironically, you often see these men with strong women who positively radiate energy. Here we have a finely tuned young man, ecologically superior to his father, sympathetic to the whole harmony of the universe, yet he himself has little vitality to offer.
>
> The strong or life-giving women who graduated from the sixties, so to speak, or who have inherited an older spirit, played an important part in producing this life-preserving, but not life-giving, man.
>
> I remember a bumper sticker during the sixties that read 'WOMEN SAY YES TO MEN WHO SAY NO'. We recognise that it took a lot of courage to resist the draft, go to jail, or move to Canada, just as it

took courage to accept the draft and go to Vietnam. But the women of twenty years ago were definitely saying that they preferred the softer receptive male.

So the development of men was affected a little in this preference. Non-receptive maleness was equated with violence, and receptive maleness was rewarded.

Some energetic women, at that time and now in the nineties, chose and still choose soft men to be their lovers and, in a way, perhaps, to be their sons. The new distribution of 'yang' energy among couples didn't happen by accident. Young men for various reasons wanted their harder women, and women began to desire softer men. It seemed like a nice arrangement for a while, but we've lived with it long enough now to see that it isn't working out.

(Bly, *Iron John*)

In such an analytic fantasy only a return to a pre-industrial world of organic village craft activity (at least in your mind) could restore male bonding, father–son relationships and a 'yin/yang' energy distribution which would restore the role of the sexes and the ecological health of the planet.

A clean break from the mother is crucial, but it's simply not happening. This doesn't mean that the women are doing something wrong; I think the problem is more that the older men are not really doing their job.

The traditional way of raising sons, which lasted for thousands and thousands of years, amounted to fathers and sons living in close – murderously close – proximity, while the father taught the son a trade; perhaps farming or carpentry or blacksmithing or tailoring. As I've suggested elsewhere, the love unit most damaged by the Industrial Revolution has been the father–son bond.

(ibid.)

From anti-industrial politics to gender politics and beyond to myth, ecological lobby groups embraced every level of activity from the simply nomadic (New Age travellers were a feature of early 1990s newspapers in Britain) to the overtly aggressive. Jonathon Porritt, a British Green activist, gives a useful checklist for 'being green':

- a reverence for the Earth and for all its creatures;
- a willingness to share the world's wealth among all its peoples;

- prosperity to be achieved through sustainable alternatives to the rat race of economic growth;
- lasting security to be achieved through non-nuclear defence strategies and considerably reduced arms spending;
- a rejection of materialism and the destructive values of industrialism;
- a recognition of the rights of future generations in our use of all resources;
- an emphasis on socially useful, personally rewarding work, enhanced by human-scale technology;
- protection of the environment as a precondition of a healthy society;
- an emphasis on personal growth and spiritual development;
- respect for the gentler side of human nature;
- open, participatory democracy at every level of society;
- recognition of the crucial importance of significant reductions in population levels;
- harmony between people of every race, colour, and creed;
- a non-nuclear, low-energy strategy, based on conservation, greater efficiency, and renewable sources;
- an emphasis on self-reliance and decentralised communities.

(Jonathon Porritt, *Seeing Green*)

A cursory glance at the list will show that one area may be profoundly disturbing to those who uphold another. What, for instance, is the implication for poorer countries of 'significant reduction in population levels' and its *moral* relationship to 'harmony between people of every race'? These things still need to be resolved and whilst environmental ideas have currency in the United Kingdom, few ordinary people know exactly what they can do to save the ozone layer, recycle old rubbish, and save the rain forests. The lowest level of expression of these ideas was John Major's call in the 1990s for a 'more caring society', a 'Citizen's Charter' and 'Back to Basics'.

All this is the general scenario of futurology as it has developed since the 1970s, been refined and focused in the market-led 1980s and reconsidered in the 'caring', 'new world order' of the 1990s. Here the battle is for the perceptual space of the individual. No more power to the worker, politics is now a project reserved not for national governance but for a personal destiny based within a supposedly 'sensible' self-imposed restriction of consumption in a world dominated by increasingly sophisticated technologies. How does this specifically relate to the future of British culture and arts?

James Robertson in 1985 saw 'miniaturisation [as] now the frontier of society' and this to be understood as referring not only to technology but also to the way computerisation had disaggregated white-collar workers, creating a workforce of more isolated workers who were compensated by a feeling of greater individual autonomy and freedom of action. And yet computerisation did not lessen the workload for those at their desks – it merely changed the rate of information handled. Yet these changes did mean that more diffuse patterns of labour had begun to appear amongst the middle classes and this added (alongside the economic fluctuations between 1979 and the early 1990s) a level of unpredictability hitherto unknown amongst professionals.

Jane McLoughlin in *The Demographic Revolution* supported the idea that demographic changes would create a society whose workforce was more self-reliant and, perhaps, (seen with no irony) more 'trained'. The demographic change which would dramatically increase the number of women in the workplace would also bring a crisis in the perception of gender roles, for 'now men and women alike [were] poised on the brink of fundamental change'. Most seriously, 'the demographic revolution [of the last quarter of the twentieth century was] the first female-led opportunity to refashion the workplace', leading to a 'feminization of the workplace'. The crisis inherent in McLoughlin's analysis surfaced, as we have seen, in the gender concerns of Robert Bly.

The changes in cultural needs for the twenty-first century will be driven, if McLoughlin's analysis is correct, by a rise in the power of women, a considerable expansion of the middle-aged and elderly population and an absolute decline (by over one million) in the youth population. For McLoughlin this will lead to a 'mature' society based on 'realism'. Such a conclusion, however, needs further investigation.

Youth has dominated our lifestyle since the sixties. Fashion, entertainment, even the lay-out of our high street shops, are geared to attract young people. This goes deeper than the outward paraphernalia of sex and drugs and rock and roll. Youth culture has for years permeated the way the middle-aged feel about themselves, their growing sense of failure as they grow older because they could not stay young for ever, resentment that at what they feel is their peak they are perceived at work as over the hill. Millions of middle-aged women have accepted without question that they should sacrifice their own work interests to serve the paramount interests of youth by putting their children first, and finding an identity through them if they can. Men and women alike have denied the sum of their experience in favour of thinking and looking as young as possible. It has not been the young who dreamed the impossible dream, but the thirty-somethings.

(Jane McLoughlin, *The Demographic Revolution*)

By the late 1990s, growth in the 'over-forty' population had, relative to youth culture, begun to create a culture of its own. Certainly, such a culture set down roots in the early 1980s and had expanded to embrace everything from insurance and private health care, to security systems, car purchasing and tourism. Older people, and especially older, economically liberated, women now expected fashion and glamour to reflect their needs and the power of their pocket.

Liberated by 1960s feminism, their own income and a confidence in their own power, 1980s British women flocked to watch 'the Chippendales', male bodybuilders who stripteased. These male strippers, banned by law from displaying an erection (sign of male sexual dominance and aggression), were the fantasy objects of women who enjoyed such displays without having their own sexual identity threatened. This was safe sex with a vengeance, one result, although unexpected, of feminism's moral distaste for masculine pornography and the fear of actual rape or sexual attack. Thus contained, male power was neutralised as female amusement. Containment and control were, despite the hysteria of the audience, the key points of a Chippendale show.

Further changes were also to be expected,

> The old and middle-aged will thus become the target market of those lifestyle trendsetters, the advertisers and the commercial people, of architectural planning, of entertainment. . . . Added to that, at the end of the century the first wave of career women launched by the Women's Movement will be gathering their harvest of occupational pensions and investments.
>
> (McLoughlin, ibid.)

However, whilst there has been relative growth in this area, youth culture, though in decline, has certainly found enough resilience and identity to retain a potent voice. If anything, the allure of permanent youth holds even greater appeal to those about to lose it.

Whilst McLoughlin highlighted the important growth in the mature population, the economic power of the 'forty-something' generation (the products of the baby boom, who were children in the early 1960s, teenagers in the middle 1960s, observers of the drug and hippy scene, recipients of 'the pill' and students in the 1970s) has increased. In the early 1990s, this generation was bringing up a young (school-age) family. They were far wealthier (relatively) than their parents and had high expectations. Family responsibility, high mortgages (having bought in the buoyant market of the 1980s before the economic slump), a need for greater levels of insurance and private security (with a declining welfare system), high consumer expectations (especially with technological goods) mixed with a relatively insecure job market, threats of redundancy (against a decline in saving) and fears about their children's future, have meant that this generation became more conservative, more private and more insular.

Products of the welfare state, this generation rejected 'bureaucracy' when at school as part of the individualistic revolt of youth (the 'pill' added to this sense of freedom). It is hardly surprising that the idealism of many sixties teenagers was individualistic, self-expressive and yet directed to conservative ends; economic well-being begins with individual self-determination. The 'hippy' mentality no less than the 'working-class' skinhead movement of the very late 1960s contained an element of rejection of all state practices. Skinhead conservatism with its vague nationalism, racism, authoritarianism and emphasis on manual labour (the dark opposition for hippies) nevertheless moved (as families grew up in Basildon, Harlow and Milton Keynes) towards a far less vehement authoritarianism and towards a belief in market forces and the image of a strong economic (and military) Britain. The C2 voters (so-called 'Essex man') who put Margaret Thatcher and John Major into Downing Street voted in a strange and yet continuing political alliance with those middle-class ex-hippy teenagers who were looking for greater wealth through self-determination and who had little faith in the system or its guardians. Alternatively, the 'yuppy' factor, based on the attitudes and lifestyles of a relatively small group of early to mid-twenty-year-olds enjoying the 1980s boom in the property and financial markets, has been a short-lived phenomenon compared to the 'deep' culture which appeared in the 1960s and matured between the 1980s and the 1990s.

The conservatism of the now 'forty-to fifty-something' generation will show itself most conspicuously in ironic nostalgia for its lost rebelliousness. As contemporary youth has moved away from the recognisable pop music culture which was the foundation of the sixties generation so the older generation has moved closer to its roots, creating for Raymond Williams, as for Jane McLoughlin, 'a culture of nostalgia' and quietism.

It is a generalization that we grow more conservative and intolerant as we age. If this is so, do we inevitably face a period of moral repression?

Certainly there will be strong pressures for more censorship of
anarchic ideas, of the sexually explicit, of artistic experimentation.

But our older generation in the 1990s are not Victorians. Those
who were young in the sixties were a fundamentally liberal generation. . . . It comes down to a question of who pays the piper. If
theatre, the cinema, art, literature, television and other media are
technically uncensored, the preferences of the audiences may tend
to act as a brake on innovation. Those preferences are rooted in
the cultural climate of their youth. . . . That nostalgic frisson per-
vades popular entertainment as well as advertising, and this may well
have implications for what we see on our screens and stages in
the 1990s.

(Williams, Towards 2000)

The growth of horror films in the 1990s and *Back to the Future* 'if only'
movies and television shows of the 1980s suggested a period of conservatism, as did the extraordinary success of British films such as *Four
Weddings and a Funeral*, *The English Patient* and *Shakespeare in Love*. It is
no surprise that the revival of D. H. Lawrence's work in the 1960s with
its liberationist sexual message was replaced in the 1990s with the
conservative traditionalist revival of the work of Jane Austen (especially
in film) and the rise of British film star Hugh Grant.

It will not come as a surprise to readers that Raymond Williams's
study in futurology, *Towards 2000*, began, in effect, with a long analysis
of the 1960s. Published in 1983 during a period of unqualified decline
in socialist political thought and activity, and viewed against the background of Thatcherite policies, this book exists more as a *cri de coeur*
than a sustained argument. Like many Marxist philosophers, Williams
saw capitalism in constant and 'endless crisis' of which the 'current
crisis' was just the latest.

In his analysis of 'post-industrial' Britain (a term he firmly rejected)
Williams was concerned to reassert a traditional Marxist model against
those models proposed by post-modernists, whether of the right or the
left. Nevertheless, such a reassertion had considerable theoretical draw-
backs as it centred debate upon increasingly marginal areas, even if, at
a glance, they still seemed indispensable elements. Thus,

the point of entry for analysis, either of the fundamental nature
of the industrial revolution or the severe crisis of industrial society
which we are now beginning to experience, is the idea of *employment*.

(Williams, ibid.)

This classic formulation grounded Williams's analysis of culture within the conditions governing economic well-being. Yet economic well-being need not be predicated on the problems of unemployment. Williams's model essentially related to the conditions governing economic well-being in the 1930s. Unemployment in the 1980s and 1990s had been accepted (even by many of those out of work!) as a necessary condition of anti-inflationary activity and therefore economic growth. Even given the extraordinary unemployment of the early Thatcher years, no social upheaval or revolutionary activity took place. The aggressive defeat of an unpopular tax ('the community charge') which united all sectors of the population, was a revolt against a particularly distasteful piece of legislation and not against the totality of Thatcherite politics (including privatisation of those industries which began their decline in the 1930s and were nationalised after the Second World War).

Williams's concern that work should not just be associated with employment seems wholly peripheral when the idea of the 'dignity of labour' was so outdated (and has never had any meaning for the modern worker in the south of England and London). Equally, such an analysis was bound to concern itself with '*forces* of production' and '*relations* of production' yet it everywhere ignored the condition of consumption and the perceptual space of the consuming citizen. This essential shift from humans as makers (however 'alienated') to humans (in the wealthy West) as consumers is hardly represented in the Marxist lexicon. Moreover it directly relates to the notion of employment *for wages* (Marxist 'wage labour').

Credit systems deferred debt infinitely and stretched money. Such purchasing power had never before been enjoyed by the working population of Britain and it increased the power of consumption *over* labour and production and emphasised the relationship (always known by the wealthy) between culture and money. Whether unemployed or employed, the ordinary person was shielded to a far greater degree than his or her ancestors from the horrors of the workhouse or the 'degradation' of the pawnshop (despite high levels of personal bankruptcy and mortgage default in the early 1990s). Unlike the age of Micawber, where debt was misery untold, the modern age became the age of debt, and money as actual cash was infinitely deferred and replaced by credit. This had consequences for both knowledge and culture.

By the 1980s, the classic socialist view of *exploitation* could only be properly applied to the growth of 'have nots', without political or economic power, who were beyond the help of the welfare state, and who were disliked by the employed working class and vilified as 'seaside scroungers' by the popular press. In the late 1990s, they were shown as dirty 'New Age travellers' by *all* of the press and television. This one estranged sector had apparently been expunged from the decision-making process, far more effectively than the attempts to undermine working-class solidarity. The employed working class in the south were Thatcherite before Thatcher.

Williams continues,

> There are very few absolute contrasts left between a 'minority culture' and 'mass communications'. . . . The privileged institutions of minority culture, bearers of so much serious and important work, have for many years been fighting a losing battle against the powerful pressures of a capitalist-sponsored culture. This is the most evident source of cultural pessimism. But its deeper source is a conviction that there is *nothing but the past to be won.* This is because, for other reasons, there is a determined refusal of any genuinely alternative social and cultural order. This is so in theory, in the determined objections to new forms of democracy or socialism.
>
> (Williams, ibid.)

Even Internet jokes shared the nostalgia Williams noted, as well as Williams's own nostalgia for a traditional explanation of the capitalist system, hence,

> This little boy goes to his dad and asks, 'What is politics?' Dad says, 'Well son, let me try to explain it this way: I'm the breadwinner of the family, so let's call me Capitalism. Your mom, she's the administrator of the money, so we'll call her the Government. We're here to take care of your needs, so we'll call you the People. The nanny, we'll consider her the Working Class. And your baby brother, we'll call him the Future. Now, think about that and see if that makes sense.' So the little boy goes off to bed thinking about what Dad has said. Later that night, he hears his baby brother crying, so he gets up to check on him. He finds that the baby has severely soiled his diaper. So the little boy goes to his parents' room and finds his mother sound asleep. Not wanting to wake her, he goes to the nanny's room. Finding the door locked, he peeks in the keyhole and sees his father in bed with the nanny. He gives up and goes back to bed. The next morning, the little boy says to his father, 'Dad, I think that I understand the concept of politics now.' The father says, 'Good son, tell me in your own words what you think politics is all about.' The little

boy replies, 'Well, while Capitalism is screwing the Working Class, the Government is sound asleep, the People are being ignored and the Future is in deep shit.'

What this all seems to prove is that late twentieth-century capitalism is even more virulent, exploitative and nasty than its earlier incarnation. Those who oppose it on behalf of high culture, do so for outdated and conservative reasons. Those who wish to create a new socialist cultural order have not thought things through. In both scenarios, modern capitalism divides and rules.

This profound *failure* in the very heart of cultural life had, for Williams, been caused by the continuing and increasing alliance between money and the arts, all tending, through sponsorship or inertia, towards a backward-looking conservatism. Newspapers and television, the life-blood of a popular mass culture (which Williams saw as the only viable modern culture) were themselves victims of monopoly capitalist manipulation by powerful owners (such as Rupert Murdoch and the discredited Robert Maxwell) and state-sponsored media art. Everything seemed infected with the contradictory cultural values of conservative traditionalism and corporate rapaciousness.

> This is where corporate production and official minority art now embrace, in the form of old displaced pieties and the resigned and accomodating versions of war, cold war, exploitation and arrogant wealth.
>
> (Williams, ibid.)

The state of culture in Britain seemed irreversibly dominated by the capitalist mandarins in a way even more disastrous than a hundred years before. Williams's last chapter, entitled 'Resources for a Journey of Hope' clung, nevertheless, to the transformational message of feminism, ecological concern and personal politics. In such a way, Williams believed late capitalism could be challenged: even returning to a more 'national' culture opposed to the internationalism and Americanism he disliked. Communist Russia still held promise of a, possibly, more equitable future.

Having recognised a 'new' relationship between consumption, knowledge, financial circulation and mass culture, Williams could not reconcile these processes, although he recognised the decline of the older forms. For Williams, as for the American 'guru' Alvin Toffler at the other extreme of the political spectrum, the age was one of crisis. But continuity was also strong amongst large sectors of the traditional British middle and working classes. Indeed, as one social survey pointed out:

> Britain is a nation in which appearances, social perceptions and traditional values count for a great deal.... The values that characterize British society are not derived from any single conflict or event representing the birth of the nation, nor are they laid down in a written constitution. For all that, they seem to be at least as robust.
>
> (*British Social Attitudes*, 5th Report)

Not least of the changes that have challenged traditional views was the new wealth of the employed working class, who, whilst they remained loyal to many views expected of their group, had a purchasing power often equal to, or in excess of, the lower middle classes (school teachers, health workers, local government middle management) and lifestyles and expectations which often exceeded in *material terms* those of many of the professional middle classes. This shift towards simple equability of economic power between the classes changed perceptual expectations (Florida became a cheap holiday choice for the AB voter *and* the C2 voter), but did not fundamentally change class relations.

Affluence, especially in the South (despite the depression of the late 1980s and early 1990s, the south of England was still relatively rich compared with a supposedly buoyant northern economy) gave the working class a confidence that meant it moved away from some older notions of working-class identity towards expectations for family, children, home, comfort and travel that were once only available to the middle classes. The important socialist measures of the late 1940s and the political consensus of the 1950s to mid-1970s (with the 'break' announced on 4 September 1974, with Sir Keith Joseph's monetarist speech at Preston) meant that the goals of the active working class were largely fulfilled. The old pride in hard labour began to give way in the 1960s. By the 1980s, young working-class men and women (those in their early twenties) had good wages, good homes (which they began to purchase), good cars and good holidays. This 'loadsa money' attitude (satirised by comedian Harry Enfield), rejected older feelings towards protective collectivised security and for critics such as Tony Parsons represented a new barbarism 'in the long spiritual decline of the working class' in which conservatism and deference (modesty) counted for nothing and where the word 'respect' was a euphemism for fear. Indeed for Parsons,

They are the real class traitors, betrayers of the men who fought the Second World War, those men who fought for Churchill but voted for Clement Attlee. But in the tattooed jungle they have no sense of history. The true unruly children of Thatcherism, they know their place and wallow in their peasanthood.

(*Arena*, September/October 1989)

The struggle of the older working class (with parents and grandparents) had been towards greater *self*-determinism both political and economic. Old age pensions, the National Health Service, educational reforms, trade union power, welfare benefits, nationalisation and even university grants (replaced by a loan system in the 1990s, ironically, by a Labour government) gave the employed working class the self-esteem and power they needed and left them free to pursue a cultural agenda separate from the middle classes towards whose lifestyle (but *not* towards whose perceptual frameworks) they aspired.

The consensus policies of welfare-state capitalism now rebounded. The workers, having gained self-determinism, eventually rejected those organisations that won them this freedom and in so doing had 'shackled' them to new trade union and state bureaucracy. The unparalleled propaganda war in most of the media against these state systems (now no longer seen as liberating but as repressive and archaic) was generally accepted by many working-class voters, as it had been already by many of the affluent *new* middle who had either forgotten their debt to the welfare state or who had bought themselves out of it. Thus public ownership (by all of us collectively) was replaced by privatisation (ownership by all of us *autonomously*). Only the National Health Service (under severe pressure although still highly supported by *all* sectors) survived this redirection of energy. Working-class power was and is based on *purchasing* power: not the right to produce goods, but the capacity to purchase them *in quantity* (i.e. cheaply) and when wanted. Thatcherism allowed them to assert the right to reappropriate their productive capacity in purchased goods and services.

Whilst the majority of voters who voted Labour in the election of 1992 were working class, their expectations amounted to a modification of labourism not a vindication of reinvigorated Thatcherite (conservative) radicalism. The loss of Tory seats was happily (for Conservatives) still accompanied by a fourth term of office *and* an extremely acceptable majority of twenty-six seats in the House of Commons. And yet the seeds of dissolution were already sown. The Social and Community Planning Research Group (SCPR) could already show in 1989 that Thatcherism had penetrated less deeply than the 'revolutionary' Thatcherites suggested.

> True ... the government ... made sweeping changes. But it has so far failed to achieve the revolutionary task that Mrs Thatcher set for herself and her administration, which involved not only the radical reform of many state institutions and their practices, but of British culture itself. The overriding aim was to replace the 'dependency culture' ... by a new 'enterprise culture'....
>
> What might the expected values of such an 'enterprise culture' be? For one thing, the public would surely regard the fruits of business investment and entrepreneurship as a legitimate reward for share-holders and top managers, not (only) for workers and customers. For another, they would support the progressive privatisation of health and of education, as well as cuts in social expenditure generally. They would frown on Keynesian solutions to unemployment, such as job creation. Yet ... only a minority of the public embraces these ideas.
>
> (*British Social Attitudes*)

Conservative Central Office could hardly fail to be aware of this prob-lem despite the euphoria of victory and the predicted demise of Labour. The *Sunday Times* crowed, for example, under an editorial written by Andrew Neil and entitled 'Socialism, RIP',

> In the end, the Tories could not even give it away, though there were times during the campaign when they looked intent on doing just that. But even the worst Tory campaign in living memory coupled with the best Labour one, the longest recession since the war, an election fought largely on Labour issues, lingering resentment about the poll tax and a bungled Tory budget could not secure a Labour victory. With so much working to Labour's advantage, yet the result a fourth Tory term, it is hard to imagine what it would take to give Labour power. The most significant lesson of the general election of 1992 is that, in its present form, Labour is unelectable. Despite four defeats in a row, Labour is still not ready to face up to this.
>
> (*British Social Attitudes*)

John Major's victory had, indeed, seemed amazing given that the pollsters had predicted either a swing of 8 per cent with an outright victory for Labour or a hung parliament with a Labour prime minister. In the event, Major won comfortably.

A caveat in the *Sunday Times* article hinted that this could have been predicted: 'But it could be that the polls were wrong all along and that a Tory defeat was never in prospect'. Ivor Crewe had made such a prediction, based on available evidence as long ago as 1988:

> Only an extraordinary turnaround of votes could bring Labour to office in four years' time. Put it this way: Labour needs a national swing of 6 per cent to win a bare absolute majority: but since 1945 the largest swing at a single election has been 5 per cent, and the largest swing to Labour a mere 3 per cent. Moreover, if the electoral system continues to lose its exaggerative properties, as it has for the past quarter century, the swing required will be larger still. The choice available to the British electorate in 1991–2 is not between a Conservative government and a Labour government, but between a Conservative government and a hung Parliament.
>
> (Crewe, quoted in Skidelsky)

Significantly, 'the working class (as traditionally understood) had become Britain's newest minority'.[1] Indeed,

> manual workers now constitute a mere 45 per cent of the labour force; exclude the self-employed, foremen and supervisors, and they dip to under a third, in the next election they will be outnumbered by the professional and managerial salariat, there will be fewer trade union members than shareholders, and owner occupiers will exceed council tenants by five to two in the electorate and by almost two to one among the working class.
>
> (Ibid.)

And finally, 'the Conservative advance ... has been entirely within the working class' (ibid.). The working classes were not only a minority but a Thatcherite one to boot, according to many observers. Yet they were mistaken, as working-class voting remained traditional and was about to deliver a surprise reminder of that fact.

The 'landslide victory' of the Labour Party in 1997 (179 majority) and the decimation of the Conservatives seemed almost inexplicable. This was not the case, for countervailing pressures on both parties, as well as 'new' thinking in the Labour Party, were making themselves felt. By John Major's second term, it was obvious that the Conservatives were a disunited party; riven by deep and unbreachable differences of opinion over Europe (especially monetary union), the party's wings pulled further apart until disaffection turned to rebellion; challenges to the prime minister's leadership exposed right-wing dislike of government policies; back-bench MPs either refused to toe the party line or simply left; every by-election was lost; the party seemed to be saturated with corrupt politicians on the take (so-called 'sleaze'); the peace process in Ireland had failed. John Major's last-minute personal appeal to the electorate failed to save the government and the party. What was left after all the Tory years was a shattered group which may take until 2007 to be in a position to challenge for government again.[2]

The origins of this change began when John Major took over from Margaret Thatcher and distanced himself from her artisanal zeal (despite her endorsement of him) in order to return to more communal politics.[3]

> He had a feeling for the public weal that repudiated the most famous phrase Mrs Thatcher ever uttered: 'There is no such thing as society'. Major's invention of the Citizen's Charter was an attempt to marry the concepts of the consumer society and customer-driven markets with the provision of services which were always going to be, in his view, public rather than private. . . . The world Major summoned up when speaking from the heart was intensely traditionalist. He liked school uniforms and the three Rs, old regiments and the Great Western Railway, warm beer and a constitution that gave Scotland nothing.
>
> (Dennis Kavanagh, in Dennis Kavanagh and Anthony Seldon)

The Thatcherite new right represented by Michael Portillo, Peter Lilley and John Redwood, were all, in Major's famous jibe, 'Bastards'.

In his anti-right swing to more middle ground, Major 'returned' the political arena to social issues and debates about values, all areas associated with Labour. After disastrously botching Britain's relationship with the ERM (Exchange Rate Mechanism), Major's government had to translate economic success with the home economy (disbelieved after October 1992 by most voters) into perceptual success: 'the feel good factor'. Relations with Europe and the question of European monetary union were less questions about financial arrangements than coded questions about national sovereignty and communal cohesion (and independence). In other words, economic issues had become social and moral issues more suited to Labour governmental policy. Major's shift back to traditional conservatism (as represented by Ian Gilmour) seemed a shift towards a middle ground of democratic socialism. His own disastrous fall in opinion polls signalled that the general public wanted a modified Thatcher with vision and morality, not a 'weak' and 'incompetent' leader and *not* a return to Thatcherite 'enterprise' zeal with social institutions.

The change is dramatically illustrated by the changing opinions of the conservative working-class and middle-class readers of Rupert Murdoch's papers:

> The largest falls in Conservative support between the 1992 election and 1993 occurred among readers of the Murdoch tabloids – *Today* (minus 17 per cent), *The Sun* (minus 16 per cent) and the *Daily Star* (minus 16 per cent) – while the smallest falls (of 7–8 per cent) occurred among readers of the non-Conservative *Mirror, Guardian* and *Independent*. It was notable that the drop off in Conservative support was smallest among readers of the *Daily Express*, the one Tory tabloid to stick steadfastly by the Government – and John Major. 'It was the Sun Wot Won It' crowed *The Sun* after the 1992 election. Two years later it was demonstrating that what Murdoch giveth he can also taketh away.
>
> (Kavanagh, ibid.)

By 1996 Rupert Murdoch had had meetings with Tony Blair, now leader of Labour, an unheard-of situation but one indicative of the new alliance between *business* and labour. It also heralded the necessary shift Labour had to make from the left to show itself able to protect the working class *and* middle class from the *excesses* of enterprise culture whilst encouraging entrepreneurial culture within a semi-protective governmental umbrella. Thatcherite changes would remain, Thatcherite mentality would not. In this Major represented an unexpected bridge back to socialism, but now socialism devoid of socialist principles. At its most extreme it can be claimed that

> Labour is now in many respects a party of European social democracy. It speaks cautiously on public spending and taxes, has abandoned unilateralism, accepted many of the changes in industrial relations, is steadily weakening its connections with the trade unions and has given up on public ownership. The leadership's rhetoric now invokes 'consumers' or 'citizens' not 'workers'. Socialism, on the rare occasions that the word is uttered, is not about public ownership but about supply side socialism, diffusing power, giving people more choice and freedom. Labour is now virtually the catch-all social

democratic party that the revisionists sought to promote after 1959, the party that the Social Democrats wanted to become.

(Kavanagh, ibid.)

Meanwhile a ruthless policy of 'modernisation' within the Labour Party itself, commenced by Neil Kinnock and John Smith (d. 1995), culminated in centrally directed change under the leadership of Tony Blair: clause 4 (the party pledge to public ownership of production, introduced by Sidney Webb) was dropped; the left wing was ostracised; the market was embraced as socialist ideas were ditched or modified; alliances were made with the city and capital; promises of low taxation (high taxation was Labour's fatal flaw) were aimed at the middle classes; decentralisation and federalism looked both to Scottish and Welsh devolution (limited assemblies) and European unity; constitutional change was to prepare the way for a radical curb to the House of Lords.

This double movement, Tory decline and Labour revival, matched to the generally felt 'need for a change' helps explain Labour's overwhelming victory and Conservatism's defeat. Just as Thatcherism stole the rhetoric of old Labourism and reinvented it as a new Liberalism, so the Labour Party learnt its lesson and reinvented itself as the party of middle England and stability, stealing in its turn the language of a certain Conservatism.

The breakdown of consensus politics which followed the economic depression and social upheaval of the late 1960s led to governments determined less by traditional party allegiance and more by a need to preserve government as an apparatus *between* party and people. As the representative and the executive of the state, governments (and especially cabinets) have progressively separated from a political and parliamentary base. Acting as a subversive authoritarian irritant to her party, Mrs Thatcher made herself into a party of *one*, opposed as much to traditional Conservatism as to old-style Labour. She effectively abrogated power to herself (as her most effective and only security) and when she could no longer control that power she found herself at the mercy of the party. Thus power existed less and less in the 'party machine' and more and more accrued to the person of the Prime Minister.

Thatcherism was, of necessity, an abrogation of power and a centralisation and accumulation of that power at the top. The ideology of individual endeavour actually weakened all other positions (through the devolution of privatisation) but effectively revitalised opposition from positions not at the centre of the state. Blairite Labourism learned the lesson well: the encouragement of devolution, nationalism and

federalism alongside the attack on traditional privilege appeared democratic but, in effect, damaged those discrete units and limited their
power in relation to the central state. The policies of national and
federal devolution were intended to ensure Labour power in those areas
rather than offer them some well-deserved autonomy.

Indeed, autonomy will precisely put areas in the clutches of big
government when resources are limited and ensure loyalty without
burdensome cost to the centre. The concentration of government
power is *increased* not lessened by this dependency of the periphery and
strengthens the hand of the prime minister. Authoritarian centralism
was bound to follow consensus as a reaction to it and its failed political
will. That will is more and more centralised in cabinet under prime
ministerial orders, effectively removing the real ideological differences
that once separated Conservatives and Labour. Blair's 'third way' was
no less than this *non-political* centralisation which has operated within
party politics but which is a pressure from without. Blair's concept of
the individual and their responsibilities (rather than rights) is closer to
Thatcher than to the idea of the community as espoused by traditional
Labour or Conservative thinking. It is no coincidence that Tony Blair
(a child of the 1960s, a Thatcher success in the 1980s and Prime Minister
at 43 in 1997) should have declared himself an admirer of the 'Iron Lady'.

For older traditional left-wing social and cultural critics these
changes, and the collapse of world communism, had left them not only
powerless but relatively speechless. Raymond Williams, as we have
seen, could show the decline in left fortunes (although he could hardly
believe it) but could suggest little to change the course of events, except
a wishful hope. Stuart Hall could offer little to compensate left activism
and Terry Eagleton was forced into a moral tone reminiscent of the
Leavises whom he had done so much previously to debunk. Of Tony
Benn, the radical left's most famous parliamentarian, little was heard
and for Arthur Scargill, leader of the disastrous miners' strike of 1984
and the left's most vociferous trade unionist, there was only defeat and
humiliation (made deeper by his marginalisation within the Labour
movement).[4]

The old left was thus routed not merely by the outdated nature of its
rhetoric, academicism and mystique of labour but it was also severely
discomfited by its own intellectual fights with post-structural theory
and with feminism. It is no coincidence that Eagleton's 1984 book
The Function of Criticism was dedicated to Toril Moi, a radical feminist
whose views, in the totality of a feminist vision, could only be *opposed*
to the economic and governmental politics of class antagonism.

Furthermore, left-wing feminist critics could not sufficiently reconcile the history of man's own oppression of women to man's aggressive relationship with man in the class struggle. Sorority opposed economic fraternity. Beatrix Campbell in her study of the unemployed in 1980s Wigan, whilst savage about George Orwell and his patronising and patriarchal brand of upper middle-class socialism, nevertheless was quite unable to offer a programme of *economic* reform consistent with gender affirmation. Her final paragraphs accept the defeat of a revolution that never happened and suggest instead,

> Most importantly, the radicals within the working class I met were mostly women; they were the most reflective and imaginative, it was they who affirmed democratic ways of working, it was they who affirmed egalitarianism, it is they who are on the move, and it is they who are being transformed by their own experience of change. The men's movement seems not to have noticed. Orwell's socialism comes out of a tradition that hasn't and won't represent women. If the men's movement is to cooperate with these women, then it must look to itself and put the reform of men on its political agenda. That is the condition of women's creative cooperation with the men's movement.
>
> (Campbell, *Wigan Pier Revisited*)

Ultimately the left could not properly predict nor account for the forms of power their opponents now commanded. Yet on the right things faired better.

The traditional establishment right is not quite what is meant here; Margaret Thatcher herself confirmed that with her hatred of 'Wets' (traditional public school-educated consensus politicians). She rooted them out. The Conservative Party itself was in transition. One index of change was in the education of its constituency representatives; of 336 Tory MPs, 47 per cent or 159 MPs had been to state schools. Moreover, almost one-third of MPs (32 per cent) or 106 MPs called themselves 'businessmen': such changes reflected and followed the rethinking of Conservatism in the 1970s. Two people exemplify this change: Keith Joseph and Bernard Ingham.

Leading this rethinking process was the Centre for Policy Studies headed by Keith Joseph, whose seminal 1974 speech had given Thatcher her intellectual creed. Joseph, son of a Jewish society family, whose head had been Lord Mayor of London, was a keen intellectual, and he rose quickly through Tory ranks (anti-Semitism seemed not to have been a handicap below prime ministerial level) but lacked the charisma or drive for ultimate office. His importance lies in the creation of a Conservative 'think tank'. In the light of what we shall see about Bernard Ingham it is not surprising that Joseph schooled himself in economic theory with a converted Marxist: Alfred Sherman. The result, as already mentioned, was the Centre for Policy Studies.

> The aim of the CPS was to get at the fairly small number of people who influence the thinking of a nation. It was comparable to the Fabian Society, almost a century earlier, which had changed the British intellectual climate sufficiently to make socialism acceptable, working through the educated classes. The major task of the CPS was to make market economics acceptable in a society that had for years taken a measure of socialism, or at least of state intervention in the economy, for granted.
>
> (Morrison Halcrow, *Keith Joseph*)

Joseph's intellectual drive was matched by the conviction politics of Bernard Ingham, a civil servant, who as Thatcher's press officer became her 'Rasputin'. Ingham was the first media civil servant, an arch and highly successful lobby manipulator who, alongside Tim Bell, gave Thatcher her distinctive 'edge' and tone.[5]

Ingham had been born in Hebden Bridge, Yorkshire, of a working-class weaver family. His father had been a passionate Labour councillor and council leader and after leaving school (and missing university) his son had become a local reporter. Ingham rose to become a loyal civil servant to Barbara Castle, but growing trade union power and the personality of his next minister, Tony Benn, made him reassess his Labour roots. Thus he emerged as a passionate socialist who felt the voice of the working man was that of Mrs Thatcher.[6] Indeed, 'he did not merely speak for Thatcher, he out Thatchered Thatcher', as Robert Harris makes clear,

> Whatever else he was, he was not Tory. But then – and this is what finally convinced him he should take the job – *neither was she*. Thatcher, like Ingham, had been born without privileges. She had never quite lost the aura of an outsider. She did not want to conserve Britain's institutions: she wanted to abolish a lot of them, or shake them up, or dismantle them. She was not a member of the Establishment. She was suspicious of it. She thought it had gone soft and let the country down. With all of this, and especially with her conviction

that an economic recovery depended on a reduction in trade union power, Ingham was in full agreement. 'I think I'll do it,' he confided to one colleague. 'The thing is: we're both radicals.'

(*Good and Faithful Servant*)

Ingham's politically canny musings and bluff Yorkshire common sense were part of a spectrum of views to engage on the right. Not only were there those of already established right-wing intellectuals nor only those of the common-sense school of lower middle-class thinkers such as Roger Scruton whose (Peterhouse Group) *Salisbury Review* was both nationalist, élitist and traditionalist, but also radical right writers such as Julie Burchill, who alongside her husband Cosmo Landesman and journalist Toby Young began *The Modern Review*, dedicated to the serious study of popular culture, anti the literary establishment, very much pro market forces and 1980s consciousness. Even so they too employed a Marxist writer occasionally. Thus the right formed a spectrum from the highbrow to the popular, from the public-school intellectual to the working-class intellectual.

To counter the political power and ideological hegemony of the Thatcherite notion of Conservatism it was necessary for thinkers on the left to revise left-wing paradigms using Thatcheristic propositions about empowerment and self-responsibility: to think through new rightism into a new left space. The central problem was how to create a coherent model of left-wing empowerment that did not diminish the intellectual gains of the 1980s right-wing think tanks but which *modified* them in such a way as to retain the concepts of individualism and capital whilst turning these to a left-wing advantage. It was essential to retain belief in self-empowerment and individualistic choice but to reinvent individuals as Labour-orientated agents: active participants in charge once the right-wing new deal of 1979 had ground to a halt ten years later. This was a matter of rhetoric and reinterpretation as well as reorientation.[7]

Seizing the opportunities offered by monetarist rhetoricians, Labour thinkers began not to talk of capitalism but of markets; not of communism but of community; not of labour but of stakeholders; not of redistribution of wealth but of fairness; not of the poor but the 'have nots' and disempowered; not of nationalisation and public ownership but of responsibility; and nowhere of class division at all. Old socialism had to go. But what was old socialism? Labour thinkers now disavowed the Marxist tradition of British socialism in favour of the *traditions* of Christian Socialism and communalism.

The starting point of non-Labour establishment left thinking began with the truism that British culture was in a deep malaise amounting at worst to a crisis in the body politic. For Peter Hain,

> This is a society, if not in clichéd 'crisis', then incontrovertibly in deep structural trouble. The next generation is going to be morally and socially poorer. And economically too. Now that the cushion of North Sea Oil revenues and privatisation proceeds has deflated, there is no other way forward than to make a break with the suffocating conventional wisdom of Thatcherite and post-Thatcherite economics; it is time to overturn a long tradition of failure, systemic to Britain.
>
> Under-producing corporate Britain, militaristic industrial Britain, over-indebted household Britain, parasitic financial Britain, impoverished public Britain and inept governmental Britain – this is a recipe for long term disaster. It cries out for a socialist alternative.
>
> *(Ayes to the Left)*

The millennial and apocalyptic ring was itself part of a political and cultural refrain that emerged at the end of the nineteenth century and again in the early years of the twentieth. Then, of course, it was the right under pressure from 'bolshevism' not the left under pressure from a 'bolshie' Thatcherite version of Conservatism. In both cases it was traditional culture that was under threat: the British organic community.

For Hain, despite its democratic credentials, British culture was still highly élitist and highly exploitative and this had been exacerbated by the changes of the 1980s. Thatcherism effectively reinforced the power of the state and its institutions. To combat this Hain proposed a 'devolutionary' model based neither on monetarist state consolidation (a paradox of the 1980s) nor Marxist–Leninist statism (as inherent in old Labour). This devolutionary model was itself inherited from an older 'dominant' Labour tradition of communalism and co-operation where the state (i.e. government) was (just as with Thatcher and Reagan) diminished to the level of a regulatory body. Wealth would have to be redistributed, inequality of race and sex dealt with and privilege abandoned by a decentralised government still able to 'direct'. In such a model local markets would be preserved (as opposed to *big* capital) and individual agency restored, avoiding 'Americanisation' and US individualism whilst based on a mixture of 'market' freedom, individual equibility and a more socially coherent community. The mechanisms, however, were far from clear and at worst sounded like the Soviet model before Stalinism, even though Hain was at pains to distance himself from collectivism. The role of the government too was far from clear as, just as with Thatcherism, it would have to be constantly on its guard to legislate, 'facilitate' (Hain's term) and proscribe.

> Without decentralisation of power, not just individual liberty but also social equality is impossible. No ground should be surrendered in the quest for a broadly egalitarian society. On the contrary, economic justice and the greatest possible social equality is impossible unless each citizen has the power – at work, in the home, in the neighbourhood, over services, as a consumer – to demand it for herself or himself.
>
> In place of the limited form of democracy inherent in the British system, the objective should be to create a 'participatory democracy' in which there is the greatest possible involvement of citizens. This will require two principal changes: making representatives much more accountable; and decentralising decision-making as far as is compatible with wider interests. It will also involve not just the democratisation of government but the whole of society. . . . Participatory opportunities and localisation of power should therefore spread into every area of social activity. . . .
>
> Effective decentralisation will require concentrations of private ownership and wealth to be broken up and spread more evenly throughout the population. It will mean national redistribution of resources from prosperous to poor regions of the country, from the suburbs to the inner cities, from the dominant to the subordinate classes, from rich to poor, from men to women, from whites to blacks and from able to disabled. There will need to be nationally established minimum levels of public provision. Minimum levels should be set for housing provision, public-transport subsidies, social services, nursery schools, day-care facilities, home helps and so on.
>
> (Hain, ibid.)

This 'new' socialism which itself was a 'return' to the *real tradition* of British socialist belief was essentially a *moral* set of concepts, just as Thatcherism had been. Hain opposed the moral imperative of new Labour to the immorality of the Thatcher years: Thatcherism was the morality of evil and greed. Both views, however, opposed mere instrumentalism.

Official Labour Party doctrine is better represented by Will Hutton, whose book *The State We're In* offered a blueprint for power by wresting both power and rhetoric from the right. In this, Hutton could not have failed but to be mindful of the influence exacted over the book by the Social Democrats of the 1980s, themselves breakaway 'right-wing' Labour members. Indeed, Social Democrat David Marquand's *The Unprincipled Society* (1988) could not have failed to be an influence in its identification of 'social and intellectual factors' for Britain's 'lagging competiveness' and 'adjustment problems' nor in its assertion that 'behaviour cannot be studied . . . in isolation from beliefs and *traditions*' [emphasis added]. Writing in *The Observer* (for which Hutton was editor) Marquand praised Hutton's 'optimism' and 'awesome' 'creativity' (a quote used on Hutton's paperback revised edition). Hutton's approach was to put the economic structure first and look at instrumental ways of improving it. For him the problem was one of mechanics, 'the case [was] technical rather than ideological'. Morality flowed from this proposition and a proper communal ethic could only return if the economic solution of Labour was applied. Instead of Thatcher's enterprise/ownership economy, the so-called shareholder market, Hutton proposed '*stake*holder capitalism', a proposal neither properly Thatcherite nor old socialist. Not the demolition of capital but its regulation was now the issue (a conceptual model reminiscent of Labour in 1945) but this no longer meant full public ownership of industrial production (clause 4 of the Labour Party's constitution).

The 'deep changes' in the deepest parts of the British psyche brought about by recent Conservative governments (crisis theory again) would only be cured by a wholesale demolition of 'the City' and 'gentlemanly capitalism' and the institutional branches of privilege and the establishment. In this Hutton sounded suspiciously like Thatcher, who hated the 'Wets' (public-school gentlemen), but unlike Thatcher, Hutton's distaste had far different consequences – not enterprise culture but a culture of shared responsibility (to replace gentlemanly patronage). To root out 'fundamental amorality' it would be necessary to tackle the ethical vacuum in the 'moral economy' brought about by *laissez-faire* attitudes. Only this would avoid 'explosive levels of stress' as Hutton put it.

Hutton's solution was a radical *republicanisation* and *federalisation* of the economy, beginning with the Bank of England redesigned on American lines:

> If it became a social partner in the republican sense, running monetary policy impartially with a democratic awareness of the trade-offs between lost output and lower inflation, the presumption would be that it would gain independence along US lines. With new

constitutional arrangements there would, finally, be a way of ensuring its democratic accountability.

(Will Hutton, *The State We're In*)

To suggest such a move broke the old Labour hostility to American ideology and at the same time strengthened the market and those that *regulated* it: the gentlemen became responsible citizens! Thus (at the time when the monarchy was under extreme pressure) 'republicanism of finance and the democratisation of welfare [were] intertwined.'

American-style finance arrangements could, Hutton believed, be aligned to welfare state-ism and traditional Labour taxation policy, hence:

The vitality of the welfare state is a badge of the healthy society; it is a symbol of our capacity to act together morally, to share and to recognise the mutuality of rights and obligations that underpins all human association. It is an expression of social citizenship.

(Hutton, ibid.)

The Labour Party, once it came to power in 1997, kept Hutton's first promise and quietly forgot the taxation of the middle classes which Hutton had proposed. Was Britain to be a United States of Britain with a federal government and a welfare state attached? Old Labour was finally dead – socialist no more.

Part II
And our Friends are all Aboard: Literary Culture

The critics of England and the authors of England are unrivalled as a body, and hence it becomes impossible to find fault with them.
William Makepeace Thackeray, *The Book of Snobs*

3
1910 was a Good Year: Connoisseurs and Book Lists

I

In 1910, Edward VII died, the Post-Impressionist Exhibition came to London and *The Bookseller*, trade paper of the literary *industry*, went weekly. Edward's death and the Post-Impressionist Exhibition seemed, by a strange coincidence, to open the way to a new modernity: the Georgian literary accession. The weekly appearance of *The Bookseller* marked a new vitality in the literary industry: the emergence of fiction as *the central* literary commodity of the pre-First World War period. Indeed, *The Bookseller* seems to have gone weekly precisely because of the dramatic increase in authors of fiction.

> By 1910, fiction advertisements largely surpassed the advertisements for new editions of classics...which had diminished greatly. The advertisements of the 1900 editions were dominated by...Victorian classics or other older work. The increase in the popularity of the sixpenny novels and other cheap editions...marked the gradual heightening of the popularity of fiction, particularly current fiction.
>
> (Elyse Deeb, unpublished research)

This extraordinary increase in the commercial power of fiction (and in particular *new* novels, rather than reprints), and its accompanying increase in new readerships and markets, was to have far-reaching effects on literary sensibility and general cultural taste. The new critical sensitivity cannot be understood except against this new broadening of fiction's remit and the essentially *anarchic, commercial, contemporary* publication of the novel. Both *The Bookseller* and literary critics tried to make sense of the changes that occurred during 1910. One anonymous critic had earlier lamented in *The Bookseller* about the ruinous levels of bad fiction being published and reviewed '[when] the taste of readers must be ... blunted and deteriorated by the amount of fiction inflicted on them'.

For Virginia Woolf looking back from the promontory of the mid-1920s, 1910 saw a division in literary taste (and therefore cultural percept-iveness). Her two camps, the Edwardians and the Georgians, were repres-ented by H. G. Wells, Arnold Bennett and John Galsworthy on the one hand and E. M. Forster, D. H. Lawrence, Lytton Strachey, James Joyce and T. S. Eliot on the other: materialists versus spiritualists, realists ver-sus real artists – Victorianism versus modernity itself. 'In or about December 1910 human character changed', she famously tells us. For Woolf, it was artistic sensibility and acumen that was at stake. The work of the Edwardian authors was finally a flawed and failed enterprise. The Edwardian serious (and popular) novel failed (for Woolf) both because of its social content and its structural imperatives (its non-holistic form). The novel of ideas was, in the strictest sense, no longer a novel at all. Wells and his colleagues were all hybrid essayists.

In an age of experimental psychology, an age, in other words, *neurotic*, Woolf could lament (and that ironically) the loss of an earlier period's wider literary field. For that loss was the price paid for discrimination in an age that had gone beyond complacency. The field could never be full again, critics could never be innocent again, reading would never again be indolent. Victorian taste becomes a type of somnabulism from which modernity had awoken, wiser and *older*.

For Woolf, the proper stuff of art was the fleeting 'reality' and flux of the ordinary but her famous phrase concerning 'an ordinary mind on an ordinary day' had little in it other than a reconfiguration of what she rejected in the Edwardians. The new experimentalism was a matter of inner exploration (psychology) not outward description (sociology) – it marked a peculiar turning away from the generally accepted determin-ants of ordinariness and ordinary concerns and the literature that expressed that ordinariness for the mass of new readers. Woolf's cham-pioning of ordinariness was a special plea for the aesthetic technicalities of revolutionary modernism, in complicity with a political conservatism which looked to an anglicised classical traditionalism, a view which she wholeheartedly embraced from T. S. Eliot.

In contrast to Woolf's belief that 'the most prominent and *successful* novelists in the year 1910 were, I suppose, Mr. Wells, Mr. Bennett and Mr. Galsworthy' (emphasis added), *The Bookseller* suggested the most successful (by which I take it Woolf meant commercial) authors were Nat Gould, E. Phillips Oppenheim and H. Rider Haggard. Woolf's 'I suppose' shows the new myopia that marks literary debate to the present day. It effectively closed down a whole world of fictional production – indeed denied it any literary status. Even Woolf herself, at the moment of her greatest advocacy for the new Georgian experimentalism, sounded a word of caution and nostalgia.

> If you read Mr Joyce and Mr Eliot you will be struck by the indecency of the one and the obscurity of the other. . . . [H]ow intolerant [Eliot] is of the old usages and politenesses of society. . . . I . . . envy the indolence of my ancestors who . . . dreamt quietly in the shade with a book.
>
> ('Mr Bennett and Mrs Brown')

The period between the 1900s and the 1920s marked a progressively discriminatory reading practice which is undiminished to the present day. Between 1920 and 1924 the critical and commercial gazes effectively turned their back on each other. English literature broke into three distinct areas: traditional (Edwardian), experimental (Georgian) and popular – but only the first two were still called literature, however.

The last gasp of the old undifferentiated literary culture found expression appropriately in the battlefields of the Western Front. The now forgotten literary broadsheet campaign of 1915 had grown out of a belief that literature, broadly conceived, had an elevating and unifying effect and that these two together with literature's qualities to entertain and relax would have a real effect on troop morale during the stalemate at the Front (the broadsheets were also given to sailors). Conceived by Bruce Richmond of *The Times Literary Supplement* and Sir Walter Raleigh, Professor of English at Oxford, as an antidote to jingoist propaganda and outright pacifism, the campaign was designed to include neutral but inspirational literature which avoided any censorship rules imposed by the Defence of the Realm Act (DORA). It was also *not* made up of exclusively British authors and it included both prose and poetry chosen from a wide historical spectrum.

Encouraged by Richmond, Raleigh was enlisted as a selecting editor. His comments are illuminating:

> I am preparing 'broadsheets' for the trenches. It's better fun than I knew. I wish you would send me references of anything that occurs to you, from bits of the Book of Job to accounts of a Prize-fight. No standard except 'good of its kind'. We shall blossom this week or next. I covet enormous variety . . . I have just put in some extracts from the

18th Cent., *Life of Elwes the Miser* – a spendid work. There is room for everyone's pets, except elephants. And (what I didn't know) there is real demand.

(Sir Walter Raleigh, quoted in John Simons, unpublished paper)

Any selection had therefore to be broad and accessible but both modernist excess and popular sensation were avoided. The result was populist and yet also middlebrow: 'good of its own kind'. Raleigh's sense of his own Englishness was also to be found in his sense of the moral significance of how English readers read: frivolous, free, non-partisan, non-Prussian (regimented, professional).

I confess I like the idea of this library. Apart from its main use it seems to me to symbolise the cause for which we are fighting. The Germans are right when they call us frivolous, if it may be permitted in the name of politeness to assume that by frivolous they mean playful. They are right; we have playful minds, and they have not, so that we have often been embarrassed in our converse with them. They are full of a simple unquestioning faith in Germany, in things German, in the great deeds they have done and the great deeds they are about to do, in all that is large, heavy, solid and persistent. . . . They do not want Heine in their trenches; there is a danger that he might not be serious. We could not think of ourselves as they do, magnificently, for years together; some one would be sure to laugh. . . . We believe in freedom and we mean to keep it. We will fight as long as we can stand, so that the world may still be a place where spontaneous and playful persons, especially women and children, may lead a life free from fear. There is no better expression of freedom, in all its senses, than English literature.

(Raleigh, ibid.)

Good English literature and healthy English culture represented the highest seriousness, that of irony and self-awareness. Such a literature was frivolous only in the most serious sense as it represented the deepest *popular* currents of British liberty, democracy, individuality and communality. In its totality, English literature was the embodiment of English sensibility accumulated over time as national character. It may be that this view of English literature was a rosy myth less true now than then but it was certainly a more honest vision than the propagandistic and patriotic attitude required by the Ministry of Information and actively sought by them amongst leading authors during 1914.

II

By the end of the war, the gentlemanly (officer class) patronage of literary taste represented by Sir Walter Raleigh at Oxford was to be challenged by the new professionalism of English criticism at Cambridge. It was to be a decisive break.

The professionalisation of literary (and later cultural) criticism during the interwar years went together with a separation between academic critics and those practising writers who indulged in critical activity (such as Eliot and Orwell). At face value, the era of the amateur connoisseur was over. Indeed, the increasing pressure of modernity seemed to make the connoisseur appear more eccentric, more isolated, more part of a receding *aristocratic* world in which the connoisseur was little more than a fop in a world of his own artificial making. Of the lifestyle of the influential art critic Bernard Berenson we are told,

> To visit 'i Tatti' is to experience more than the pleasure of stepping into the frame of a Renaissance painting. It is to be transported into a dreamland of the aesthetic imagination: Altamura. To Bernard Berenson and those friends who imagined it at the turn of the century, Altamura was to be a monastery, but one devoted to the Spirit of Delight, to the arts of living.
>
> This villa, transformed from a modest farmhouse on the hills of Settignano not far from Florence, was the setting in which its inhabitants might 'dwell in the contemplation of eternal essences ... behold Beauty with the eye of the mind and ... feed on the shadows of perfection.'
>
> (Meryle Secrest, *Being Bernard Berenson*)

Nevertheless, both at Oxford and Cambridge, the scholarly or connoisseur tradition continued to be an important *institutional* force and a potent intellectual position. The belief that connoisseurship was superseded because it had nothing to say, was élitist and had no relevance in an age of *scientific* criticism was only partially true. Its denigration was to have considerable consequences.

As early as 1921, in a series of lectures delivered at Oxford (at the invitation of Sir Walter Raleigh), John Middleton Murry could point out:

> It is, I believe, a fairly common experience for those who have been engaged for a good many years in the profession of literary criticism, to slip, almost unconsciously, into a condition of mistrust of all their

most familiar and general terms. The critic becomes dissatisfied with the vagueness of his activity, or his art; and he will indulge the fantastic dream that it might be reduced to the firm precision of a science.

And, as a writer, Murry added:

> Whether it is with the vain hope of giving to the language of criticism, like the symbols of mathematics, a constant and invariable significance, or with the more reasonable aim of gaining a more exact control over the instruments of his craft, the critic is preoccupied by an ideal of definition. If he cannot legislate for the republic of letters, and determine the sense in which terms of criticism must be used, he can try to discover and distinguish the senses in which they are used. He invariably finds that the confusion is great.
>
> (John Middleton Murry, *The Problem of Style*)

Murry's book that emerged in 1922 as *The Problem of Style* can be read in light of the then current debate around the definition of modernism and should be especially judged against T. S. Eliot's strictures on the poetic imagination, as rendered in 'Tradition and the Individual Talent' (1919), in which Eliot was concerned with the personality of the artist-creator now represented analogously in the language of Imperial Chemicals.

> [A]s that of [a] catalyst.... two gases... mixed in the presence of... platinum ... form sulphurous acid.... The mind of the poet is the ... platinum.

The poet's personality was therefore,

> [I]n fact a receptacle for seizing and storing up ... particles which can unite to form a new compound.

Murry's answer was part of the long struggle between professionalised modernistic-technological criticism and ethical-holistic 'amateur' connoisseurship. Against Eliot's wholesale attack on the unique personality and its consequent 'perversity' (i.e. romanticism) and aberration, Murry elaborated a thesis of 'Wholism' [*sic*] and unique particularism:

> A true style must, therefore, be unique.... A style must be individual, because it is the expression of an individual mode of feeling. Some styles will appear more peculiar than others, either because the

writer's mode of feeling is unusually remote from the normal mode, or because the particular emotional experiences he is seeking to convey are outside the ordinary range of human experience. . . . The test of a true idiosyncrasy of style is that we should feel it to be necessary and inevitable; in it we should be able to catch an immediate reference back to a whole mode of feeling that is consistent with itself.

(John Middleton Murry, op. cit.)

At the centre of a book on 'style,' Murry posited the preconditions of authentic subjectivity. His quest was technical and ethical at the same time, something that Eliot's essay was also despite its reference to 'depersonalisation' and its preference for technical *process*.

In an age in which ethical issues could soon be subverted into propaganda for left or right, many academic critics turned to technical and formal exposition (especially the New Critics in the United States) as a way to *disengage* art from various forms of totalitarian struggle and capitalist exploitation. Caught between American New Dealism (possible US socialism), Soviet centrism and bolshevism and Italian, Spanish and German fascism, cultural critics attempted to provide a space where propaganda held no sway. That place was literature. Techno-formalism ironically freed criticism from overt ethical considerations and therefore rendered its judgements both *neutral* and *disinterested* (indeed healthy). Criticism could thereby serve democracy.

During the interwar years, the connoisseur approach was still nevertheless able to mount a lively defence, as can be seen from Sir Arthur Quiller-Couch's lectures and articles of the 1930s. Quiller-Couch had been a successful author writing under the *nom de plume* 'Q' and a Fellow of Jesus College, Cambridge, where he was now King Edward VII Professor of English Literature.

Like Murry at Oxford, Quiller-Couch was keen to defend the connoisseur tradition against the new professionalism and scientism of current literary critical practice, hence:

Few can admire more than I the hard thinking put into their work by some (and notably here in Cambridge) of the new race of 'psychological' critics as I may call them; or hope more of their earnest sincerity. But the vocabulary of their science is not yet determined; they invent new words and locutions as they press along, and in such haste that *B* may too easily mistake what *A* precisely means by this or that abstract term, even if *A* shall have fixed it to his own mental satisfaction. Further, this concentration on Æsthetic tends more and

more of late to distract the attention from the essential in any given
work.

> (Sir Arthur Quiller-Couch, *The Poet as Citizen*)

By such comments Quiller-Couch distanced himself from both the
'new' psychological approaches of I. A. Richards and the psychoanalytic
approaches of the 'ego' critics. Again, the 'essence' of literature had
apparently been obscured by an avoidance of the literary question itself.
Moreover, the scientific method when applied to literature seemed to
breach even good manners; definitions, like bad manners, willfully
ignoring the communalism that made for civilisation itself.

> To me definitions, in life, and more particularly in literature, are the
> devil in a world hag-ridden just now by scientists, and as little applic-
> able to the understanding of life *or* letters, as a book of *Rules of Etiquette*
> to the unconsciously acquired habits of good-breeding.
>
> (Quiller-Couch, ibid.)

At first glance, then, pronouncements such as this seem lost in a haze
of port and cigars and country-house *bonhomie*, a suspicion made more
concrete by Quiller-Couch's ideal student: a public-school-educated
Cambridge man, who loved poetry, read for the classical Tripos but would
have read the English Tripos had it existed, who would join the civil
service and spend as much on his children's education as his parents
had on him. In other words, this was aimed at the upper middle-class
male of the English establishment. Yet a closer reading reveals that, for
all its class bias, Quiller-Couch was attempting to talk to 'any cultivated
man [*sic*]'.

It is this approach that marks Quiller-Couch's arguments off from
mere snobbery or thoughtless intuition. Published as *The Poet as Citizen*,
Quiller-Couch's lectures and articles were designed to consider 'the right
place of poetry in a well-ordered Commonwealth, and the right value of
the Poet as a citizen'.

The preface to the collection was itself dated, significantly, Trafalgar
Day, 1934. Quiller-Couch's purpose, then, was twofold: both an attack
on 'ego' criticism in literature and an attack on ego politics in Europe:
'in nation after nation there is revolt against Government by reasoned
consent and clamour for a dictator, a superman: in education, a theory
...that every child should...follow his own bent without restraint'.
The duty of a poet was for 'Q' a *civic duty* against which egocentrism was
merely perversity.

One might have believed that Quiller-Couch would follow Eliot's own line in 'Tradition and the Individual Talent'. This was not the case. By the 1930s, Eliot was both the boldest and most dangerous critic in the English-speaking world. His attacks on romanticism and 'egocentric' perversity had hardened into a dangerous right-wing ideology. Hardly surprising that Quiller-Couch, like Murry before him, had to engage directly with Eliot's views. Just like Eliot, Quiller-Couch also deplored the new egotism, but 'Q' was determined to defend the liberal tradition of humanism that Eliot's classicism opposed. In a choleric note, we are told that Eliot's latest essays tended towards a dangerous dogmatism, less about literature than about what it meant to be civilised.

For in my search after what [T. S. Eliot] means by Orthodoxy in literature I find him continually sliding off into theology.

And in a sneer at Eliot's New World asceticism,

Scarcely had the Pilgrim Fathers landed on Plymouth Rock before they started to build an orthodoxy of their own at least as repressive and rigidly tyrannous as anything they had fled from. Escaping across the Atlantic for liberty of conscience they ... ran to and fro burning 'witches'.

(Quiller-Couch, ibid.)

In Eliot's writing of the 1930s, Quiller-Couch rightly discerned (because of his own connoisseurial ethical bias) a tendency, previously latent, towards a theological authoritarianism, a dogmatic assertiveness and an inquisitional determination precisely akin to the political fascism abroad. Eliot was essentially a person who *subordinated* his ego to orthodoxy (authoritarian) and Quiller-Couch rightly understood the mechanism of Eliot's dislike of Western liberal democracy.

I do not thank him for the rhetorical sleight of hand or series of ambiguities by which he palms off this ego-worship as identical to 'Liberalism'.

Under extreme pressure from the professionalism of Cambridge criticism and the political developments of Europe, Quiller-Couch's belief in the civilising and civic role of the poet may appear naïve (it was to find success in the film work of John Grierson, however), his appeal to 'good manners' and 'good breeding' simply risible and his pacifist attitude worrying (a confused peace through armed *opposition* to fascism: hence, Trafalgar Day). Nevertheless, he urgently addressed the moral and critical problems of 'culture' at a time when these issues were confined to left-wing critics (politically hoodwinked by Stalinism) or right-wing critics (politically hoodwinked by Italian fascism). By the middle 1930s, not only literature, but liberal humanism and democracy were under severe strain. Thus, 'Q' defined and catalogued English Literature and its essential temperament, upholding that '"Liberalism" which questions dogma'.

III

Another set of critical maps to the definitive authors, books *and characteristics* of English literature can be obtained from student textbooks and guides: surveys of the significant works and thematic patterns designed to acquaint beginners with a ready topography of the literary scene. Such general textbooks abounded after the establishment of English Studies and give an excellent overview of the current critical temper and the authors recognised by that temper. Here, academic sensibility and prejudice were perambulated for the beginner. As such, these guides are conservative in nature and cautious in tone; slightly behind avant-garde debate but guardians of the current line. By the late 1920s, English Literary Studies had a clear pantheon of contemporary authors worthy of notice. In 1928, for instance, A. C. Ward, tutor at the City Literary Circle evening classes, published *Twentieth-Century Literature* as a guide to the then current authors of note. The volume is subtitled 'The Age of Interrogation', indicating the role taken on by artists since the late Victorians, as questioners of artistic and social norms and practices. Ward's pantheon of major novelists (for instance) included H. G. Wells, Arnold Bennett, John Galsworthy and Joseph Conrad but it also noticed the rise of younger writers (from 1910 to 1912) such as Compton Mackenzie, Hugh Walpole, J. D. Beresford, Frank Swinnerton and Francis Brett Young and the emergent D. H. Lawrence. There also were to be found Elizabeth Robins, Mary Sinclair, Sheila Kay-Smith, Rose Macaulay, Dorothy Richardson and Virginia Woolf. James Joyce was also noted. There was absolutely no place now for such contemporaries as Nat Gould, H. Rider Haggard or E. Phillips Oppenheim.

What is noteworthy here is not that Ward displays a catholicism of taste amongst those he considered 'serious' writers and an awareness of the emergence of voices from the literary avant-garde (both male and female equally), but that his critical viewpoint, essentially formal and moral, was quite capable of recognising the 'necessary' changes occurring in the experimentalists, notably Richardson, Woolf and Joyce, of whom Richardson was considered the best. What is of interest is his judgement which recognises the eclipse of Mackenzie, Walpole, Beresford and Swinnerton but also predicted that:

> The difficulty of preserving a sense of proportion in a survey of twentieth-century fiction is aggravated by the trend of contemporary criticism. Starting from the assumption that the traditional forms of fiction are exhausted and that new methods must be found, reviewers are disposed to give more prominence to what is new than to what is normal. Yet whatever patience and sympathy may be brought to a consideration of new movements in fiction, the traditionalists do 'satisfy,' whereas the modernists do not. Much of the 'new fiction' is laborious to read, and impossible to re-read; it creates a distaste that can be removed only by turning to more normal writers. The idols of the *intelligentsia* are not the idols of the majority, but both sets of idols may be equally hollow. By 1950 Dorothy Richardson will no doubt rest 'quite, quite forgot' in company with Ethel M. Dell, and Virginia Woolf with E. M. Hull; while a novelist so little trumpeted as the author of *Elizabeth and Her German Garden* may be among the survivors.

Ward's critique of modern reviewing and academic bias makes quite plain the problem of laying out what exactly constitutes English Literature at any one time, what exactly constitutes its boundaries and what its extensions. Mention of E. M. Hull and Ethel Dell remind the reader of the ironies wrought by time on all levels of taste but it also reminds us that by the 1920s popular fiction was no longer considered literature at all and that if Ethel Dell may have vanished Agatha Christie certainly has not and may outlast 'better' writers. Ward's book is instructive in its eclectic vision and its awareness of tradition and change.

By 1941, *The Concise Cambridge History of English Literature*, edited by George Sampson, could call upon the wisdom of critical debate and academic education in English Literature to delineate major authors. John Galsworthy, Henry James, George Moore, Arnold Bennett, Rudyard Kipling and Joseph Conrad represented the late Victorian and early modern movement, as did Somerset Maugham, E. M. Forster, Frank Swinnerton, H. G. Wells, D. H. Lawrence, James Joyce and Hugh Walpole; Virginia Woolf joined Dorothy Richardson, Rose Macaulay, Mary Webb,

'Elizabeth' (whose *Elizabeth and Her German Garden* we encountered in Ward) and Katherine Mansfield. Moreover, Sampson also noticed minor humorists and stylists: F. Anstey, Jerome K. Jerome, Kenneth Grahame, W. W. Jacobs, 'Saki' and P. G. Wodehouse.

Sampson's choices were, to a certain extent, consistent with Ward's made some two decades previously. Here too are recognised the 'traditionalists' and 'experimentalists' but now all are 'backdated', as it were, in a chapter headed 'Late- and Post-Victorian Literature'. Moreover, there is one extraordinary omission: *Heart of Darkness*, a work now considered Conrad's most significant, was left wholly unmentioned in Sampson.

English literary criticism and especially literary history becomes, to all intents and purposes, always something *other* than it is, always, to a later generation, *exclusive* and blind. How else could Sampson praise 'Elizabeth' as by right of 'seniority and quality' greater than Woolf or Richardson? Indeed, how do we account for the inclusion of Mary Webb as an equal of Katherine Mansfield? Sampson's judgement may or may not be faulty but it cannot be faulted except on grounds of 'value' claims (this work lasted because it was better quality) or ethical grounds (this work lasted because it was ethically more useful). In both cases it is our own judgement which has dismissed the taste of the past as *insufficient*. Yet 'Elizabeth' has not been judged and dismissed by the present but actually *forgotten*, despite the fact that

> 'Elizabeth' was never a narrowly 'feminist' writer but no one knew better how to make a conquering male ridiculous.

The extravagant claims made by modern critics for Virginia Woolf might well be tempered by her own contemporaries.

> [Her] ... Novels ... are the attempts of an essayist not instinctively a novelist to use fiction as a means of expression. [She] has small invention and her characters are the transient and embarrassed phantoms of her ideas.

Sampson's critical acumen was the received acumen of his peers (which should humble our own originality of thought) but it had penetration especially when comparing Woolf to Richardson, whose limits he also noted,

> But at least Dorothy Richardson had an impulse to fiction and was not a literary women attempting to make novels.

Referring back to the First World War, Sampson finally concluded on a sour note in relation to modernist experimentation, for 'what was the use of a new technique applied to compositions of no vitality?' For Sampson there was no such thing as 'new fiction'.

Ward and Sampson may have had limited vision but it was a vision which also noticed what we do not. If both dismiss or ignore the issues we now cherish this is not to diminish their own tastes, for their vision acts as a critique of ours; their inclusions are glaring omissions in our own reading and values. A mere glance at the poets Sampson finds worthy of attention shows how we have reduced the range of authors we could read (and thereby diminished the range of reading we might experience).

Walter Allen's classic account of English fiction, *The English Novel* (1954), included not only the writers already mentioned by Ward and Sampson, but expanded the list to notice such writers as Arthur Morrison, Barry Pain, Israel Zangwill, W. Pettridge, Edwin Pugh and Frank Swinnerton. *Heart of Darkness* was now acknowledged as Conrad's masterpiece. Wells, Bennett, and Galsworthy begin to fade in importance.

Of the writers of the new Elizabethan Age, Allen noted only Graham Greene, Joyce Cary, Elizabeth Bowen, Henry Green, Anthony Powell, L. P. Hartley, James Hanley and P. H. Newby. Joyce, Woolf and Richardson, we are told, still awaited final judgement. Of popular novelists there was simply silence, a silence which denied any status to such work (in a book called *The English Novel*!) and which was even more discriminatory than the work of a previous generation (A. C. Ward). For Allen, *Ulysses* stood out as the great modern novel and Joyce a central figure alongside Lawrence, Richardson and Woolf. The modern pantheon was complete.

His treatment of Woolf was nevertheless revealing both for its (not so) unconscious sexual imagery in describing her prose and for its concern over her use of grammar in its relationship to meaning.

> Much of her fiction [is] marred by portentiousness....Nor do the moments of revelation...always seem illuminative...but rather a succession of short, sharp female gasps of ecstacy; an impression intensified by [the] use of the semi-colon where the comma is ordinarily enough.

It would be easy to dismiss Allen's orgasmic language as sexist and juvenile if his point about semi-colons didn't make sense as a criticism of Woolf's actual performance.

Allen's inclusion of some authors and exclusion of others, his dismissal of the 'minor' authors of the First World War and his exclusion of all popular novelists demonstrates the necessarily vicarious nature of literary debate. If some authors now emerged as major figures (Joyce) others were newly championed (Lawrence: dismissed by Ward and Sampson; the latter stating that Lawrence was a mere case of pathology), others remained problematic (Woolf). Equally, modernism had now emerged as *the* major strain of fictional production. But this was tempered with Allen's own worry about an age's shortsightedness, revealed in his comments on the forgotten late nineteenth-century author William de Morgan: 'today, though it is possible to see why he was praised, he is *unreadable*' (emphasis added). In part at least, the unreadableness of a book was also the unreadableness of its context (historical and cultural).

Allen's comment opened the question of literary longevity and of the nature of fiction's limitations. If a book becomes unreadable how do we *now* 'read' its readers – how do we judge without diminishing the necessary *relationship* between value (transhistorical qualities) and ethics (historically particular qualities)? The vicarious limits of contemporary criticism become the pronouncements that limit the *actual* space of literary production.

Ward, Allen and Sampson, in their attempts to guide the reader through English Literature, illustrate the problems of proscription and of inclusion. If certain figures remain, others vanish or still others take their place. A certain level of personal choice creeps in – names lost to history retain, in these pages, a certain significance. What is aimed at in these writers is *critical* stability (argued as tradition, development and change within *the form*) in the face of an historically unstable entity: English literature. The rigid exclusion of all popular fiction was a necessary move to stabilise the field. The concentration of debate around traditionalists and experimentalists (realism versus psychology) was a further move to stabilise the serious novel. It is no coincidence that 'serious' novels that follow neither path were dismissed even though they may represent the most 'famous' novels in the English language. Hence, as late as 1973 in the revised edition of *The Penguin Guide to English Literature* (originally published in 1961) Gilbert Phelps could state that:

> As for George Orwell's *1984*, it is surely by now apparent that a good deal of the excitement it aroused when it was first published (in 1949) was related to Cold War fever. Although it can still produce its *frissons* of horror, the writing is frequently slack and tired compared to that of Orwell's earlier books (including the far more vital and effective fable, *Animal Farm*, published in 1945), the tone is

frequently shrill and hysterical, and the characterization notably wooden.

Not only popular fiction, but serious novels of ideas had no place in the critical vocabulary of the mainstream literary guides of the 1960s and early 1970s. What these guides illustrated was that in their choices there was necessity but not inevitability. Technical felicity and moral appropriateness were the keystones of novels accounted significant, and expressly Leavisite values now determined inclusion in the literary pantheon. *The Penguin Guide* not only included a chapter on the centrality of Leavisite attitudes (attitudes absent in the work of Ward and Sampson) but also chapters by authors highly influenced by Leavis's views: Raymond Williams and Raymond Hoggart, founders of the British version of cultural studies.

IV

The mobilising of anti-humanist and neo-Marxist critical approaches which paralleled and then superseded the *Penguin Guide's* approach to literary history did not radically alter the trajectory of the critical vision despite reams of argument to the contrary. Rather the nature of English was *atomised* into discrete canonic projects, primarily directed either by redistribution or by creating new nomenclatures. And such redistributions were themselves predicated unwittingly on those of the past: Edwardian and Georgian (Woolf) replaced by traditional and experimental (Ward) replaced by Victorian and Post-Victorian (Sampson) etc., and thence belatedly to modernism and post-modernism (current). Thus Joyce's work became post-modernist (i.e., up-to-date) whilst Lawrence and others simply remained modernist (outdated) and Wells, Galsworthy and Bennett found silence and oblivion.

Feminist, ethnic and gay critics have all reconstructed English Literature to their own tastes and agendas, agendas essentially determined by ethical issues predicated on the problems of representation. Whereas the older humanist histories (and Marxist, too) saw the community as made up of a number of individuals, newer approaches using deconstructive techniques see the individual as made up of a number of cultures: the self also becomes atomised. Whilst the readings of newer critical schools claim to disestablish critical boundaries, they have nevertheless stabilised their own critical views around certain types of text: Marxists favour realism; feminist and gay critics favour books which represent gender issues, especially those dealing in biology and culture; ethnic groups are concerned with post-colonial and 'black' writers ignored by traditional critics; post-structuralists concern themselves with work which highlights language and grammar and the problem of 'reading', especially in fantasy, detective fiction and the surreal. Across all, popular fiction has been brought to prominence – at least, apparently.

The emergence of English literatures rather than merely English Literature has undoubtedly revealed new possibilities and new areas but it has avoided any direct investigation of the total field (something that the older histories, however limited, attempted to do).

The newer critical practices have, therefore, effectively particularised their historical perspective and in so doing lost the opportunity to find or create a comprehensive understanding of literary production. The actual, historical, anarchic nature of print was given a veneer of stability by critical particularism and exclusion rather than by the interrogation of an inherently unstable (yet total) field. The move into cultural studies was not therefore an inevitable move but instead a blindness to the work left to be done amongst the archives of cultural history. Cultural studies abandoned history in favour of linguistics and in so doing trapped itself in an ever-expanding contemporariness. The dynamics of historical change and expansion were lost in ahistorical formalisms (readings) which were rarely re-attached to a contextual base.

V

The question 'What is English Literature?' is interwoven with the question of 'What is history?' and more particularly how can we now, after post-structuralism, talk of 'literary history'? The abandonment of historical inquiry in cultural studies has effectively shut down an essential component of literary inquiry. This has occurred under the very name of history itself: new feminist, ethnic and gendered histories. The linguistic assault on historical methods (historiography) reduced it to a rhetoric essentially literary (a genre). Abandoning history and historical method was at once liberating (for minority interests) and debilitating. The death of grand narrative leads not merely to relativism but to parochialism. The end of 'English Literature' in our progressive universities is unsurprisingly accompanied by the end of history. The death of both is seen as a triumph of progressivism and an unmasking of fraudulence, but it is also a tragedy.

The field of English Studies was effectively opened up by post-structuralism only the more effectively to shut it down. The political vocabularies of liberation now employed are little more than the sophisticated rhetoric of academic Newspeak.

The irony is that cultural studies brings to finality the inherent conditions we can see in earlier literary study: concerns for themes, structures and canonicity all attempted to bring into some order the 'chaos' of literary production. This chaos could only be rendered clearly by the historical perspective long suppressed by the contemporary gaze of literary critics. Cultural Studies is not opposed to English Studies. It is the rightful, fruitless, inevitable result of a history of decisions based on contemporary values. Even as we enter a new century of professional criticism, there is neither will nor wish to reconcile literary sensibility with literary sales. Our culture is diminished as a result.

4
Eyes on the Prize:
Booker and the Orange People;
Joan Collins in Court

Do as I do; read all the reviews, neither buy nor borrow any
of the novels. You can dine out forever on your knowledge
of the current literary scene without having to wade through
the junk that passes for literature today in the English-
speaking world. After five years, if people whose judgement
you trust are still talking about the book, get it and read it
– it's probably worth the effort. And remember, buying the
books, like feeding stray cats, only encourages them.

Letter to the *Sunday Times*, 24 April 1994

I

The last chapter was concerned with the origins of twentieth-century
canonic and scholarly taste in Britain and its political, cultural and commercial contexts. It concentrated on the contrast between commercial
values and cultural values and looked at how they are formed and
reformed by professional literary critics. Above all it was about the often
difficult negotiation between anti-commercialism and anti-philistinism
and the very market forces that allowed these attitudes to flourish. This
paradoxical position is nowhere more obvious than in the corporate
sponsorship of contemporary national art prizes and those prizes aimed
at literature and especially new fiction. It is here that corporate culture,
literary values and political expediencies are most closely tied. Prizes are
not new to literature nor are they a novelty in the arts. Pulitzer created
his prize in 1917 (first awarded in 1918), Nobel in 1901, the Goethe Prize
appeared in 1927 (first awarded in 1928) and the Prix Goncourt in 1903.[1]

Signs of national and imperial pride, these prizes were also the expression of corporate values reworked as cultural criteria.[2] Moreover, many of the most distinguished awards are centred around fiction, especially new serious novels which are themselves usually the standard bearers of a long tradition of humanist moral enquiry. The short-listing and prize-giving belong to a process that validates such a tradition: the literary canon as an unbroken moral project and the serious novel at its centre.

In Britain, there is the Booker Prize, which carries a substantial monetary reward and a guarantee of fame and further royalties for its lucky winner. Both Thomas Keneally's *Schindler's Ark* and Michael Ondaatje's *The English Patient* (award winners in 1982 and 1992 respectively) were the causes of a process of cultural validation which led to still more prestigious prizes and other corporate ceremonies, Stephen Spielberg and Anthony Minghella both collecting Oscars at the Academy Awards: another stage in a saga at once market-led, popular and respectable – an ironic alliance of opposing terms.

It is no coincidence that the years which witnessed the appearance of the modern corporate business were also the years that saw the fragmentation of culture and the appearance of the most acute forms of the class system. Just as classes separated, so taste was divided and redistributed amongst the deserving. In this new world, old categories were relentlessly broken down and professional interest groups whose powerful opinions determined market reaction replaced communities of readers. Just as surely as the older communities were moulded by and reacted to the market so too came the now familiar stratification of economic groups into low-, middle- and highbrow tastes, born together out of a desire for a form of recognisable cultural stability in an age of inherent instability.

Where money alone ruled, the cultural niceties were no longer paramount, perhaps no longer recognisable. Taste alone would make culture safe and would, above all, preserve civilisation – for Matthew Arnold in the 1880s as for Frank and Queenie Leavis in this century in Britain, this was the overriding obsession. The cultured person, not market forces, would now make the world civilised. But if the cultured person stood against the market-place (and the very success of entrepreneurs was proof of their lack of culture) then it was certainly paradoxical that only in the market-place could good taste be properly validated. The literary prize is nowadays the most overt form of that validating procedure.

The prize-awarding process is essentially concerned with reconciling opposites: good taste and commercial success; to do so in such a way that good taste is made democratically available to all (who may wish to read the award-winning book) and yet keep the élite nature of the prize's rationale intact. What emerges is 'serious' commercial fiction aimed at middle-to highbrow readers: a literary genre as much as a recognition of well-trained reading habits.

For an author honoured in this way the consequences are immediate and concrete: a reasonably substantial cash award designed to aid the process of a professional writing career but actually a token of the potentially huge royalties generated by sales; film or television adaptations or other offers; promotional tours; possible interviews and articles; a guaranteed publisher and rights scramble for the next work; honours and further prizes; academic recognition and awards. Such possibilities completely curtail the arduous processes of a life in writing and confer a dangerous and seductive comfort on a lucky winner.

For the publishers of such a book the consequences too are immediate and concrete: the author becomes a 'hot property', a commercial *focus* in which 'author' signifies as only one form of commercial possibility and that the least significant. There are considerable rewards: greatly increased hardback sales through booksellers and book clubs; the acceleration of the paperback appearance and increased print runs of both hard- and paperback units; hard sell in the United States and the expectation of translation rights; increased personal promotion and market management; film and television rights; guaranteed sales on a further book and increased 'investment' in the property and its merchandising potential; finally, recognition that their author (only one aspect of the property) is of importance and that the author confers upon the publisher a type of professional status now recognised by others in the industry and by reviewers, critics, etc.

For critics, reviewers and hangers-on there are immediate and concrete consequences: newspapers run articles and features both before and after competitions on the authors and their publishers; books are debated, praised, demolished, analysed, consigned to oblivion or to Olympian heights as matters of immediate public concern; the process is decried only in order to promote it; by promoting books reviewers promote careers; newspapers promote sales; television promotes the product through the televising of award ceremonies where previous winners, publishers, journalists, critics and hangers-on are elevated to expert status as they opine on the outcome.

Judges themselves are also former winners, reviewers, critics and publishers – validators of their own culture, lifestyle, tastes: a magical, charmed circle into whose thought processes we are invited for a vicarious few moments but from whose social milieu we are rigorously excluded. The masons of serious literature have an occasional and much publicised open day for the (paying) general public. We witness the auguries, the sacrificial rites and canonic procedures not only of literary value but also of commercial nous (except the latter is never mentioned). And if we are lucky we may witness masonic dissension, the judging panelist who publicly dissents from his or her colleague's view or the accusations of plagiarism aimed by unknown academics at the very books to which others of greater stature have awarded the laurels. A major literary prize is a loop of opportunity for all.

Minor literary prizes, or important but less publicised and prestigious prizes, also take their validation from the process of the grand prizes, despite disclaimers to the contrary or a belief that the minor prize is of greater moral value because of less commercial worth. Such attitudes are simply reverse snobbery (indeed, actual snobbery) in which the grand prizes are accused of merely pecuniary importance and actually antagonistic to good taste. Here, good literary taste, when not determined by subjective waffle on 'style', 'technique', etc. is often underwritten by an antagonism to commercial value and therefore the propensity to value the unprintable (therefore, ironically, the commercially *second rate*).

Such an ironic position would horrify many judges but it cannot be discounted. Nor can it be discounted that minor prizes given to 'amateur' writers are overtly democratic whilst covertly determined by methods and prejudices attached to preconceptions about good taste and good form which are, of necessity, underwritten by notions and hierarchies themselves antithetical to the democratic widening of access to amateur authors who might wish to become professional authors in pursuit of major prizes.

The minor prize circuit itself become a means by which 'amateur' authors or genre authors can compete for the allocation of resources to enable them to enhance their writing career – a precarious means to a very modest supplement to their living where sales cannot be boosted nor publishers found. The minor prize circuit is itself a loop of local status enhancement (good taste) and professional enhancement (money) which nevertheless proceeds outside the necessities and pressures of international commercial competition, publishers' deadlines (here, the publisher may be the author) and sales considerations. Here, too, taste and commercialism (masquerading as its opposition) intertwine and proliferate.

The prestige prize is not therefore an aberration determined by cynical commercial interests but *the* condition towards which all other prizes for literature tend. It underwrites minor prizes and validates the proliferation of the entire prize industry in promoting 'culture'. In Britain the greatest of these prizes is the Booker.

II

Just as with book reviewing, it is important to recognise the cultural role played by the Booker Prize and its offshoots (such as the live televised broadcast of the awards ceremony) in promoting fiction (or at least certain examples of it) and in bringing the event, the authors and the novels to the attention of a wider public.

The stated aim of the Booker Prize is that it should be awarded to 'the best full-length novel of the year', and it is intended to 'reward merit, raise the stature of the author in the eyes of the public, and increase the sale of books'. But whatever the role of the Booker Prize may be, it is clear that its high profile makes it newsworthy as far as the media are concerned, interesting and intriguing for many readers of fiction and an important annual event for publishers and booksellers alike. It is not without its detractors but as Martyn Goff, administrator of the Prize since 1979, suggests,

> The Booker Prize ... has contributed to raising the profile of serious fiction during its twenty years of existence. It has helped to restore confidence in the form ('Is the novel dying?' has ceased to appear as a regular Sunday newspaper article); it has boosted writers in their need to find an audience; and it has acted as a signpost to the general reader indicating the more worthwhile books published every year. It does not, and indeed probably cannot, always get it right. It is hard on the non-winning, short-listed authors. It focuses too much attention on the autumn publishing season. Even then its benefits clearly outweigh its drawbacks. It has led to a number of other prizes. It has helped to raise the status of Commonwealth fiction; and it has given great pleasure to writers and readers alike. That surely is enough for the first twenty years.
>
> (Martyn Goff, *Prize Writing*)

Goff makes a number of substantial claims for an event which many consider to be a rather cynical marketing exercise, and it is therefore perhaps not surprising that he is someone so closely involved with organising and presenting the Prize. However, Goff also raises a number of questions which highlight most of the specific issues relating to the ways in which fiction is judged in this particular context. One of the reasons that the Prize has had such a visible presence in recent years is due to its symbiotic relationship with the media: events and individuals related to the Prize have been presented as being newsworthy, and the media attention they have attracted has made the Prize itself more important – and hence itself more newsworthy.

The Booker Prize is not by any means the only literary prize for fiction awarded in Britain; the Book Trust's *Guide to Literary Prizes, Grants and Awards in Britain and Ireland* lists a total of over two hundred entries, with prizes ranging from £50 for the book which has made the most distinguished contribution to folklore studies (The Katharine Briggs Folklore Award) to £25,000 for the best work of non-fiction (NCR Book Award). Several, notably the *Sunday Express* Book of the Year (£20,000) and the Whitbread Prize (£21,000) do receive public and media attention, as does the recent Orange Prize, but it is undoubtedly the annual award of the Booker Prize (for £20,000) which in the 1980s and 1990s had become the most important literary prize in Britain, arousing tremendous media interest (it was until recently the only literary prize-giving ceremony to be covered live on television, which it has been every year since 1981) and moving literary debates off the Book Pages and into the public domain.

The Booker Prize was launched in 1968 as a result of a collaboration between publishers Tom Maschler and Graham C. Greene from Jonathan Cape Ltd and the Authors Division of Booker McConnell Ltd (which later became Booker plc). Booker plc had established what was to become their highly profitable Authors Division in the mid-1960s in order to buy the copyrights of authors such as Ian Fleming, Agatha Christie and Dennis Wheatley. Chairman Charles Tyrell and Managing Director John Murphy were then approached by Greene and Maschler, who were seeking sponsors for a literary prize which could match the Prix Goncourt in France for both reputation and as a stimulus for book sales. Their suggestions were welcomed and, with the backing of the Publishers' Association, a committee was set up to organise it. Initially dominated by Maschler and Lord Hardinge of Penshurst (literary adviser to Booker), the form of the Committee was formally organised in 1979 into one which specifically encompassed all areas of the publishing industry: an author, a paperback publisher, a hardback publisher, a writer, a bookseller, a librarian, Chairman of Booker Sir Michael Caine, and Martyn Goff, administrator of the Prize (who during his career has been an author, a publisher and a bookseller).

Since 1971 the administration and publicity for the Prize has been handled by the Book Trust, an independent charitable trust which aims to promote reading. The first Booker Prize in 1969 was worth £5,000; this has since been increased a number of times and its current value to the winning author is £20,000. A number of coinciding events in 1979 and 1980 may possibly explain the increasingly dominant role the Booker Prize now plays amongst literary prizes in Britain and throughout the world.

Firstly, in 1979, Sir Michael Caine, Chairman of Booker McConnell Ltd, took over as Chair of the Management Committee for the Booker Prize, and it was from this time that the more formalised committee membership dates. Secondly, in the same year, bookseller and Management Committee member Ian Norrie made what became a crucial suggestion: that details of the winning novel should be withheld until the ceremonial presentation of the Prize. In previous years the name of the winner had been known up to a month previously in order to give the publisher sufficient time for reprinting. Since the inception of the Prize, one of the stated intentions of the organisers had been 'to arouse speculation and interest in more than one book and one author' by announcing the short list several weeks in advance. Norrie's suggestion aimed at capitalising on this pre-existing speculative mood by creating and maintaining suspense about the identity of the winner from a known set of possible choices, creating a lucrative and speculative competition.

Both of these decisions served to establish the Prize as an event as far as literary and publishing circles were concerned, but it was with the run-up to the 1980 Prize that it began to get media attention. As Martyn Goff pointed out,

> two giants, Anthony Burgess with *Earthly Powers* and William Golding [with *Rites of Passage*], were clearly seen battling for the winning post – and the public were enthralled. The press reported that Burgess would not come to the awards dinner unless he won and that I had a private line to his room at the Savoy Hotel. The truth was more mundane: I phoned him on a public line to say that Golding had won … whether it was the sense of two giants battling against each other or just that the seeds planted over 12 years of the Prize's running had at last taken root, there is little doubt that the contest started to matter not just to literary circles, but to a huge number of ordinary readers, whether they were book buyers or library borrowers.
>
> (Interview, 24 July 1991)

Exactly why the Prize had started to matter appears to be two-fold. On the one hand, the two literary heavyweights Golding and Burgess were perceived as being in contention, on opposing sides of an, as yet, invisible evaluative divide, and this sparked off a debate about the evaluation of literature which continues to gain momentum. On the other hand, this signalled the beginning of what have become known as the 'scandalous' incidents which caught the attention of the media and hence of the public: the élite of the literary establishment were perceived, perhaps for the first time, as being vulnerable to public – not merely academic – scrutiny. Whatever the reason, the impact of the Prize has been considerable, and not only in terms of its finding an audience. Ion Trewin, Editorial Director of Hodder & Stoughton, commented on the extent to which authors and publishers have also been influenced by it:

> at the end of the seventies, before the Booker Prize had really taken off, serious fiction was in a commercial decline . . . Nadine Gordimer, . . . she won the Booker Prize in 1974 (in those days I was literary editor on *The Times* and I was Chair of the Booker judges), Cape couldn't find a paperback publisher for [her]. *This* is how things have changed.
>
> (Interview, 8 August 1991)

In recent years the cultural and commercial significance of the Prize has become so great that the Book Trust now declares that being short-listed not only 'enhances an author's reputation', but also that it '*guarantees* [emphasis added] a considerable increase in sales, with spectacular world-wide demand for the winner'.

The 'Booker Year' commences with a meeting of the Booker Prize Management Committee immediately after the presentation in October in order to discuss any problems which have arisen with either administration of the Prize or media (particularly television) coverage for that year's award. The Committee is also responsible for finalising details affecting the rules and for appointing the panel of judges. When these decisions have been concluded the administration of the Prize is managed jointly by Martyn Goff (overseeing the judging process) and the Book Trust (known as the National Book League until 1986), who collect and despatch the books to the judges and organise publicity.

Submissions for the Booker Prize must be full-length novels written by citizens of the British Commonwealth or the Republics of South Africa or Ireland, which have been scheduled for first publication in Britain between 1 October in the preceding year and 30 November in the year of the presentation. The judges attend a preliminary meeting in April or May, where they are introduced to each other and where the dates of future meetings are arranged. Towards the end of August each judge gives a list of six favourites; these are then assimilated by the chair, and at a further meeting these are whittled down to produce a short list of between three and six titles. The climax of the process comes in late October when the judges (plus Martyn Goff and a representative of the Book Trust) meet privately to select the winning novel. The Prize is presented at a formal dinner at the Guildhall later that day when Sir Michael Caine presents a cheque for £20,000 to the author. (Until 1991 the short-listed winners also received a leather-bound copy of their own novel; in that year the bound editions were arranged by 'designer bookbinders', each designer producing a specially bound copy which 'interprets the novel in the binding by means of graphics, colour and materials'.)

The Management Committee comprised in the 1990s, Sir Michael Caine and Martyn Goff, Antony Haines (Non-Executive Director of Booker), P. D. James (author), Matthew Pritchard (Chairman of Booker Entertainment, previously known as the Authors Division), Alison Shute (Devon County Librarian), Peter Strauss (Publishing Director, Picador), Ion Trewin (Editorial Director, Hodder & Stoughton) and Tim Waterstone (bookseller). The main functions of the Management Committee were, and remain, to consider and, when necessary, revise the rules of the Prize, and to select the judging panel.

The total number of books considered by the panel for the Booker Prize ranges from eighty-five to 110 and one of the more contentious rules is that which controls the number of titles which can be submitted by each publisher. This has been revised over the years but currently stands at two per publisher plus any novels by previous short-listed authors or winners, plus a list of up to five additional titles which the publisher suggests warrant particular attention, and from which the judges make a further selection. In 1987 no titles from these lists were called in by the judges and as a result in 1988 a new rule was introduced compelling the judges to call between five and fifteen of these titles and requiring publishers to include a brief outline explaining their reasons for putting the books forward. In addition, judges may include eight to twelve titles which they feel should have been included. It is felt in some quarters that the major publishers are unfairly disadvantaged because the number of novels they are allowed to submit is the same whether they publish nine or ninety-nine novels per year, rather than being a proportion of their total output.

The Prize rules also specify that a book will only be considered eligible if its publisher agrees 'to spend not less than £1,000 on direct, paid-for media advertising of the winning book, including a winning poster or showcard, within the three months following the announcement of the award' and 'to contribute £3,000 towards general publicity if the book reaches the short list'.[3] These conditions of entry pull into sharp focus the perceived importance of publicity surrounding the Prize, not just for the winning novel but, as stated, also for those on the short list. Winning literary prizes can be big business – the prize luncheon is never free, even if the price is token.

Other rules (the restrictions on the nationality of the author, for example) would seem to be somewhat arbitrary: the United States and Europe are excluded, while South Africa is included, but on the whole there have been few serious challenges. When there are, or when it is felt that the rules are open to interpretation and need to be clarified, the judges can be offered advice by Martyn Goff or the Book Trust, although any suggestions which might be put forward are not binding. And it is when questions of interpretation arise that some of the most interesting issues, both technical and aesthetic, are spotlighted.

In 1991 two novels were submitted which generated debate around the question of exactly what constitutes a novel. The first was *Happenstance* by Carol Shields, which was written in two sections: 'The Wife's Story', which starts at the front and runs halfway through the book, and 'The Husband's Story', which is then read by turning the book upside down and starting from what was the back. This was written and published to be read as one piece only, each reflecting on the other, although they can be read independently (and in fact one section was published first in Canada). It was agreed that as they had been intended to be read as one novel, that decision should stand and it could be submitted as such. By comparison, William Trevor's book *Two Lives* was judged to be two novels (*Reading Turgenev* and *My House in Umbria*), partly due to the fact that on the flyleaf the publisher had announced that '*Two Lives* comprises two major new novels by William Trevor'. It was agreed that only one of the two could be considered, and in fact *Reading Turgenev* went on to become one of the six short-listed novels that year.

In 1982 the prize-winning novel was *Schindler's Ark* by Thomas Keneally, which was published in Britain as fiction but is categorised by the Library of Congress in the USA as non-fiction. It is the story of Oskar Schindler, a Polish industrialist who protected and rescued Jews in Nazi-occupied Poland during the Second World War, and Keneally uses what he describes as 'the texture and devices of a novel to tell a true story'. After short-listing the book, however, the judges (Brian Aldiss, Joan Bakewell, John Carey, Samuel Hynes and Hermione Lee) reconsidered their decision regarding its eligibility: whether it was in fact a novel. In this instance the decision was effectively reached by default: the act of short-listing the novel was deemed sufficient to confirm its eligibility as fiction as it could not have been short-listed if it were not. Nevertheless, although the judges were therefore not formally required to address the questions directly, the episode did succeed in provoking debate about the nature of fiction and 'faction'.

The most important meeting for the members of the Booker Prize Management Committee is the one held regularly each February, when a list of possible judges is considered. The composition of the judging panel has changed considerably since the inception of the Prize. In the earlier years, the panel of between three and five judges was heavily weighted towards authoritative academic figures. The first panel, for example, was chaired by W. L. Webb and included Rebecca West, Stephen Spender, Frank Kermode and David Farrer. Later panels included George Steiner, Saul Bellow, Richard Hoggart and Karl Miller. More recently the panel has consistently comprised a chair and four judges, usually a mixture of academics, authors and literary critics. In 1990, for example, the Chair was Sir Denis Forman (Chairman of Granada TV), and the judges were Susannah Clapp (Deputy Editor, *London Review of Books*), A. Walton Litz (Holmes Professor of Literature, Princeton University, on sabbatical as George Eastman Professor at the University of Oxford), Hilary Mantel (novelist) and Kate Saunders (journalist and writer). And in 1991 the Chair was Jeremy Treglown (writer and ex-editor of the *Times Literary Supplement*), Penelope Fitzgerald (novelist), Jonathan Keates (author and teacher), Nicholas Mosley (author and biographer) and Anne Schlee (novelist).[4]

The list of candidates proposed by the Committee is augmented by suggestions from outsiders: 'People like Melvyn Bragg and Michael Holroyd, the latter once on the Committee himself'. Three possible chairs are then proposed and contacted in order of preference, and the Committee, in consultation with the chair, then puts together a panel of judges. Referring to this process, Martyn Goff has commented that 'inevitably the panel will be quite different if the chairman is Fay Weldon than if it is Norman St John-Stevas'. It is because of statements such as these that questions about the validity of the judging panels can seem justified. Such comment ('people like') implies that the Booker organisation uses and is in cahoots with a group of people who have some element of power and control of literary issues, perhaps because of the fact that they are either specifically 'media figures' such as Melvyn Bragg (novelist and presenter of *The South Bank Show*), or that they have a high profile in literary circles, such as the author and biographer Michael Holroyd. Although Goff does justify the second name ('once on the Committee himself'), nevertheless the way in which 'outsiders' appear to have a profound, albeit informal, influence on the decision-making process appears somewhat insidious, especially when such care has been taken to construct the formal procedure for managing the Prize. Furthermore, acknowledging that different chairs will 'inevitably' make for different types of panel denies the opportunity for truly objective judging even before any discussion about whether objectivity is possible or not. 'Differences' in panels presumably means differences in literary preferences and in criteria, and one can only assume that this would result (if the different panels were judging the same batch of books) in a different novel winning the Prize.

However, Goff does appear simultaneously aware of potential difficulties such as partiality and prejudice, and has commented that the Booker Prize

> has gained an extraordinary reputation and it really means so much more than any of the other prizes [because of] the total integrity of the judges. We've achieved this by first having different judges every year. With the exception of years one and two ... we have never repeated a judge. And that is very important indeed, because once judges are doing it year after year they take into account each other's prejudices, foibles and so on: 'It's no good me pushing X because Y won't like it' and so on – that doesn't exist. We work very hard to balance the judges ... We try to mix an academic with a writer or two who hasn't got a book coming, with a literary editor or two and a reviewer ... We had an experiment as you know for some years which I happen to have been against but Bookers were really keen on the 'man in the street' thing, which was quite ridiculous because there isn't such a person.
>
> (Interview, 24 July 1991)

Clearly the Committee does take precautions intended to pre-empt accusations of unfairness, etc., and it is evidently very important that 'integrity' and 'balance' are seen to be vital considerations. The 'man in the street' experiment refers to a decision in 1976 to include in the judging panel someone who would represent the ordinary reader and who was not part of the literary establishment. The Management Committee, noting that the Prize was becoming 'too highbrow, too divorced from the common reader', decided to introduce one judge to represent 'the man in the street' in an attempt to make it more accessible and more relevant to the general public who make up the bulk of the book-buying public, and who needed to be attracted to the Prize. The first of the individuals selected in order to redress this balance was, somewhat paradoxically, Lady Mary Wilson, the wife of the Prime Minister and a published poet, and she was followed by media personalities such as the actress Joanna Lumley, radio and television presenters Robin Ray and Benny Green, and the newscaster Trevor MacDonald – the experiment was hardly representative of 'the common reader'.

Recent panels have been widely criticised for the narrow range of interests they represent (particularly those of what has become known colloquially as the 'Hampstead literati') and for promoting only the works of their friends and colleagues. This has been strongly denied by both Goff and Jeremy Treglown who assert that the extent of disagreement between the judges clearly frustrates this argument, stressing that the initial meeting is held with the express – and usually crucial – purpose of introducing the judges to each other.

> [In 1991] Jonathan Keates and Ann Schlee were not known to Penelope Fitzgerald. Nicholas Mosley I don't think had met anyone. Jeremy Treglown knew a lot about them, because after all he had been editor of the *TLS*, but he hadn't actually met them all either; he certainly hadn't met Ann Schlee and I'm not sure he'd met Penelope Fitzgerald. This shows you that when an author wins, even an author anti-prizes and anti-Booker like Kingsley Amis, it is of tremendous value, regardless of the 20,000 quid, regardless of all the nonsense: they have been judged at what is for them a particularly high level, in a way that nothing else quite does it.
>
> (Goff, interview, 24 July 1991)

Goff's assertion that the judges were not chosen from some pre-existing literary clique is possibly persuasive; he also claimed that the 1991 panel was not unusual in any way and therefore could be seen as representative of other judging panels. Nevertheless, it becomes apparent that the reason why it is so absolutely vital that the panel is believed to be impartial is the *integrity* of the Prize as a literary and cultural thermometer. Only if the process is *believed* by its audience to have been absolutely fair (and a group of judges who disagree with each other would sustain this expectation) can the competition maintain its reputation for verdicts that are at 'a particularly high level' and thus the final result can be appreciated as a reliable indicator of literary achievement – and it is at that point that its 'tremendous value' really does become conspicuous, as Treglown commented after the presentation of the 1991

Booker Prize which generated, relatively speaking, a tremendous furore because of the resignation of one of the judges, Nicholas Mosley.

Not surprisingly, Treglown later spoke rather defensively about the process with which he had recently been so closely involved (as chair of the judging panel), arguing that even members of a literary 'clique' may differ substantially in what they consider to be 'the best', but that there is also an element of inevitability in the composition of any panel.

> The interesting thing to me is that there you had a group of people who absolutely conform to the kind of either *Daily Mail* or *City Limits* stereotype . . . We were all if not actually Oxbridge, Oxbridge-ish; we were all middle class to upper-middle class; we were all white and as you say a good number of us lived in north-west London. And yet when we went in there we couldn't have had more dramatically contrasting views of what was and wasn't good. Now, having said that I don't deny for a moment that there are people, groups of people, who exert stronger cultural influence than others, and it does tend to be the case that they tend to congregate in various ways: they drift towards the metropolis . . . and they meet each other socially . . . at launch parties. What's wrong with this argument . . . is first to suggest that there isn't a complex filtering mechanism which is tending to favour people who know what they're talking about, and I do think there are some people who have read more and better than others . . . secondly, the argument against this forgets or chooses to ignore how many contending worlds there are within that world which are arguing for all kinds of different books, all sorts of writing. It's hard to think of a social group that was excluded by the shortlist. Now you might say, well, that's an example of Hampstead and High-gate repressive tolerance at work.
>
> (Jeremy Treglown, interview, 28 November 1991)

It is hard not to be impressed by the sincerity those connected with the Prize take to the judging process. Admittedly, much of it is defensive, in the face of considerable criticism not only about the 'cliqueyness' of the judges but also about the sort of literary novels which, it is suggested, tend to win. Even though the motivation behind such self-conscious analysis may simply be to satisfy the vested interests in Booker being seen to be run fairly and with integrity, one of the results is that a great deal of thought and effort is put into trying to achieve exactly that.

Jeremy Treglown, nevertheless, clearly stops short of examining the assumptions he makes about contrasting views held by the various judges. His presentation, for example, of a group who 'drift' powerlessly towards particular areas of London and who meet socially more by chance than design, emphasises merely the inevitability of the situation whilst it denies the crucial factors of cultural and material influences. Similarly, despite acknowledging the existence of what he refers to as a 'filtering mechanism' which excludes those who don't 'know what they're talking about', he fails to note the possibility of any correlation between this 'mechanism' and the one which controls the socio-geographical 'drift'. What results is a paternalistic view fit to oversee a procedure which is judged, as Treglown sees it, mainly on the results rather than the process. If those results are perceived to be satisfactory (which might be reflected by Treglown's assertion that 'it's hard to think of a social group that was excluded by the shortlist') then no deeper or more probing analysis of the process is deemed to be necessary.

This concern about exactly what is being judged was at the heart of a number of the 'incidents' connected with the Booker Prize and was central to what became by far one of the most public literary debates when (in 1991) judge Nicholas Mosley resigned after the meeting to decide the short list. This event resulted in Nicholas Mosley and his fellow judges Treglown, Penelope Fitzgerald and Jonathan Keates, along with Allan Massie (the author of *The Sins of the Fathers*, the novel which had been rejected by all the judges except Mosley, thereby prompting his resignation) all defending their decisions and explaining their position in articles in the British national press. In addition, the incident was referred to in leaders in *The Times* and *The Independent* and in substantial pieces by distinguished figures such as A. N. Wilson (author and literary editor for the *Evening Standard*), Lord Gowrie (ex-Arts Minister and Chairman of Sothebys) in the *Sunday Telegraph*, and Bryan Appleyard in the *Sunday Times*. The scandal of literary tastes, however, is always good for business.

What can be learned from such special pleading? Those involved felt they needed, for whatever reason, to express their opinions publicly (when the judging is traditionally a confidential process). As articles written by those involved were accepted for publication, newspaper editors obviously believed that such articles were 'newsworthy' and of interest to their readers. Indeed, it was deemed appropriate that assertions and arguments be answered and rebutted in the same medium and in the style of a correspondence.

A total of 109 novels were submitted for the Booker Prize in that year. Each of the five judges read the books, and after two meetings to discuss them each judge put forward a list of the six favoured titles. Some overlapped, and so there were a total of twenty-seven novels from which a short list of six was to be produced. The books were re-read, and the procedure for final voting was that each judge then listed the novels in order of merit, giving six votes to the first, five to the second and so on. The six receiving the most votes would constitute the short list. In the event, three tied for sixth place: *The Tax Inspector* by Peter Carey, *Time's Arrow* by Martin Amis and *The Sins of the Father* by Allan Massie. The chair of the judging panel, Jeremy Treglown, had the casting vote. He was strongly in favour of the Amis novel, and also felt that 'if I had a chance to put Martin Amis onto the shortlist and to break this kind of taboo against having him on the shortlist, I should do it' (interview, 28 November 1991). Therefore, after what he felt what due discussion with the rest of the panel, he chose *Time's Arrow* and the novels by Peter Carey and Allan Massie were put aside.

It was at this point that Nicholas Mosley resigned. His stated reasons for doing so were that Massie's novel was 'by some distance' his first choice for the prize, that none of the six books he had chosen got onto the short list, and that he was left with no book that he 'cared deeply about'. The resulting flurry of articles focused on the significance of the notion of the 'novel of ideas'. Mosley wrote in *The Times* that:

> the other four judges complained that my chosen books were novels of ideas, or novels in which characters were subservient to ideas. This was held not to be acceptable. My point was that humans were beings who did have ideas, who were often influenced by ideas, to whom ideas were important. If they were not, then there was some lack in being human.
>
> (*The Times*, 26 September 1991)

In *The Daily Telegraph*, he added that

> There was a moment when the chairman of the judges quoted the last line of Allan Massie's novel with the aim of making a decisive point against me. [Massie's] last line was 'What about me? What about us? What about humanity?' My fellow judges seemed to feel that a novel that had such a last line could not be a serious contender for the prize. I said that such questions were implicit in any good novel.
>
> (*Daily Telegraph*, 26 September 1991)

It is evident that some very personal and heartfelt grievances were being expressed in these articles, but most importantly these complaints all concerned what it is in a novel that is to be sought and rewarded.

Jeremy Treglown responded in *The Times* by asserting that

> no-one who has read Martin Amis' *Time's Arrow* or Timothy Mo's *Redundancy of Courage* ... will take seriously Nicholas Mosley's claim that the judges are uninterested in ideas. Our argument was about whether the particular 'novel of ideas' favoured by Mr Mosley is well written and imaginatively stimulating.
>
> *(The Times*, 28 September 1991)

In *The Daily Telegraph* Treglown re-emphasised his criteria, explaining that he didn't disapprove of asking the questions 'What about me? What about us? What about humanity?', but rather that he and his fellow judges preferred such questions to be asked in what he termed an 'imaginatively striking way' (*Daily Telegraph*, 28 September 1991).

Three important features become apparent when comparing these comments. Firstly, the number of points on which the two appear to agree: on the relevance of the 'novel of ideas', for example. Secondly, that they both found it necessary to made public statements, by means of articles written for publication in specific newspapers. And thirdly, that the difference between them is that only Treglown identifies the criteria for a winning novel – preferring it to be 'well written and imaginatively stimulating'. Treglown actually said '*we* prefer it to be asked', referring to the judges who agreed with Treglown that Amis's novel should go forward, and thus excluding Mosley.

It is important to note, however, that the rush to set pen to paper on this subject was by no means simply a personality war or point-scoring contest. The serious concern with which the issues raised by Mosley's resignation were discussed was exemplified in the leader column of *The Independent*:

> The great glory of the form is its infinite variety and versatility. To say that novels must be about ideas is like saying omelettes must contain eggs. What matters is the form in which those ideas are clothed, and whether the novelist endows his or her characters with sufficient life and vitality to carry the reader along. Great novelists succeed in creating a world that enriches the reader's understanding of human nature, of personal relationships and, in many cases, of history. However big the idea, it will make no impact if it is not incorporated into a convincing structure compounded of characterisation and story-telling.
>
> *(Independent*, 27 September 1991)

It is plain that the author of this piece was engaging in the debate by making oblique reference to remarks published, for instance, by Nicholas Mosley ('To say that novels must be about ideas . . .'). But the fact that these comments were published in the leader column of a national newspaper also reinforced the idea that the author also saw such observations as a contribution to a quite different dialogue, suggested by the proposition that certain individuals and institutions regard themselves as 'guardians of culture' – that they have some degree of responsibility for maintaining the standards of the 'cultural canon' to which they adhere. And there is, additionally, the question of vested interests: newspapers may address issues such as Mosley's resignation from the Booker judging panel in a serious and intellectual way in order that they are *seen* to be contributing to, and hence being part of, the debate. The more important the debate is in cultural terms, the more important their role as participants.

Personal and professional vested interests were at issue. It was not a coincidence that aside from Jeremy Treglown, the other four judges that year were all novelists. They were not only commenting on their personal reading of the novels, but in so doing they were also reflecting on their own profession, their own craft, and that the points at issue had particular and acute relevance to them. Jonathan Keates wrote an article for *The Observer* which illustrated both the issues and the problems:

> The point of the division becomes clear. Mosley evidently believes that the very nature of the question 'What about humanity?' places its use in a serious novel beyond the reach of criticism. Play safe and keep your utterances momentous. The concept of fiction as art, its inventions redeemed and enhanced by imagination, graces of style, dialogue, characterisation and description, is to be rejected in favour of the novel as conceptual vehicle, scorning those shifts of emotion and circumstance which bind or divide individuals, and searching instead for patterns of meaning in grand abstracts and world-shaking ideas. Thus, presumably, no *Mill on the Floss*, no *Great Expectations*, no *Sons and Lovers*. Can Mosley seriously want this? If he genuinely asks 'What about humanity?' he might do worse than look again at our shortlist, whose novelists celebrate love, hope, the endurance of human dignity and the conquest of fear. He might also ask himself whether these things, transfigured by fiction, do not in the end matter more than all the portents of history, politics or science.
>
> (*The Observer*, 27 October 1991)

Keates's comments amply demonstrated the extent to which great passions had been aroused by the debate, fused by strong personal beliefs which served not only to intensify the argument but also to support the more theoretical elements of it. No doubt this was to some degree because those involved, being authors themselves, had a great deal invested in such discussion, but regardless of this there remained a distinct and specific technical emphasis on the more detailed analysis of literary form rather than how judging panels should be organised in the first place.

It would appear from the degree of commitment expressed by the various lobbyists that there was and remains no agreed code by which fiction can be judged in this or any context. It is perhaps to the credit of the organisers of the Booker Prize that their encouragement of such a debate has been so successful in making it a more public discussion, even though the issues remain obtuse and confusing.

Jeremy Treglown responded to the furore in 1991, which had broken out even before the Prize was awarded, by describing his experience of another prize:

> I've found myself feeling nostalgic about another prize I once judged, the Cheltenham Literature Festival Prize. The organisers choose one judge, who chooses one book, which wins. The Booker Prize is more complicated. It has five judges – at least to start with. They mostly disagree. Later everyone disagrees with them. Why does anyone take any notice? First, because most of the judges are likely to have interesting views about fiction: this year, all of the judges, apart from me, are themselves novelists. Second, the arguments are about very good books. Of the 110 novels we read, over a quarter were thought by one or other judge to be serious candidates for the prize.
>
> (From speech announcing winning author, 22 October 1991)

Undoubtedly in Treglown's opinion there seemed a way to avoid the furore which the Booker Prize inevitably generated as a result of its organisation. But at what cost? Avoiding the fuss and the controversy, and hence at least some if not most of the publicity, was not necessarily desirable and could prevent the goals of the Prize being achieved if its significance as an annual cultural and media event was diminished. This was clearly at odds with the idea that the reason people take notice of the Prize is because it involves people with 'interesting views about fiction' arguing about 'very good books'. It is perhaps not surprising that, while the organisers will acknowledge that controversy is an essential element for the success of the Prize, those who are closely connected with the judging of it insist on stressing those factors which support their personal and professional investment in it. Penelope Fitzgerald, for example, commented in *The Times* that she didn't believe 'it is to anyone's discredit that we [the Booker judges] cared so much about the present and the future of the novel' (23 October 1991). Correspondingly, Jonathan Keates wrote about his experience, highlighting the intensity of the judges' passion for fiction:

> Pure objectivity is an *ignis fatuus* at the best of times, and each of [the judges] shamelessly trumpeted our madder enthusiasms ... If there is any message from [the short-listed novels] and from others almost as good, it is surely that English fiction keeps on disdaining schools, dogmas and systems in favour of extravagant offshoots and out-growths, a wild garden which long ago got the better of well-meaning attempts at containing it.
>
> (*Independent*, 27 September 1991)

The reason there was and remains so much disagreement is due to there being no codified set of criteria which can be universally applied. As the leader writer in *The Times* put it, 'the whole point of creative writing is not to conform, but to break boundaries. No wonder judges of literary awards have a hard time: they have no agreed standard against which to judge their material'. If there were, it is likely that the Booker Prize would be a much 'quieter' event, if only because the personal and public defences would be unnecessary, although the organisers would have failed in their mission to encourage people to argue about books.

Anthony Curtis, a judge in 1984, asked:

> What does the word 'better' *mean* when you are dealing with novels by different writers with utterly different aims? ... The truth is that novels are not like athletes competing in a race where you can take out a stop-watch and measure who performs best.
>
> (*Financial Times*, 28 September 1991)

Paradoxically, if there *were* a code or agreed set of criteria then it would be much more difficult to make the Prize into an event which people, whether professionally involved or not, could be engaged with or participate in because of the lack of 'space' for their own contributions and their own opinions. The non-existence of defining criteria could thus be seen as permitting and encouraging the validity of the individual opinions offered by non-professional readers. Indeed, if a set of criteria did exist, the Booker would be a much quieter event and the controversy and enjoyable bickering of judges lost, as a result of which there would be no publicity for the prize, no kudos for the organisers and no benefit for the book trade.[5]

One organiser has referred to the judging process as one of 'formalising emotional reactions' (Treglown, interview, 28 November 1991). This is a crucial phrase because it describes how two sets of personal and discrete criteria can be assimilated. The first set could include individual preferences, instinctive reaction, even prejudice; the second set would then moderate these responses and involve a more analytical and objective approach, enabling verdicts to be supported and justified. Many of the critics interviewed for this book who are professionally involved with assessing contemporary fiction, such as book reviewers, publishers, prize judges and the like, have had great difficulty expressing exactly what it is that makes them decide whether a novel is good or great or not, and why, and they tend to assert that it is reliant on gut reaction or instinct, based on personal preference and experience. 'Formalising emotional reactions' is the process of analysing that verbal stumbling and gut reaction so as to be able to express an authoritative opinion.

The prize judges, when selecting books for the short list, effectively have to lobby on behalf of their favourite novels, putting forward arguments as to why they should be supported by others. However, although a great number of articles have been published about the judging process, very little has been recorded about how particular books are selected: the authors tend to be long on principle but short on specifics. Perhaps this reflects how vital it is that the judges' meetings are held in private, because this allows initial responses and opinions to be instinctive, personal, conversational, even humorous or prejudiced, and it is only once such reactions are brought out into the open that they can be analysed and explored. This would appear to be exactly how the concept of 'formalising emotional responses' operates.

During the latter part of the 1990s, the tendency to present all manner of cultural ephemera in terms of competition or league tables had become increasingly evident. One very visible addition to the contemporary literary scene was the Orange Prize for fiction written by women. The prize had a propitious start, having been initially sponsored by the Mitsubishi Pencil Company who then quietly pulled out, allegedly due to the potentially contentious nature of the prize (which still excludes writing by men), although it was not long before a new sponsor, Orange, was found. An anonymous donor covers the impressive £30,000 first prize (the biggest literary prize in the UK).

The prizes were targeted at women writers who might otherwise be overlooked, but established writers (such as Anita Brookner in 1996 and Nadine Gordimer in 1998) refused to have their titles submitted for the prize due to its discriminatory nature and the quality of the writing also came under suspicion, epitomised by the *Daily Telegraph*'s headline (quoting one of the judges) declaring the submitted work as '[o]bscene, brutal, boring and dreary drivel' (*Daily Telegraph*, 15 April 1996). This was further reflected in the attitude of the chairs of the judging panels. In 1996, Lisa Jardine criticised women's writing for being too parochial, and Lola Young claimed, in 1999, that British women authors were too insular and too lightweight, although Elaine Showalter, chair of the panel in 1998 and commenting in 1999, suggested that these criticisms implied a bias against female subject matter and female subjectivity.

The Whitbread Prize, which has in the past tended to be a rather more subdued event, had also begun to demand its share of attention. In 1999, the award ceremony was televised for the first time, producing a clumsy copy of the Booker event, likened to a game-show. As Alain de Botton noted in *The Sunday Telegraph*, 'this created an awkward contrast with the rather sombre subject matter of many of the short-listed books ... [which] included John Bayley's account of his wife's battle with Alzheimer's disease, John Diamond's account of his battle with cancer, Ian Kershaw's biography of Hitler, and Giles Foden's novel about Idi Amin's reign of terror in Uganda' (17 February 1999).

Meanwhile, the Booker has continued in very much the same vein as previously. In 1998 the attention of the media was drawn to the short-listing of Magnus Mills's novel *The Restraint of Beasts*, for the simple reason that he was a bus driver, and the tone of the coverage was one of astonishment that a bus driver could achieve such a thing. Following the announcement that the prize was to be awarded to Ian McEwan, the media reflected Beryl Bainbridge's (alleged) disappointment at losing after being short-listed for the fifth time.

As the century closed there appeared a *fin-de-siècle* anxiety manifested through an increasing preoccupation with lists, league tables, books of the century, the nation's favourite poems, the debate about the new poet laureate. In 1997, there was even a world poll of the world's favourite books (repeated again in 2000 on World Book Day). Literary league tables offered something that seemed to fill a need to put the century's cultural works in order. And the media, book sellers and publishers were happy to enable any such schemes which boosted their profits.

The machinations of the Booker Prize during the 1990s brought into acute focus the conditions governing public taste and ratified, even in contention, the guardians of that taste. It was this annual (stage-managed) contention that reconciled the very unvisual nature of print with the very visual televisual medium. The award itself still cannot translate the impervious nature of print into action so instead it promotes *around* print the dimension of spectacle using the glamour of the award ceremony itself as a focus. Here, print becomes *theatre* dominated by the clash of personalities, a product itself of division, confrontation, humiliation and human interest. Judgement, too, becomes a mode of action, an *event* rather than a process of discrimation and in so doing confirms that taste is always a matter of *antagonism* and refusal: a landscape of struggle and dispute. Together, spectacle and action combine to make the literary award the equivalent of a *sporting* event (bookmakers have long offered odds) in which competition is accentuated and winners defined. Good taste becomes partisanship and touting; authorial practice now a refined form of entrepreneurial activity.

The prize ceremony is the most evident point where one can see literature accelerated into event, into a space neither literary *per se* nor spectacle but which is designated as the site of the *literary* proper. The status of serious fiction is confirmed in selection and contendership. As such, literature is not an end in itself nowadays but a *pause* before conversion into other media and other significant spaces, where the literary can be confirmed in what it is not: television and film.

This is exactly the point with the late twentieth-century craze for Jane Austen adaptations. In such ways 'serious' fictional literature is always not quite itself, always awaiting adaptation, always a scenario rather than a novel. But this *pause* is what recognises serious literature *as* serious – its untranslatable nature (its *quality*) captured in the infinite care of authorial expertise (the novel's very 'style'). Such a paradox acts as nostalgia for the days when print was an end in itself, and the contemporary serious novel performs (in its very resurgence) a homage to the nobility of print and its inherent moral purpose. Serious novels are, even as they sell in their thousands, anachronistic in form. The very resurgence of serious novels during the 'philistine' 1980s was a peculiar instance of the simulacrum: print as the *sine qua non* of the novel's ontological condition, at the very moment when the conditions for the novel's success were predicated on non-literary foundations. At such a point, print again took on value as the exemplary condition of culture's expression: its guarantor.

Yet this was a false perspective – a self-induced hallucination of literature's guardians. In the nineteenth century the novel called to the impresario and the theatrical agent. Now they call the television or movie producer. What has changed is not the speed of adaptation but the expectation of adaptation. Serious fiction is the hallucination of the fixity of print confirmed in the equivocal nature of literary prize fashions and presented in the ephemeral space of film and television.

If it takes an author to write a book, it takes an industry to make it public and an entire culture to confirm its status. 'Fickle' public approval and critical fashion nominate and then confirm the eternal qualities of art even as those qualities are 'denied' in the very structure of the judgemental process in which literature is a compliant servant.

The arbitration of newspaper reviewers in matters of artistic and literary taste is rarely a case of only determining the commercial success or failure of the latest novel. If, at the most basic level, the reviewer's duty is to inform and guide the consumer, at its highest it assumes the level of an ethical practice determined by civic duty.

This civic duty, apparent in the criticism of an F. R. Leavis, a Bernard Levin or a John Carey, takes culture as a given and the culture of the remnant (as Matthew Arnold called the guardians of civilisation) as the standard. The formal properties of high culture are a continual refusal of excess, vulgarity, noise, violence, sexuality and consumerism, replaced instead by restraint, coolness and irony.

In deciding the relative technical merits of a theatrical production or novel the reviewer's relationship to ephemeral taste (to the latest fashion) is tempered by an often unspoken allegiance to tradition and continuity, to organic community and to the moral trajectory of humanist literary production. As such, the reviewer takes on a role, which requires him or her to be objective, professional and technically knowledgeable. This creates a certain paradox, as the critic must be seen to be an expert only in as much as he reflects the amateur status of his readers. The critic then becomes a trusted friend of the reader rather than the managerial professional that he or she is. This is the mark of the 'gentleman' reader (and the 'lady' reader), always on guard against the shrillness and excitability of feminist, ethnic and other ethically committed positions.

Yet the reviewer is also and primarily a connoisseur, someone whose inherent good breeding is essentially trustworthy (because natural) and therefore actually opposed to professionalism (technocratic training). Culture can only be defended by nature – by the good-taste gene: upper middle-class and Anglo-Saxon in essentials. Critical 'disinterest', whilst the outcome of intense training (usually at the best universities) must appear to come from the antithesis of training, inherited sensibility appropriately displayed in exquisite particularity, articles thrown off as entertaining bravado for a public that needs to be kept amused. The commercial book review, in Sunday newspaper or even literary magazine, is therefore, in essence, a hybrid and problematic exercise.

Books for review usually come into the hands of a literary editor in one of three ways: direct from publishers (or PR consultants) as a result of being on a mailing list; by special request, because the editor and his or her staff have consulted the publishers' catalogues; or as a result of recommendations from friends and colleagues.

Given the number of novels published each year it is very unlikely that most of them will be reviewed even once, and those which are may have to wait many months after the date of publication. The *Times Literary Supplement*, for instance, estimates that it reviews approximately 400 novels per year. Decisions must therefore be made about which books will be selected for review and which won't, and it is notable that one of the most important criteria is that reviews earn their place in a publication by being 'newsworthy' (even if it is a rather long time after 'the event' or publication date).

This concept of book reviews as 'news' is one which commonly gets little consideration, probably because anything to do with the arts is perceived as being in a different category, almost a different world, to that of everyday concerns. From a newspaper's or magazine's point of view, however, one of the principal ways by which book reviews (along with, for example, fashion or health stories) justify their existence is by being 'news' – albeit of a rather different nature to 'home', 'foreign' or 'sports' items. Anthony Burgess noted of the job of a reviewer that, 'the task is a typical newspaper one of turning books into a kind of news. Of the millions of events that happen daily, some are more newsworthy than others... and so some books are more newsworthy than others.' The job of the literary editor is to decide what 'newsworthy' means in terms of books, and which books fit the criterion. In the event-hungry late twentieth- and early twenty-first centuries, 'Book pages have to justify their existence as lively journalism in a world in which journalism becomes livelier every day. Your hardened journalist begrudges the precious space given to book reviewing', suggested Philip Howard, former literary editor at *The Times* (in A. J. Walford, *Reviews and Reviewing*). Publisher Anthony Blond noted in the 1990s that 'literary editors [were] journalists first and foremost and [got] paid to fill their columns with good copy' (see *The Book Book*).

One of the ways by which 'newsworthiness' and 'good copy' are translated into a visible presence on the book pages is described by Penny Perrick (of the *Sunday Times*), who indicated that amongst her choices would 'obviously be the new Martin Amis', one of her criteria being that 'if it's not by an established name that has to be treated as news, it's not sent out [to individual reviewers]' (interview, 9 December 1992). Amis is a significant figure in the cultural world as understood by Perrick's *Sunday Times* readers: a review of the new Amis novel would therefore be 'expected' by them. Many literary editors cite a similar 'benchmark' author, and each expresses similar views about their duties and responsibilities in relation to books and readers. At the same time, however, it is hard to overlook their rather self-important view that everyone will obviously agree with their selections. Opinions run from,

I can't ignore the next Milan Kundera novel, even though I know everyone's going to review it, still it wouldn't be fair to our readers ...we owe it to our readers to review the important and good novels ...

(Lola Bubbosh, interview, 28 February 1991)

to,

Apart from the obvious ones that one simply had to cover ...you'd be doing something pretty perverse if you didn't want to review the new Umberto Eco ...

(Alan Jenkins, interview, 18 April 1991)

to,

[Even though it is not good fiction], *Ambition* is a novel by Julie Burchill and therefore you cannot ignore it: it's a big deal, everybody's going to want to read it because it's a novel by Julie Burchill ...

(Jenny Turner, interview, 18 February 1991)

Each editor feels that they have a duty to provide reviews of particular books, either because readers want them or because certain novels are believed to be important and have therefore somehow earned notice. The belief system which underpins this supports the attitude of self-importance expressed in distinctly paternalistic tones by several editors who describe how they provide not only what their readers want (there seems to be no question that they do know what this is) but also what is 'good for them' – what they should know about.

The role of the serious reviewer, if that of an educator and informer, may include supporting serious neglected, underrated or new authors but rarely runs to the point of acknowledging genre fiction. If popular fiction is reviewed it is done under the pretext of newsworthiness rather than as literature worthy of notice. Where a popular author is reviewed it may well be simply to burst their bubble of pretension. Usually such fiction is simply dismissed because not part of the same 'serious' culture. Genre fiction (a.k.a. popular literature) elicits quite different responses from serious reviewers. Alan Jenkins, for instance, has suggested that he would 'certainly review [John le Carré's] novels because he takes himself so sodding seriously...he actually asks for critical attention' (interview 18 April 1991). There is a clear implication here that Jenkins believes le Carré's work to be good enough to merit a review but that the review itself would almost certainly take a dismissive or ironic position in order to diminish le Carré's self-importance ('he takes himself so sodding seriously'). Of Julie Burchill's novel *Ambition*, which became a bestseller, Jenkins has only this to say about the reason why he did not review the book, 'it was', he tells us, 'just too god-awful stinking bad'. Indeed, 'why review that?' (interview, 18 April 1999).

Another prominent reviewer explains,

> I'm going to have slightly different criteria if I'm given a novel that is said to be 'the best novel of the year' and it turns out just a thriller. Whereas if I was given it as a thriller then I would evaluate it as such, so it partly depends on how the publisher presents it. If they present it just as 'a novel' then I'm probably judging it on the harshest characteristics, I want it to have all sorts of things from the liberal literary critical tradition: depth of character, tautness of plot and so on. Whereas perhaps if the way it was presented was slightly narrower then I would narrow down my criteria...if it was presented as a thriller than perhaps I would be more interested in the plot being efficient and suspenseful than in the depth of character or in the inventiveness of the language.
>
> (Greg Woods, interview, 18 April 1991)

When is a novel not a novel? Apparently when it's 'popular'.

Anthony Burgess correspondingly detailed why he had a narrower set of criteria for judging thrillers:

In a sense it is quite impossible to review a novel by Frederick Forsyth, because it achieves perfectly what it sets out to do. *The Fourth Protocol* is perfection...The perfection depends on limitation...it does not share the properties which we find, say, in William Shakespeare – complexity of character, difficulty of language, the exploitation of ambiguity.

(*The Observer*, 30 August 1992)

There are notable resemblances between these two sets of criteria, particularly between their references to character and language. Most importantly, however, their approach to such literature is similar and can be best illustrated by comparing Burgess's comment about *The Fourth Protocol* – that it 'achieves...what it sets out to do' – with the previous, comment that the plot should be 'efficient and suspenseful'. In other words, popular genre fiction must be technically efficient and, therefore, must have a utilitarian function. As such, it is opposed to the liberal, literary (critical) tradition against which it is both judged and diminished.

For some reviewers, popular fiction not only requires different criteria but those criteria must cease to have any connection to the literary at all. Many reviewers accept that there is something like a two-tier system for judging either serious or popular writing, which seems to require different sets of evaluative criteria. Alan Jenkins happily endorses the view that one is duty bound to uphold such a position. With regard to the reviewing of historical romance he expounds that, 'you're reviewing a genre, you're not reviewing an individual novel, you're reviewing a formula'. Against such reviewers, popular fiction (popular enjoyment) has no court of appeal – the more successful it is, the more damned; the more popularly successful the author, the less likely to write in an individualistic manner!

Jenkins adds,

We will always review the best and the most deserving cases in science fiction, that have come out of the closet [*sic*] or out of the margins or off the margins or whatever...it is a truth universally acknowledged...that the intellectual's idea of a holiday is to open a crime novel.

(Interview, 18 April 1991)

Popular novels are not merely the antithesis of *the novel*, they are also the antithesis of the tradition in which the novel has flourished and is critically supported. Popular fiction provides a type of negative space in which the literary and literacy are negated. In such escapism as the popular novel offers we take a vacation from the very processes that we are engaged in pursuing, those of reading and evaluation. By avoiding reviewing popular fiction, the serious reviewer proclaims his or her credentials. The serious novel requires the reader to make strenuous efforts to be educated and informed. This is not merely work but *vocation*. To suggest that reviewing novels for a living is itself a continuous, delightful holiday for the connoisseur, dilettante and journalist is perhaps to hammer home an irony that only the crass reader of popular fiction might find amusing.

III

Nowhere is this more clearly demonstrated than in the tawdry, awful and hilarious proceedings that began one freezing day in New York City in Supreme Court 60. The case (which opened in October 1994) centred on *Dynasty* star Joan Collins.[6]

Collins had had a long and varied career since starting as a Rank starlet in the 1950s. Following a lull in her film career, the leading role in *Dynasty* made her an international star and this had allowed her to branch out into popular fiction. Her sister, Jackie Collins, had been a consistently popular writer since the 1960s and Joan and her publishers had soon realised her own potential. Her publications, though not as successful as her sister's, had, nevertheless, already sold 50,000 copies in Britain and America, but with 'Joan Collins fever sweeping the UK' (as one publisher put it at the trial), any new work was set to be the biggest blockbuster *of all time*, surpassing even Jackie's extraordinary sales. A two-book deal with Random House having been brokered, Collins was the recipient of advances worth $4 million, to be paid in stages as manuscripts arrived.

The case revolved around one of the manuscripts, *The Ruling Passion*, that Random House asserted had been delivered 'unfinished' (i.e. not a complete manuscript) and which Collins and her attorneys argued had been delivered finished and complete as required under the contract. Random House, eager to recover half a million dollars paid out on a worthless collection of disconnected pages, sued for breach of contract at the Supreme Court, New York. The argument was clear: when is a manuscript 'complete'?

The question in law was one of contractual obligation, but it could not be resolved 'in law' without a lengthy courtroom debate determined by questions of narrative, style and literary 'quality'. Indeed, the legal niceties of the case turned precisely on the relationship between business and aesthetics – the entrepreneurial authoress versus the corporate giant, the qualitative value of a narrative and its quantitative presence (as a delivered manuscript). Just what, in anybody's opinion, constituted a properly delivered novel? Was it the author's opinion or the publisher's? Was a *finished* manuscript an object or an aesthetic judgement, or both? Here, the judgement of law met the judgement of literary criticism (itself doubling as good *business* acumen).

It is true that there may have been little to debate, if Joan Collins's agent had not, with uncanny prescience (both of aesthetic judgement and business sense), renegotiated contractual obligations so that the US contract required only that the manuscript of *The Ruling Passion* be delivered *on time* and regardless of quality! If Collins met those requirements Random House would have no right to withhold payment of advances even if they thought the manuscript was 'rubbish'! Random House's interpretation of this clause was that a *complete* manuscript was one ready for editing and then publication: a complete narrative without narrative gaps or gaffes produced to the author's 'best efforts' and agreed by all parties as ready for a public readership. Thus, Collins's attorneys, led by Ken Burrows, argued that *full* was a quantitative term referring to a delivered object whilst Random House's attorneys, led by Robert Callagy, argued that full meant *complete* qualitatively (i.e. publishable). When is a novel a novel and when does it become a blockbuster? The next days would decide.

The trial witnesses, almost all of whom were Random House employees, were all quizzed on the 'state' of the delivered work. What, in their opinions, was the status of the delivered manuscript? How, in short, could one separate a qualitative and aesthetic judgement about fiction from a legal and contractual question determined by money? For Random House and its editors, the answer lay in the aesthetic values and technical skill displayed in the writing – the definition of popular fiction itself. Joanie Evans felt the work, 'over-the-top, dated, melodramatic [and] not credible', the writing 'jumbled and disjointed' and of Collins's previous manuscript of *Hell Hath No Fury*, that it was 'alarming, frankly'. Leah Boyce could see nothing but 'tangles' that were 'far from resolved', a story without coherence and reliant on a mess of 'genres'. Rosemary Cheetham, Random House's British representative, found merely 'disjointed scenes', adding that Collins had chosen subject matter she knew nothing of: 'magazines [and] the New York business world!' Moreover, Collins's setting was also problematic as 'none of [them] knew anything about Monaco' (a comment which drew laughter).

With the appearance of Lucianne Goldberg, Collins's agent, questions of literary value turned rapidly to farce. Asked about narrative inconsistencies, which she could not answer, Goldberg parried with wit. Of one character's drug habit, which was suddenly dropped in the narrative, she replied 'it's a miracle'! When the same character (Desirée) contracts cancer but is later suddenly cured, Goldberg was asked, almost facetiously, by Random House's attorney Robert Callagy, when chemotherapy had occurred. Her reply that 'she (Desiree) must have been very sick. She didn't tell anybody!' brought further humour to proceedings, as did her ironic insistence that all inconsistencies be put down to divine providence – yet 'another miracle!'

Defending Collins's integrity as an author, her attorneys were happy to concede that she was 'not James Joyce or Proust' and that her intention was to write 'commercial fictions . . . like . . . Jackie Collins', intended to have 'fancy and fantastical plots', and be obsessively concerned with 'money, sex, power and sex, and intrigue and sex'. Indeed, when Collins herself took the stand, indignant, hurt and self-consciously 'English', she freely admitted her work was 'over the top', 'melodramatic' and 'more colourful'.

When is a novel a novel? When is a manuscript complete? Summing up, Judge Ira Gammerman found no grounds to suggest that Joan Collins had welched on her contract even if it needed 'editors', 'book doctors' or 'ghost writers'. A novel is a novel when it is delivered on time, when complete means a coherent (or semi-coherent) narrative, and when 125,000 words is not mere gibberish. Random House was ordered to pay Collins $1 million and Dutton published her ninth book, *Infamous*, during March 1996. The multi-million dollar advance blockbuster had ceased to exist, but Joan Collins hadn't. Her personal triumph was also something more. Acquitted by a female literate jury it was also the vindication of the popular. Marry me, Joan Collins!

Part III

Under Dreaming Spires:
The Academic World

5

The Nature of the University at the Present Time

Far from the popular image of a timeless, unchanging guardian of cultural standards, the university also has a history of change. Like all other social institutions it is bound by the economic, social and political pressures it is subject to and which it helped to shape. Most obviously, women and many ethnic minorities have only had access to this white male world for a relatively short time and working-class school leavers, whether male or female, are still grossly underrepresented in the more prestigious of our institutions of learning. What then constitutes a university becomes a question with important ramifications.

Citizenship and culture seem to be at the centre of this question, but neither citizens, cultures nor democracies have ever needed universities, such places enjoying privileged status under many types of government. Indeed, it should not be forgotten that universities in Britain became what they are today relatively recently: no earlier that the 1960s and perhaps as late as the 1980s.

The nineteenth-century liberal university, dedicated to disinterested or impartial knowledge (a relatively modern concept) coincided with the opening of education to Nonconformists, Jews and women and the appearance of a model of disciplinary and objective study: inorganic scientific inquiry. All the human sciences necessarily conformed to this model of inquiry, which itself was a factor in the opening of educational opportunity; the two were inseparably and paradoxically joined: method as enlightened liberation and education in preparation for service to the state, its civil and diplomatic needs. Here the methods of the physical sciences, with their quantification, measurement, experimental approach and belief in progress were the informational expression of political enfranchisement (and co-option) and democratic involvement in an age of rapid industrial reorganisation and expansion. Scientific inquiry seemed to have the impartiality that recognised neither gender, race nor class position. No cultural inquiry could *exist* outside such a paradigm and sociology, psychology, anthropology, archaeology, social geography and finally English Literature all conformed to the scientific liberal model.

The role of the university was once crucial to the production and definition of official cultural *identity* (it has always been irrelevant to the lived *vitality* of a culture). It is this role we must next consider in the wider context of culture as a system open to both cultural analysis and intellectual control and direction.

In an age of disestablished certainties we are entitled to reopen the questions regarding the conditions governing the organisation, management and dissemination of knowledge in the first world – a question which is crucial to the survival of (academic) inquiry for the next half-century. This question of the relationship between data, data management and the status of information production is nothing if not central to the provision of academic disciplines and the codification of cultural inquiry. At the centre of this problem is the nature of the privilege accorded the university in the creation of knowledge and the position and status of academics, whose role is no longer clear, within organisations whose charitable status belies their market-led business aggressiveness.

The most important business of business in the early twenty-first century is the management and control of information, processed and systematised into knowledge paradigms (that is, into *economic* units). The university is one such producer of knowledge, whose position is now threatened by the proliferation of other information processing businesses. Governed by economic targets and endless constraints (student demands, employer demands, government demands) the university has been revealed (in its macro-organisational structure) as one *business* amongst others. It is a knowledge business, dedicated to the organisation and systematisation of information. A university is a privileged, diversified information business.

In 1937, Queenie Leavis wrote a famously vitriolic review of the work of Dorothy L. Sayers. In it she attacked the diminution of standards in the academy and deplored the 'invasion' of popular culture, misrepresented (as she saw it) as legitimate literature by those who should have known better – the academics themselves. The *moral* decline of the university was partly to be explained by the philistinism of academics, but that was just a symptom which could be explained by the university's degradation into 'trade'. Mrs Leavis concluded,

> In fact the more one investigates the academic world the more striking appears its resemblance to the business world (I recently met someone who had collected a lot of data showing this, he was distressed). Here, too, to be disinterested or unconventional is to be eccentric and dangerous; here, too, to be materially successful you must be a good herd member; here too, the trade union and the club spirit obtain.
>
> (Q. D. Leavis, Scrutiny, vol. 4, 1937)

What Leavis regretted was not Sayers's false romanticising of the dreaming spires, but that it were ever *true* – for Mrs Leavis the world was already old, corrupt and riddled with self-interest. The Arnoldian virtues were a mythic ideal; her 'investigator' was morally defeated ('he was distressed') by his findings and so was she, offering instead an alternative university, uncorrupted and dedicated to universal truth and enlightenment. For her, the university existed only as a pastiche of itself; as business, something it should not have been.

Leavis's retreat from the modern world, her implied distance from any form of *mass* cultural experience (which she saw only as false and debased), also cut her and her husband off from the very things they wished to engage with more closely. More particularly, and leaving aside her dislike of business as a simplistic snobbism, (indeed a distaste for her own class, as had her husband for his own family's class of small traders), Queenie Leavis saw no difference between the dissemination of knowledge by a teacher and the management of knowledge by a university organisation. Her distress at the debasement of educated taste was based on an attack on a chimera of her own making, and not on the realities of a historical situation.

Mrs Leavis's incidental comments were taken up again by her husband in his attack on C. P. Snow's Rede Lecture of 1959, 'The Two Cultures'. Snow's lecture, and subsequently published essay, argued that an unbridgeable gap had appeared within the university between its scientific and literary specialists. This *knowledge gap* had split the cultural homogeneity of Western countries in the same way as cultural homogeneity had been split in the nineteenth century between the rich and the poor (Disraeli's 'two nations'). For Snow, the crucial point was not just the knowledge gap (amounting to two irreconcilable languages) but that those empowered to *manage* knowledge were wholly ignorant of the meaning of that knowledge, being educated outside of, and subsequently contemptuous of, scientists and their methods. Snow argued that this amounted to a cultural crisis whose epicentre was the university itself.

> I believe the intellectual life of the whole of western society is increasingly being split into two polar groups. . . .
> Literary intellectuals at one pole – at the other scientists, and as the most representative, the physical scientists.

The problem as Snow saw it was that 'literary intellectuals' following T. S. Eliot (whom he took as an 'archetypal figure') abrogated to themselves the guardianship of a culture they could not command or direct, in short, a common culture of endeavour they could only wish out of existence. Indeed 'they still liked to pretend that the traditional culture was the whole of "culture"', he complained,

> Furthermore, if we forget the scientific culture, then the rest of western intellectuals have never tried, wanted, or been able to understand the industrial revolution, much less accept it.

Snow concluded that 'intellectuals, in particular literary intellectuals, were natural Luddites'. Regardless of the virtues of science and the vanities of literature, Snow did notice the conditions governing knowledge and the *management* of knowledge yet he failed to give sufficient emphasis either to the processes of scientific production (its discursive space) or its context of managerialism. And so he tells us without further explanation,

> If the scientists have the future in their bones, then the traditional culture responds by wishing the future did not exist. It is the traditional culture . . . which manages the western world.

Snow saw the gulf between the scientists and the literary critic, but he failed to identify the two emergent areas that would change the outlook of both: management and computerised automation.

Of these two poles, management was the emergent area in the 1950s. Yet management belonged to the world of business that Snow, like Leavis, could not address. Also, and perhaps from a psychological point of view more importantly, its theorists usually emanated from the United States, a country then dismissed as uncouth and common by English cultural thinkers.

Snow's arguments were predated by Peter Drucker's *The Practice of Management* (published in 1955). Although unrelated to the question of academic culture, Drucker's book set out the necessary conditions for successful organisational management. His argument essentially offered a philosophical rationale for management and shifted the emphasis from traditional concerns over 'labour' to contemporary hopes for managerial productivity. Such a shift de-emphasised the exploitation of proletarian resources and placed the onus on business and on *wealth-creating* management. This argument, whilst influential in business debates, was ignored by sociological debates obsessed with labour, exploitation and marginality and alienation. Drucker's humanism led him to limit the remit of management and restrict it to the business sphere proper. However the ramifications of his theory were pertinent to any managed organisation seen *as a business*.

> The manager is the dynamic, life-giving element in every business. Without his leadership 'the resources of production' remain resources and never become production. In a competitive economy, above all, the quality and performance of the managers determine the success of a business, indeed they determine its survival. For the quality and performance of its managers is the only effective advantage an enterprise in a competitive economy can have.
>
> Management is also a distinct and a leading group in industrial society.
>
> (Peter Drucker, *The Practice of Management*)

The historical emergence of management marked the appearance of truly modern Western society, but this was predicated on a view which gave the term 'management' to a movement in thought which expressed a fundamental shift in Western ontology and epistomology.

> Management also expresses the basic beliefs of modern Western society. It expresses the belief in the possibility of controlling man's livelihood through systematic organisation of economic resources. It expresses the belief that economic change can be made into the most powerful engine for human betterment and social justice.... This belief that the material can and should be used to advance the human spirit is not just the age-old human heresy 'materialism'. In fact, it is incompatible with materialism as the term has always been understood. It is something new, distinctly modern, distinctly Western. Prior to, and outside of, the modern West, resources have always been

considered a limit to man's activities, a restriction on his control over his environment – rather than an opportunity and tool of his control over nature. They have always been considered God-given and unchangeable. Indeed all societies, except the modern West, have looked upon economic change as a danger to society and individual alike. . . .

Management, which is the organ of society specifically charged with making resources productive, that is, with the responsibility for organised economic advance, therefore reflects the basic spirit of the modern age.

(Drucker, ibid.)

The paradigm shift Drucker described has two phases: the first is the simple exploitation of large amounts of raw material. For the eighteenth century, the abundance of nature was an *infinite* resource. For our ecologically minded age this is not so, but Drucker's paradigm embraces the second model of *finite* resource. Whereas once, in the early industrial revolution, large amounts of raw material yielded relatively low returns, now small amounts of raw material yield relatively very high returns. The management of resources, however defined, is the question here, not their abundance. Consequently, the management of resources does not merely move those resources around, process them and distribute them, it also *defines* resource in the first instance: all else is consequent upon that primary definition. Thus information *recognised as economic wealth* is an *infinite* resource and cannot be reduced by usage (it circulates and changes). Indeed, it exponentially increases by usage, as no other material can, as Toffler was to point out over a decade later,

The shift to this new form of capital explodes the assumptions that underpin both Marxist ideology and classical economics, premised alike on the finite character of traditional capital. For unlike land or machines, which can be used by only one person or firm at a time, the same knowledge can be applied by many different users at the same time – and if used cleverly by them, it can generate even more knowledge. It is inherently inexhaustible and nonexclusive.

(Alvin Toffler, *Power Shift*)

It is not necessary to insist that Drucker had begun to define most of what needs to be applied to the business of knowledge and specifically to the university, but we can see that 'management as such is the management of a *business* enterprise' and it is judged by 'the economic results it produces'. The university deals in knowledge and knowledge *is* economic power. As such, despite Drucker's scrupulous division of 'achievement' (business) from 'knowledge' (the academy, the church, etc.), those divisions produced by . . . humanist scruples no longer hold totally true. Consequently, Drucker's argument that

> The skills, the competence, the experience of management cannot, as such, be transferred and applied to the organisation and running of other institutions. In particular a man's success in management carries by itself no promise – let alone a guarantee – of his being successful in government. A career in management is, by itself, not a preparation for major political office – or for leadership in the Armed Forces, the Church or a university.
>
> (Drucker, op. cit.)

holds true only in the narrow practical sense and not in the *wider* philosophical framework governing attitudinal change in modern Western thought. Such an insight comes close to surfacing in consequent paragraphs, hence:

> The scope and extent of management's authority and responsibility are severely limited. It is true that in order to discharge its business responsibility management must exercise substantial social and governing authority within the enterprise – authority over citizens in their capacity as members of the enterprise. It is also a fact that because of the importance of the business enterprise, management inevitably becomes one of the leading groups in industrial society.
>
> (Ibid.)

The final factor is the notion of profit: universities are businesses in as much as they limit their growth only in relation to economic endeavour (by private and governmental grants, endowments, etc.). For Drucker, profits are *not* the sole or main purpose of a business, rather,

> It does mean that profitability is not the purpose of business enterprise and business activity, but a limiting factor on it. Profit is not the explanation, cause or rationale of business behaviour and business decisions, but the test of their validity. . . . For the problem of any business is not the maximization of profit but the achievement of sufficient profit to cover the risks of economic activity and thus to avoid loss.
>
> (Ibid.)

Just like any complex organism, an organisation's prime function is to survive, adapt and master its environment. Just like many complex organisms, the destruction of competition may itself be detrimental to its well-being. Thus brute competition and the elimination of competitors is not the prime object of an organisation but a *consequence* of *mediated* external circumstances. This is, of course, true of the university, which, with its managerial structures, corporate missions, objectives and programmes of staff appraisal is a curious blend of 1950s managerialism and 1990s information culture.

Snow was concerned directly with the academy, Drucker less so, but both taken together shift the emphasis from 'culture' towards *knowledge management*. This ugly formulation is nevertheless far closer to the truth of liberal universities as historically formed macro-organisations (determined actually by active *achievement* rather than by passive 'knowledge') than Queenie Leavis's idealist myth of cultural guardianship. The culture of business in its *widest* sense is the same culture shared by universities: the creation of productive citizens and the circulation of goods and services for the benefit of all. The very best altruistic academic *qua* academic, in as much as he or she serves the concerns of the university, is no more, *nor any less* than an enlightened specialist whose relationship to the student body and to research will always be based on achievements. The passive reception of knowledge cannot be seen as knowledge at all in any real sense. Knowledge is not merely currency because it involves an *act of volition*.

II

Our discussion of management has suggested certain organisational principles behind the modern university but it has not yet brought into play the nature of knowledge nor the relationship between information and knowledge. The third volume of Alvin Toffler's *Future Shock* trilogy marks out clearly the relationship between 'money' and knowledge in the late twentieth century:

> Thus agricultural-era money, consisting of metal (or some other commodity), had a knowledge content close to zero. Indeed, this First Wave money was not only tangible and durable, it was also *pre-literate* – in the sense that its value depended on its weight, not on the words imprinted on it.

Today's Second Wave money consists of printed paper with or without commodity backing. What's printed on the paper matters. The money is symbolic but still tangible. This form of money comes along with mass literacy.

Third Wave money increasingly consists of electronic pulses. It is evanescent . . . instantaneously transferred . . . monitored on the video screen. It is, in fact, virtually a video phenomenon itself. Blinking, flashing, whizzing across the plain, Third Wave money *is* information – the basis of knowledge.

(Alvin Toffler, *The Third Wave*)

Nevertheless, information transformed into knowledge will not act effectively unless structurally organised. Such structuring turns the commodification of knowledge into a fluid exchange mechanism. But, and most importantly, this fluidity is realisable in a multiplicity of *simultaneous* returns. Knowledge as sacred object (as in theology or any discipline with a canonical body of information) is thus replaced with knowledge as a fluid exchange mechanism. Yet the exchange is not *directly* in goods but comes in the form of further processed information. Goods and other tangibles come only secondarily and then they too act as *symbols* and not as objects *qua* objects.

This new system for making wealth is totally dependent on the instant communication and dissemination of data, ideas, symbols, and symbolism. It is . . . a super-symbolic economy in the exact sense of that term.

(Ibid.)

This saturated system is governed by the circulation and return of knowledge and breaks with the 'narrative' progress of a knowledge consisting of discrete objects whose individual trajectories are linearly organised and realisable only sequentially (as one unit *after* another unit). Bureaucratic specialisation, by which the liberal university may be clearly recognised as an organisation, acts to reinforce this linearity and does so by condoning information groups and procedures. Thus 'bureaucracy . . . is also a way of grouping "facts"' (Peter Drucker, *The New Realities*).

III

We have now grouped the main elements that hold a university together as a structure. These organisational considerations determine the totality of the university as a part of the knowledge industry. Universities remain (at the moment) a relatively privileged part of that system but it has been shown that this privilege is based on certain misunderstandings and certain misconceptions and a certain level of nostalgia. As one component in the knowledge system, the university acts in order to manage, organise, direct and disseminate knowledge as an economy of information. In the modern world this firstly parallels, then displaces and finally *re*places the flow of capital and the transfer of money. None of this is directly obvious at the level of individual teaching, but it becomes increasingly visible at the level of research, income and faculty or college organisation and where university budgets are counted in tens or hundreds of millions of dollars, pounds, yen or marks.

Knowledge transforms structurally; structure changes the basis of the knowable; managed information is knowledge structured. These three concepts – structure, management and information – determine knowledge. They are integral to the question of knowledge itself and were always inherent in those conditions governing the modern university and its place in advanced, industrial, capitalist countries.

It was in the United States in the nineteenth century that the relationship between business and knowledge was first explored and its language expressed within the demands of Jamesian pragmatism. The key terms were 'process', 'verification' and 'satisfaction', the last itself similar to Drucker's idea of 'achievement'.

> The truth of an idea is not a stagnant property inherent in it. Truth *happens* to an idea. It *becomes* true, is *made* true by events. Its verity *is* in fact an event, a process: the process namely of its verifying itself, its *verification*. Its validity is the process of its validation . . . [Concepts being] true in so far as they help us to get satisfactory results.
>
> (William James, in Bertram Russell, *Philosophical Essays*)

Pragmatism also recognised the relationship between knowledge and capital. Hence: 'Our account of truth is an account of truths in the plural . . . having only this quality in common, that they *pay*' (emphasis added).

In the creation of 'new value', the university is no different from the commercial world but equally the commercial world of information management (at the end of the twentieth century) came closest to the world of unaligned knowledge in the university itself. Kenichi Ohmae's definition of a consultancy agency in New York, London or Tokyo now sounds strangely similar to Queenie Leavis's ideal university:

My own firm ... has long experimented with this form of global organisation. The centre provides only a few 'corporate' functions. All of our work with clients around the world is carried out through a network of offices and entrepreneurial individuals, connected to each other by criss-crossing lines of communication rather than lines of authority. These multiple linkages make possible the dissemination throughout our firm of important new learning in any one part of it. Equally important, these linkages mean that creative work can happen – and be recognised and celebrated – anywhere in the network. There is competition in the sense that all our professionals want to provide exceptional value for clients, but there is no conflict because no one instance of first-rate performance detracts from or makes less likely or less visible any other. What holds this network together is our shared sense of identity, which is supported in turn by our commitment to a shared set of values.

(Ohmae, *The Borderless World*)

Such a situation led Alvin Toffler to enthuse:

Many American managers still think of the organisation as a 'machine'. ... This is the bureaucratic metaphor. By contrast, many Japanese are already using a post-bureaucratic metaphor – the corporation ... is a 'living creature'.

(Toffler, *Power Shock*)

And yet, it is precisely now, at the moment of the realisation of multiplicity within homogeneity (the organic metaphor of the living biological structure), that a 'shared sense of identity' and a 'shared set of values' collapses, requiring constant tinkering and attention through 'mission statements' and codes of practice designed to reinforce managerialism and paternalism. All common ground was stripped away, almost as if it was, or had always been, a hallucination.

For Ohmae and Toffler the ideal information organisation was one that follows a neurological or organic pattern. As information providers, the university and the consultancy were essentially equivalent organisations determined by similar attitudes, work ethics and goals. This model assumed that organisations were analogues of human interaction, especially biological interaction. Such a notion had its heyday in the late 1970s and early 1980s and replaced an older model, which *separated* the human participants from their designated roles within a structure. Biologism assumed that personnel could be equated with organic function and that each organic function enjoyed a direct relationship with the organism's health. The organic/symbiotic model took little account of bureaucratic organisations which are founded on an inherent, internal disjunction. Such an organisation is a university in which the structure of knowledge is at odds with the production of knowledge.

The nature of this problem was noticed as early as the 1960s – the culmination of a long period of soul-searching over the nature and function of bureaucracy. One writer, for instance, begins by comparing the organisation and decision processes of humans and bureaucracies.

> The behavior of both individuals and organizations changes constantly. However, during any given period when some elements are changing, others must remain stable, or there will be a loss of identity. For example, the specific behavior of an individual or bureau may be quite different on Tuesday from what it was on Monday, but the rules governing that behavior may be the same on both days. . . .
>
> Each individual's goal structure contains different layers of goals, varying from profound to shallow ones. Since the individual's behavior reflects his goals, we can identify the depth of his actions by relating them to specific layers in his goal structure. In this way, we can conceptually distinguish what depths of actions or goals are involved when an individual undergoes change.
>
> Similarly, organizations have different structural depths.
>
> (A. Downs, in F. G. Castles *et al.*, *Decisions, Organisations and Society*)

Yet this writer soon relinquishes this model in favour of a non-biological one in which disjunction plays a vital role. Hence,

> As each official goes through the decision and action process, he behaves somewhat differently from the way he would if his goals were identical to the formal purposes of the organisation.
>
> (Downs, ibid.)

The reasons for this are evident when one looks at a comparative list (drawn up as early as 1967) of decision making procedures which is then produced as a consequence of such deliberation (see table on p. 135). The model is ostensibly about time in relation to decision making and especially the problem of lead-in times; nevertheless it highlights the division between local and global knowledge production in a bureaucratic structure. Moreover, it is determined by the antagonism generated in any organisation divided between departmental long-term goals and managerial short-term goals; the needs of the organisation to react to short-term fluctuations and the innate conservatism of departments resisting disruptive change.

Policies that tend to extend degree of search and increase diversity of alternatives considered	Policies that tend to contract degree of search and narrow diversity of alternatives considered
Allow a long time before conclusions must be reached	Enforce a very short deadline
Bring many people into decision making	Restrict decision making to a small number
Insure that those involved have a wide variety of views and interests – even conflicting	Insure that those involved have similar views and interests
Reduce number of persons to whom final decision must be justified or intelligibly communicated	Increase number of persons to whom final decision must be justified or intelligibly communicated
Increase proportion of analytically skilful or highly trained persons participating, or to whom it must be justified or communicated	Decrease proportion of analytically skilful or highly trained persons participating, or to whom it must be justified or communicated
Isolate those making decision from pressures of responsibility for other decisions, especially short deadline ones	Assign the decision to those immersed in making other decisions, especially short deadline ones
Reduce proportion of extremely busy persons to whom decision must be intelligibly communicated	Increase proportion of extremely busy persons to whom decision must be intelligibly communicated

(from Downs, ibid.)

What is curiously clear from the two methods of decision making is that the left-hand column relates to the production of local knowledge, corresponding to the individual disciplines, their subject problems and research possibilities, and that the right-hand column deals with the general problems of managing a large organisation. This itself corresponds to the function level associated with non-academic policy makers and institutional functionaries. Added to this is the peculiarity of the university's make up: that it requires for its prestige (its rationale) a group of specialists whose loyalty goes *beyond* the institution and associates itself with 'pure' knowledge. There is at this level no possibility of loyalty, as such loyalty would diminish research ideals to local business practice.

No talk of mission statements, teams, interdisciplinarity, task forces or democratic management, etc. can reduce this attitudinal gap as it is precisely this gap that allows the university to succeed and compete in the first place. The attempt to mask such problems in order to widen access has the potential to erode the meaning of a university in the first place. By 1975, on the eve of the expansion of higher education, critics were already asking, 'on top of doubts about how higher education is to be financed, there are serious doubts about quite what its purposes are' (A. King, in Castles *et al.*). Such questions remain difficult to answer and are increasingly responded to by vocational promises.

IV

The plain fact of the matter is that no one can exactly define the function of a university but its discrete local disciplines can all be defended *individually*. At best, the university is a conglomeration of discrete entities, which functions to maximise the opportunities for those discrete entities. At worst, the university is an amalgamation of contradictory impulses. Yet this is precisely what provokes dynamism at the local level – the level of knowledge – and must continually be reined-in at the structural level, that is, at the level of general management. This reining-in is a bureaucratic function, which determines the level of knowledge production and therefore the amount of allowable structural or organisational fragmentation. When the modern university ceases to have a direct cultural and ideological relationship with state policy then the nature of the university's role is put in crisis.

When the university no longer functions to create civil servants for the state, rulers for the Empire or clerics for the church it falls back upon its technocratic and instrumentalist possibilities as a training ground for a merely generalised managerial class. The university will attempt to create (through government coercion) a rationale for its disciplines that fits governmental and industrial policy. At the local level of knowledge production within the disciplines this ought to provoke a *resistance*, in which repositioning is questioned. In the last twenty years disciplines not purely vocational or managerial in tone have been forced to reassess their rationale, shifting from talk about the subject to talk about talk about the subject to talk about the possibility of a subject: displacement of a displacement of a displacement.

Critical breakdown is the necessary and normal framework for cultural thinking when contemporary life becomes both the standard of measurement and the subject matter of enquiry and when vernacular language and concerns become the medium of enquiry. When archaic, *set* standards are dropped cultural enquiry can do little more than freefall: hence its weaknesses, hence its power. What appears in its stead is the *control* of the present, its regulation; thus management, technicism, professionalism. The proper study of culture is now no longer enquiry into the forces of civilisation but the management of democratic *production*. *Management studies is the new humanities* bereft of its liberal component.

In the 1990s, Sir Douglas Hague (then associate fellow of Templeton College, Oxford) highlighted the threat to universities from other knowledge businesses. He suggested that 'the current stage of economic development [was] strongly based on the acquisition, analysis and transmission of information and on its application', and that 'universities will be forced to share, or even give up part of, their role as repositories of information and powerhouses for ideas' (*Times Higher Education Supplement*, 13 November, 1998). Peter Drucker had prophesied some years earlier that 'lessons from the United States's experience show ... that once for-profit providers gain a foothold in the education market, the risk to non-enterprise-like, more traditionally, organised providers rapidly escalates' (Drucker, *The New Realities*, op. cit.). For these reasons, management studies has increasingly became the discipline and the practice through and in which the 'humanities' acquire recognition, impact and relevance.

Humanities, forced to re-evaluate its scheme of accepted values, became unsure of itself and became a permanent opposition. An ironic sign of democratic participation in a benevolently authoritarian universe, humanities is the necessary sign of democracy within the university. It is the sign of civilisation without the substance. Managerialism, professionalisation and technology invade the new liberal arts – the essence of modern civil pride: prestigious, acclaimed and rewarded. They alone employ the powerful and acknowledged tools of enquiry. To compete, traditional humanities either have to succumb or stay in permanently induced crisis, the crisis of opposition without power.

Private, virtual, mega- and corporate universities have recently been formed in association with an increasingly growing number of existing academic institutions. Six now exist in the UK. The growing 'awareness' that universities *are* businesses and that they must compete or align themselves with corporate training has meant that the humanities have also realigned themselves along such lines. Yet this alignment is precisely what cannot be achieved without the humanities becoming managerial, metamorphosing into management studies offering training, technology and professional courses, led by university marketing departments acting under the vague remit of government pressure rather than student demand.

In the United Kingdom the alliance between New Labour and Thatcherite Conservatism is nowhere more apparent than around the question of 'innovative knowledge management' which to be successful requires that 'enterprise extends from companies *into* universities... across *all* disciplines' (emphasis added) – a demand made by Labour's Secretary for Trade and Industry, Peter Mandelson (disgraced for mortgage irregularities and forced to resign in 1998).[1] Mandelson's views seemed to be little more than a softening-up exercise in advance of David Blunkett's demand that humanities courses include a vocational work placement element.[2] It is hardly surprising that the (socialist) Labour Party that introduced tuition fees should also be the party to have revived the canard that a liberal education is a waste of tax payers' money unless allied to a vocational (instrumentalist) element, nor is it surprising that the discipline targeted was history.

The relationship between the teaching of the modern secular university and the requirements of the modern secular democratic state was and remains obscure. It is not sufficient to argue that the university creates 'thinking citizens' as both thinking and citizen change their meaning over time. Democratic higher education is an essential luxury, conceived by the state as an absolute good and a problematic inessential according to the changes in state needs. As such the formation of the university is determined by two distinct *political* frameworks. At the local level these are motivated by the local community of scholarship and voluntarism, but the higher one goes (the more global) these local levels are flattened to conform to certain state demands (on vice-chancellors). Thus knowledge is determined by the methods of anarcho-communism (locally) at the service of state-aided capitalism (globally). Clearly a contradiction! Gains on behalf of women, gays and ethnic groups *locally* determined by knowledge production at the lowest level becomes coercive politically correct policy *at* the highest level. Real knowledge and the equality that comes from it soon becomes *unequal managerialism* (political correctness) into which more women, gay people and ethnic minorities are drafted.

The intellectual, in as much as he or she works in a university, is both an intellectual *and* a bureaucrat and as a bureaucrat their position is essentially *economic*, determined by trade union negotiation over pay and conditions. As an intellectual, whose responsibility is to knowledge, they have a *political* relationship to the university structure. This dualism is *not* reconcilable despite the traditional role assigned to teaching. The act of teaching does *not* reconcile knowledge and training as they are distinctly different modes of cultural awareness.

In the late 1980s and 1990s, under the pressures of Thatcherism and Blairism, the concept of 'competencies' started to replace older humanistic concepts of a cultural or ethical nature. These 'outcome' determined ideas fitted perfectly the managerialism of a technological determination.

Obsession with the management organisation and function of knowledge and information whether in a consensual or antagonistic model, upholds the purpose of the technocratic machine – to preserve itself in infinite renewal and metamorphosis. Seduction plays its part – it is the driving force behind the obsession in the capitalist age both as a going beyond and behind and as an organiser of those deep principles found beyond and behind (Marxist class, Freudian libido, feminist gender, etc.). But seduction dispossesses structural analytic strategies, takes away their threatening applicability. As a set of explanations of the greater system they act systematically as upholders and carriers of the message of the system. Here they function within a crossfield of systems *designed* to articulate capitalist enterprises – the human sciences act not as explanations, but as legitimations of the system's understanding of itself. The revolutionary potential of such explanatory subsystems is to read just that part of the system which allows it to function more successfully and renew itself though quasi-discrete interventions. In this way the analysts of the system are its servants and the analytics they employ are always on the level of the adjectival.

V

We live in an age of superstimulation. This sensory bombardment modern commentators call the age of the hyper-real. In such an age as ours, objects, so silent in themselves, participate in a kind of communal frenzy of informational output – it is this mass effect, a blinding to the difference between the real and the simulated, that brings in the age of the simulacrum. Nevertheless this stimulus is not fake, for all stimulus is real in its effects.

The age of monuments has passed, shifting to an age of impermanence, where permanence can exist only as an aesthetic pastiche, which is also political pastiche. What remains is the authoritarian benevolence of management and its gurus (the political spin doctor). An age of the ephemeral, with its 'worthless' endless productivity and *experiential* material is backed by a massive technology dedicated to the *recycling* of human experience as pure groundless commodity: purposeless information devoid of even the last vestige of the moral utility that at least made the nineteenth-century bourgeois feel guilty. And yet, at every point values still intrude and barbarism (no less or worse than before) has still not swamped civilisation. The condition of the old and the demands of the new find their reconciliation somewhere amid the mutating value systems of such an age in the materiality of the historical processes of change.

Thus we live materially and intellectually in a period of profound transformation and dis-ease, not for the vast majority of humanity but for all those forced by temperament to be obsessed with knowledge. It marks the end of the 'bourgeois' period and the 'bourgeois' consensus (and its opposition). It also marks the end of those certainties that sustained the human sciences in their quest for knowledge and its grounding: the codification of modern practice at all levels of experience – sexual, political, economic, ethnic, biological.

The nineteenth century was fundamentally a critical period – marked by the act of criticism. Even now, almost two centuries after its beginnings and even as it ebbs, the force of the critical act marks this period out. This fundamental function has sustained the momentum of the industrial age, both in its representation in the novel and in the appearance of its analytic tools, the human sciences. The critical act was sustained by a mechanistic tension that was progressively reinforced in its potential for survival through the relationship between organisational analysis at one end and functional or purposive analysis at the other. These two poles were crossed by cultural and societal ones: liberal consensus and socialist antagonism. In all spheres of activity the critical eye upheld the momentum of the industrial age. This critical principle found its expression in the 'realisms' of nineteenth-century art as well as the abstraction of twentieth-century art and in the quantitative mechanisms of science. Everything was subordinated to the quantifiable and the quantifiable was tied to a real and very material world. Within this world everything was subordinated to the imperious gaze of the human. Modern discourse was, of necessity, neurotic as the solidity of the world slowly slid away in the lengthening shadow of the twentieth century.

Language analysis and the analysis of discourse then began to function in the ruins of cultural and sociological science. Thus language replaced political intervention on all levels of human action. Instead what was left were games (Lyotard), narratives (Jameson) and simulations (Baudrillard) in the empire of signs, floating in Ferdinand de Saussure's binary divide.

The profession of literary criticism as it is practised in the universities is in crisis. This is not peculiar to literary criticism, but to all the liberal and human sciences. It has been this way now for many years. Indeed, it may be said that this is now the natural state of the humanities in the advanced cultures of the West: a movement from enclosure and emplacement to one of disjunction and displacement. What consequences can be drawn from this? Here we must attempt to come to grips with a problem central to liberal educational practice today and in a wider context the problems now endemic to cultural criticism as it is practised in the late twentieth century. What must be said of the crisis in humanities' subjects and the implications of that crisis?

This critical juncture is itself a symptom of the age of post-modernism, as suggested in Jean Baudrillard's invocation of *simulacra*:

> Baudrillard extends, some would say hyperbolises, his theory of commodity culture. No longer does the code take priority over or even precede the consumer object. The distinction between object and representation, thing and idea are no longer valid. In their place Baudrillard fathoms a strange new world constructed out of models or simulacra which have no referent or ground in any reality except their own. A simulation is different from a fiction or lie in that it not only presents an absence as a presence, the imaginary as the real, it also undermines any contrast to the real, absorbing the real within itself.
>
> (Mark Poster, introduction to Jean Baudrillard, *Selected Writings*)

Umberto Eco makes a similar point about modern culture: 'To speak of things that one wants to connote as real, these things must seem real. The "completely real" becomes identified with the "completely fake". . . . The sign aims to be the thing, to abolish the distinction of the reference, the mechanism of replacement.' In the land of supersaturation that we inhabit signification breaks down and systems with 'meaning' content cease to function 'naturally' and take on instead a strange half-life in which meaning systems *counterfeit* the roles they once had.

In this supersaturated world, in an age dominated by the pulse of electronic instantaneity, we find ourselves 'obesely' replicated in the consuming and consumed environment in which the object can no longer bear the full weight of its significance. Instead, the object (as subject of analysis) weightlessly floats into the space of simulation. Simply, the intellectual space is overstocked and the currency devalued. The situation replicates capitalist excess in an age of inflation.

The humanities founder at the end of the liberal project. Disciplines crash, and all the recuperations fail because grounded in the very processes of dissolution that they unconsciously represent. Instead of radical departures, there are only conservative recuperations dressed as challenges. Its other and its double is not the old bourgeois philistinism of the nineteenth century, nor the popular culture of the twentieth but the unchallenged managerialism of the twenty-first. This is why much left-wing thought becomes conservative recuperation: a wholesale attempt to hold back the future but now couched in the language of the communal values of corporate responsibility, 'ownership' and stake-holding. Such managerial conceptualising is all the more fearsome because capable of infinite adaptation to the conditions of managerial requirement with which values will be created and confirmed.

We need not, however, fear for the continuity of humanities subjects. In a heritage society the archaic functions as the present, and the present unites the archaic to function as if always new: Baudrillard's totally saturated society. New technologies will always allow for the escape of outdated systems which will function as living archeological sites, sites for the indulgence of nostalgia. Existence as 'the remnant' is faced by those humanities subjects which cannot easily be co-opted by vocationalism or managerialism and which will function to hierarchise museum culture over heritage culture and which signify, for the moment, political and cultural stability.

The pioneers of the social and human sciences all saw themselves in heroic terms. All these pioneers had a purpose: the discovery of that which was hidden and needed uncovering. Once the sciences had stabilised, this quest was replaced by an internal inquiry as components became interchangeable. At this point, what had once appeared as simply a means to an end now replaced that end. Study of the organisation of components and their composition replaced the purpose of finding authority in an originating moment. Such change was central to the very nature of disciplinarity and the subsequent displacement of knowledge into meta-knowledge and meta-language. Social scientists and cultural analysts changed their attention from the teleological to the regulatory, replacing the idea of origin with the idea of system. Origination and its exploration was replaced by circulation and its surveillance: the displacement of a displacement. The search for authenticity was replaced by the management of information.

In an age when the purpose of the intellectual seems both romantic and outdated and when big theory seems to amount to only partial and local lobbying on behalf of interested parties, no more difficult job exists than that of an independent thinker. Ungrounded thought is the condition of modern life and thought. It is, however, the only realm left for intellectual thought. In the ruins of collapsed dualism there must be more than a reconstitution of the rubble, and that task belongs to the radical intellectual.

Part IV
Canned Heat: Resistance

Who'll be my role model now that my role model is gone!
Paul Simon

The future isn't written yet.
  (Tony Blair, *New Labour/New Britain Centenary Membership* leaflet)

6
The Sixties in your Head: An Aborted Experiment?

What is the constitution of avant-gardism? The revolutionary avant-garde was a product of the nineteenth century, constituted by the politics of socialism and the advancements of technology. It was specifically determined by its struggle with the liberal state and the economics of capital. The struggle between revolutionary avant-gardism and reactionary avant-gardism constitutes the history of the avant-garde in its most dynamic and theoretical form.

The avant-garde was the permanent, marginal base of oppositional culture dedicated to the *struggle* to free the morally self-contained subject into a space of *liberated self-fulfilment*. In so doing it fought against capitalism; the state; militarism; institutionalism; religion; managerialism; racism; imperialism; sexism; autocracy; totalitarian authority. It was, in essence, and at every moment international; emancipatory; existential; theoretical; syncretic; technological; utopian; anti-conservative; anti-aesthetical; anti-banal; proletarian (urban and rural); anti-exploitational. Its heroes were as much Darwin as Freud; Marx as Bakunin; Engels as Thoreau; Max Stirner as Kropotkin; as much the masses as the egotistic self.

The means of the avant-garde enshrined themselves in the proliferation of critique: pamphlets; fly posters; manifestos of every shade and – 'ism'; acts of violence; disgraces and outrages; theoretical outbursts and spectacular demonstrations, all in order to embrace rupture and disjunction (especially with history, and art traditions, with consensus, with bourgeois sentiment, with the banal). The aim – to make us see otherwise and through alienating activities abolish alienated subjectivity.

Avant-gardism was dedicated to a future not yet realised – the future of itself *as* realised. But this realisation was the impossible moment of the avant-garde for avant-gardism was always a potential not a realisation.

It was precisely the premonition, anticipation and inauguration of itself, the declaration of its own beginning prior to its actual beginning. It could be traced only in manifestos and declarations of intent. This was not a failure but exactly as it should have been. Avant-gardism was the process of *defeated becoming*; realised *in history*, it nevertheless opposed the historical only in order the more to determine it. Avant-gardism 'suspend[ed] linear time, and its excess constitute[d] ecstatic time' (Paul Hegarty, unpublished research paper). Ecstatic time became the time of suspension between the defunct past and an unrealised future. As such, ecstatic time was not merely the present lived forever (as suspension of history and therefore the defeat of avant-garde aspiration) but an abysmal moment in which history was liberated on behalf of the FUTURE.

The sixties revolt was the culmination of the *nineteenth*-century struggle against liberalism, parliamentary democracy and gradualist reform. The year 1968 saw the culmination of the activities of the nineteenth-century avant-garde movement. It marked the end of the transcendent libertarian avant-garde and its socialist double, the end of a dual movement which was politically anarcho-communist and personally individualist and egostistical. The struggle for all forms of political and personal freedom conducted under the banner of these ideals was defeated as much by outside pressures as by internal contradictions: the realisation of the avant-garde was also the abolition of the avant-garde by forces both beyond itself and at *its own hand*.

The FUTURE as an ideological project finished in 1968 and gave way to frustration – the politics of art gave way to acts of terror and futility. In the ashes of art were born the movements of terrorism: the Simbionese Liberation Army; the Red Army Faction; Weatherman Collective (later Weather People); Manson Family; Molotov Cocktail Party; Motherfuckers; Angry Brigade.

Is the project of the avant-garde finished in the collapsed categories of late twentieth-century capitalist chic? What might be retrieved and used again from the aborted experiment of the 1960s, abominated by conservative reaction throughout the seventies and eighties, travestied by New Labour in the nineties, an embarrassing adolescent memory for its ageing participants at the millennium? What is the nature of the condition known as the sixties. Where is the sixties condition situated? Who feels it? Who owns it?

The 1960s was both an historical period and a mythic moment – a time out of time, during which to have 'been there' was *not* to have been there – in which if you remember the sixties you couldn't have taken part. The sixties exists as a memory of a blank more positive than action. The sixties was the moment of forgetting historical memory in order to act in history. Yet this history was always enacted as myth – as heroic altruistic action both bereft of and obsessed with memory, the past as historical burden. This sixties is a moment not just a decade, a condition of history not merely a moment in history. As such it cuts into history and myth – its narration is that of an ontological condition not a chronicle of days. The sixties was the cancelling of history on behalf *of* history: a move into history on behalf of liberation from the past, from memory, from the violence and oppression of historical narratives – from the older generation. This double movement as process, and *condition*, *out* of which process was generated, was the haunting shadow of *theory's progress*: from existentialism to structuralism to postmodern deconstruction: it continues to haunt ethnicity and feminism.

The sixties was also the refusal of a certain presence caught thirty years ago in the cacoon of itself – sealed in the vacuum of rebellion and licentiousness. Its siren allure is its call to the past *through* the present. It is a condition of a certain self but also the history of how that self came to be: a movement of myth and history. Thus we speak of the swinging sixties, sixties radicalism or the spirit of the sixties. The sixties is an ontological syndrome and an epistemological conundrum.

For Jean-François Lyotard, '1968 was an *abyss* in which the genre of democratic liberal discourse seem[ed] to disappear' ('The Sign of History'). The abyss: from which history was extruded but into which it cannot return, now unable to put back or explain the abyss. The abyss is death – a black hole of signification and distruption but also generator of the future from a silent past; a break, rupture, condition of history but not in history. It constitutes a mythic sublime and beatific point of validation for the speaking of history, and it remains in effect a hallucination recognisable in its effects (i.e. historical process and change) but without a proper past to itself or a future (it remains unchanging and remote – only yesterday – but . . .). It is the moment of myth. This sublime moment is the empty miraculous – voiding the contents of its own space into a moment *after*, from which and only from which, it can be viewed. For Lyotard it is the unspeakable from which the heterogeneous emerges.

For Jean Baudrillard, the sixties represented the brink of ecstasy in which 'the grand epoch of subjective irony or radicality ha[d] come to an end' somewhere around 1970. This is the moment of crystallisation, 'the crystal' as Baudrillard calls it – 'the pure object' and 'the pure event, . . . no longer with any previous origin or end' (Jean Baudrillard, *Revenge of the Crystal*). Here is 'something that disappears without a trace, that erases its origins and its end, and that is no longer caught up in linearity' (Baudrillard, ibid.). The *crystal* is the *object* of post-modern hyper-reality and thus the 1960s becomes the infinitely consumed post-modern object – signifying only the *now* of its presence and bringing *no* history with it. An *abysmal* or sublime effect of itself.

The emergence of theory during the decade of the 1960s coincided with the end of 'history'. For Baudrillard theory, unlike history, now became *narrative*: a 'departure' from history *per se*. It was in this atmo-sphere that around 1970 both Marxism and Freudianism 'buggered off' in the total 'confusion of things', as he put it. For John Lennon, disillu-sioned after a long decade, it seemed that all that occurred was that 'everyone dressed up but nothing changed' (in Ian MacDonald). It was Michael Foucault, who in 1972 noted that the old project of the avant-garde had 'collapsed', generating in its place 'new zones' of activity, 'that [perhaps] no longer conformed to the model that Marxist tradi-tion had prescribed. Toward an experience and a technology of desire that were no longer Freudian.... the combat shifted and spread into new zones' (preface to Gilles Deleuze and Felix Guattari, *A Thousand Plateaus*)

The collapse of the old order of the avant-garde led to a 'new' version of subversive activity, for if reality had itself collapsed into simulacrum the only subversion was now that of acts of *displacement*. To ask now, in the twenty-first century, whence does the revolution come, who makes history and in what way does *myth* generate the subversive act is to ask questions that seem redundant. And this sense of critical redundancy is itself a legacy of the rejection of the sixties ethos, a rejection which was ironically generated from within the original milieu. This redund-ancy is rather the result of a refusal to reopen the case of the sixties and to reconsider its questions, those questions and attitudes assigned either to a nostalgic but irrecoverable past or to a past seen as anything from slightly embarrassing to disastrous. The point is not to see the sixties as merely historical enactment but to reassess the potential the project of the sixties has for a reconstituted avant-gardism. If the sixties is an ontological experience then it is not only the experience of refusal for those of a certain age but it is also part of a historical dynamic whose consequences we live now.

The intellectual of the sixties was embarked on a quest: to find the ideal agent of 'permanent challenge' (Marcuse) whose refusal of the consensual status quo would start the revolution. From the beginning the quest was frustrated by an inability to identify the insurrectionary class or clearly theorise its role after the initial act of insubordination.

Who could act as the ideal social mutineers? If the student body, with its heightened awareness, was to act as the vanguard, a 'detonator' of change (as in France) or the precipitating factor (as in Britain) it was nevertheless true that they were too young and too poor to create lasting change. As transitional workers, students had neither a permanent stake in change nor a traditional nor stable economic base. Only the organised working class could offer these, but these traditional agents of change were also agents of stability and conservatism, in cahoots with capital itself. Indeed, the very egos of the traditional working class rattled with internalised capital.

The old avant-garde came from Europe. Hitler and Stalin put an end to that. The fulcrum of sixties radicalism was the United States. Everything sprang from there and reflected back to there. It was the site and generator of the sixties experiments and Europe reflected nothing less than the subsequent shock waves which stirred European radicals to action. Such radicals were bound therefore to have a different sense of themselves and radicalism itself soon ceased to have a direct connection to its origins in the struggles of the past. For Abbie Hoffman, the proletariat were essentially irrelevant to the insurrection of the New Left alliance as anti-authoritarianism was individualistic not class-based. Ridicule not respect was the order of the day – the laughter of carnival its signature. Indeed, Hoffman was happy only to embrace the socialism of the Marx Brothers' variety (including Karl) and during the May Days of 1968, posters proclaimed the Marxism of the Groucho variety!

Habituated to inactivity and reaction, the working class had become respectable, had a stake in society and embraced the bourgeoisie. The temporary alliance of students and workers was little more than an illusion in Europe and non-existent in America. The old white, territorial, *closed* working-class community was to be opposed by the new *post*-proletarian organic communalities based on gender ambiguity, ethnicity and youth. The perforation line split history into pre- and post-World War mentalities. This 'revolution of *and in* the common man [sic]' (Ian MacDonald, *Revolution in the Head*) would bring liberation despite Marx not because of him.

For many intellectuals and radicals, especially those from the margin, Marxism simply had failed to offer a correct analysis of the late twentieth century. It seemed to be unable to account for advanced capitalism, lack of revolutionary activity in advanced capitalist states, the 'absorption' of the working class into the structures of capitalist reaction and the rise of consumerism; it failed to account for co-option, had an outdated idea of the intellectual and a sinister respect for the party machine. Moreover, it had no psychology to match its critique of political economy. In the United States this led the New Left towards the abandonment of *theoretical* positions in an open set of alliances without ideological frameworks or conceptual preconditions.

The beyond of Marxism – its supercession in the contemporaneous – would lead radicals to re-examine new sources of possible rebellion and assertion. For many American intellectuals and radicals such assertions could be drawn more effectively from American soil than European. American New Leftism was much more likely to be inspired by anarcho-libertarianism or rural communalism than Marxist-Leninism.

The widespread belief that there is only one revolutionary politics of the left, and that that is essentially Marxist–Leninist has obscured the importance of other radical political positions which were repressed in the East yet continued to flourish inside capitalism as both critiques and positive alternatives. The opportunity was thus lost to create a wide spectrum of left-wing beliefs which would include anarchist socialism and anarchist libertarian thought and practice. This narrowing of focus, the domination of Cold War politics and the dominance of party-led oppositional forces, as well as the often violent repression of left-wing alternative movements, policies and actions, has restricted the knowledge of the nature of the left and those debates that might have flourished if its leaders and thinkers were as well known as Marx in academic and political circles.

Historians of the left too easily dismiss anarchist politics because they failed to conform to the Marxist–Leninist model, whereas it was precisely this model that failed. Anarchist tendencies, with their spontaneous, amorphous, popular, untheoretical, individualistic, local and self-help approaches and values are central to ecological, feminist, gender, ethnic and devolutionist debates and are the backbone of charitable organisations working against world hunger, poverty and disease. They are also to be found in the animal liberation movements and in 'spontaneous' demonstrations against authority and the state. Anarchism, rather than Marxism, has proved to be more flexible in its practical opposition to capitalism and the state, and, because it retains a strong belief in the individual, it has proved it can work in the *interstices* of capital as a moral force.[1]

Abbie Hoffman (writing as 'Free') would encapsulate the idea of New Leftism as a 'second American revolution,' Bobby Seale would demand 'constitutional rights' under the First Amendment and Tom Hayden would talk of 'the principles embodied in the Declaration of Independence' and all could claim that 'the root concept of the American Revolution remained: "power to the people" – a claim made concrete by its reference to the First Amendment.'

Much of this 'left' non-Marxist radicalism could trace its source back to debates over hipsterism and the extreme nonconformism of the underground in the 1950s. For Norman Mailer the hipster, living on the margin, like the black jazz musician was a 'philosophical psychopath,' whose religious purpose ('one must be religious') was the 'existential' conquest of the borderland. As 'a frontiersman in the Wild West of American Night Life' the hipster fought totalitarianism, conformity and co-option in order to release the sensual transcendent ego.

Whilst the New Left would have scoffed at Ayn Rand's hysterical fear of 'full totalitarian socialism' in the United States, it was quite happy to exercise its own fear of full totalitarian *fascism*.[2] It is not surprising then that many New Left and hippy leaders came closer to Rand's analysis and conclusions than they might have wished to admit. For Rand's 'psycho-epistemological' approach, the only answer to 'Atilla' and 'the witchdoctor' (i.e. totalitarianism) was free market capitalism – a wholesale return to the pioneer-entrepreneurialism of the early republic, hence:

> The professional businessman and the professional intellectual came into existence together, as brothers born of the industrial revolution. Both are the sons of capitalism – and if they perish, they will perish together. The tragic irony will be that they will have destroyed each other; and the major share of guilt will belong to the intellectual.
>
> (Ayn Rand, *For the New Intellectual*)

It cannot be overemphasised that the contradictory position of the New Left forced it to embrace both the 'fully integrated' personality of the intellectual in 'the freedom of the market-place of ideas' whilst rejecting the same for actual businessmen or for the market-place of economic goods.

> A society based on and geared to the *conceptual* level of man's consciousness, a society dominated by a philosophy of reason, has no place for the rule of fear and guilt. Reason requires freedom, self-confidence and self-esteem. It requires the right to think and to act on the guidance of one's thinking – the right to live by one's own independent judgement. *Intellectual* freedom cannot exist without *political* freedom; political freedom cannot exist without *economic* freedom; a *free mind and a free market are corollaries*.

The unprecedented social system whose fundamentals were established by the Founding Fathers, the system which set the terms, the example and the pattern for the nineteenth century – spreading to all the countries of the civilised world – was *capitalism*.

To be exact, it was not a full, perfect, totally unregulated *laissez-faire* capitalism.

(Ayn Rand, ibid.)

The rejection of *laissez-faire* capitalism either forced radicals back into a defence of gradualism and reform or turned their intellectual market zeal towards anarcho-communalism and small-scale eco-politics (and the entrepreneurial self-sufficiency that would lead many to become millionaries by the 1980s).

Revolution was, in essence, the realisation of capitalism's once *repressed* potential in its pioneering phase before the intervention of the *state* and the *corporation*. It is no surprise that the 'contradiction' implied by its definition of the market was one that was *not* a contradiction outside Marxist circles. The tradition of refusal in American radical individualism and communalism was a tradition of 'leftism' happily devoid of Marxist-Leninism and closer to Emma Goldman, Alexander Berkman or Rudolf Rocker. Left anarchism always (ironically) found a welcome home in the United States, compatible as it was with much of that country's tradition of seditious free thinking. Theoretical anarcho-communism was the unconscious of left-radical politics in Europe whilst lived out in practice by an American refusnik youth. Utopian socialism and practical communalism found a ready home in the land of Fourierism, and agrarian communalism.

For Carl Oglesby the new way of the left would be 'radical democratic communitarianism', for Jack Newfield there 'seemed something Emersonian about the SDS', and even Eldridge Cleaver could argue that the role of the Black Panthers was as instigators of a new 'American revolution', whose credo included a return to the centrality of self-determination. For Cleaver, as for American liberal democrats, 'liberty [was] indivisible'.

This was the left without Marx, a tradition that emerged in Europe too in the actual *practice* of insurrection. Indeed, the New Left, in its non-compliance with the 'old' left ideology found itself unwittingly bypassing Marxist doctrine and rediscovering (albeit most unconsciously) a European tradition of anarchism that had largely arrived in the United States during the earlier half of the nineteenth century and which gathered itself in Chicago and New York amongst Jewish, *mittel*-European and Slav immigrants. It found its most vociferous voices in Emma Goldman and Alexander Berkman.

These Russian exiles, with their *melange* of theoretical influences from Proudhon, Herzen, Kropotkin, Bakunin, Tolstoy and the novelist Chernyshevsky (author of *What is to be Done?*), as well as their debt to Narodnik agitation, became the most famous (and perhaps notorious) anarchist voices of America. They exemplified *oppositional culture*. Nevertheless this opposition was never fully expressed as a theory of revolution, rather it was an attempt to produce a life of *virtue* based on political struggle dedicated to the *negation of politics* (i.e. the power of the state). Their blend of communist-anarchism always hovered between community and individual demands, demands that they felt were neither addressed by Marxist-Leninism (despite Goldman's problematic dalliance with the idea of a 'vanguard' party) nor by the extreme individualism of Max Stirner nor the utopian religiosity of Tolstoy.

For Alexander Berkman, anarchism meant 'Life without compulsion [which] mean[t] liberty; it mean[t] freedom from being forced or coerced, a chance to lead the life that suits you best' (in Kenneth A. Wenzer, *Anarchists Adrift*). And Emma Goldman could sum up her philosophy by explaining that 'civilisation [was] to be measured by the individual, the unit of all social life; by his [sic] individuality and the extent to which it [was] free to have its being, to grow and expand unhindered by invasive and coercive authority. [And because] all forms of government rest on violence, and [were] therefore wrong and harmful they [were] always opposed to free individuality' (Wenzer, ibid.).

From Kropotkin, they took the evolutionary idea of 'mutual aid' rather than survival of the fittest and from a host of historical influences they argued that co-operation amongst humans (the production of mutual-aid communities) always led to virtuous individualism, provided impediments such as the state were not allowed to take root. For Goldman, the future was a return to an organic past. 'In his [sic] natural condition, man existed without any State or organised government. . . . Human society then was not a State but an association; a voluntary association for mutual protection and benefit' (Wenzer, ibid.).

The central importance of the individual ('the centre of gravity in society is the individual') could lead to Max Stirner's form of 'owness', exemplified by individualist-transcendentalists like Ralph Waldo Emerson or David Thoreau, but it could equally lead to Tolstoyan 'unity and love'. In language more suggestive of theosophy than revolution, Berkman and Goldman could exhort followers 'to be like [the] God whom we know only through love and reason . . . in order to be rid of suffering, to be tranquil and joyful [and] open . . . *the divine life which is in us'* (Wenzer, ibid.). For Alexander Berkman, this all meant freedom of expression and art, 'freedom from compunction (from whatever quarter), equal rights and liberties, brotherhood [*sic*] and harmony' (Wenzer, ibid.).

Both Berkman and Goldman wavered in their original anarchistic beliefs, Goldman lost faith in the spontaneous action of the proletariat and slowly turned against the unimpressed masses of America, but both retained a fear of, and distaste for, Marxist-Leninism and especially Bolshevism.

The New Left retained Berkman and Goldman's fear of all authority, whether it came from the state or the party, the government, the military or organised religion. New Left radicals shared a hatred of monopoly capitalism and exploitation too and just like Berkman and Goldman they supported individualist freedom based on free association. When it came to its ambivalent attitude towards the intellectual 'vanguard' the New Left agitated and demonstrated only in the hope of a spontaneous uprising. For such an uprising, 'politics' as traditionally practised would be abolished, replaced by ethical individualism and virtuous communal responsibility. For Alexander Trocchi this amounted to an 'invisible insurrection' (Sigma 2), a revolution in the 'broad sense cultural', not a *coup d'état* but a *coup-du-monde*. Indeed 'political revolt' was nothing less than an anachronism in the face of 'coming revolution and buddhism' (Gary Snyder) and the 'cosmic buzz' (Dave Stevens).

If the 'ethical revolt' had by the late 1960s become *political*, it retained its appeal to non-political disaffected groups and outraged individuals. Open and 'ecumenical' movements called to those who wished to demand freedom for the self above all else. Distrustful of intellectuals, the American New Left never created a stable and coherent theory of revolutions nor did it feel the need for one.

Even in Europe the relationship between the left-wing revolutionary and radical subversion and Marxism was far from clear. In 1969, Herbert Marcuse claimed that as capitalism had 'invaded' the mind, the young were now the new psychic proletarian warriors. Yet he could also argue that it would be 'refusal' and 'rebellion [distrustful] of all ideologies, including socialism' which would bring the 'self-determination' that was at the centre of radical struggle (*New Left Revue* 56, July/August 1969). A year previously *Black Dwarf* (July 1968) saw the students as a 'revolutionary vanguard' even if, as Ernest Mandel demonstrated, the 'university was bourgeois'. If the aim for Danny Cohn-Bendit was the 'overthrow [of the] regime' yet the means were not clear. Alain Geismer (who had not yet read Marcuse in May 1968) felt that one could not rely on Marxism as it had no theory of advanced capitalism and as such the revolution would be made spontaneously 'as one goes'. For J. Sauvageot the uprising of 1968 was the direct result of 'the heritage of the [continuous] French Revolutions of the nineteenth century' – Proudhonian rather than Marxian.

The practical and piecemeal nature of the revolution were at one with its *necessary immediacy* and exuberance. Danny Cohn-Bendit proclaimed that 'our movement's strength is precisely that it is based on uncontrollable spontaneity' (in Hervé Bourges, *The Student Revolt*), a variation on Carl Oglesby's formulation of the 'permanent terror of the accidental' and yippy theatrics. It is hardly surprising that student action in Europe rarely met with communist party approval or union co-operation. The spontaneity of the revolution precluded the traditions of opposition in both party and union which lent themselves to conservative hesitation and bureaucratic proceduralism. The spontaneous insurrection required the urgent re-evaluation of Marxist analysis, a project which occupied Louis Althusser from the early 1960s through to his incarceration in a mental hospital. Quite simply, there was never a structured attempt by any group to seize political power from the government: the revolution was as much 'in your head' (Hoffman) as on the street.

Technology too, whilst *essential* to revolution, was also too easily tied to current oppression – an oppressiveness seen not in the oppression of production but rather in the hallucinatory goals of consumer goods. The revolution was not to be anti-consumption but it was anti-consumerist, attacking the 'obscene' (Marcuse) society of over-consumption of unnecessary goods, of the banal and spectacular (the Situationists). Any political revolt had also to be an aesthetic revolt, a turn against the *banal* and a return to authentic sensual pleasure. The technology of self (drugs) and the technology of communication (media) all, sooner or later, would be used to attack the technology of production.

Technology always remained an intractable and double-edged problem. On the one hand, in the possession of the establishment, it was a tool of repression – as demonstrations at Berkeley proved in 1966 and 1967. On the other hand, certain forms of technology could be utilised on behalf of liberation. For Abbie Hoffman the 'only pure revolution [was] technological', speeded up by the *release* of innovations (on behalf of leisure) that had been artificially restricted to increase capitalist exploitation (both of class and world). It was technology, after all, that created LSD, itself exploited by the 'Merry Pranksters' and Timothy Leary.

Electronic media, especially television, could be put (*unwittingly*) to the task of *publicising* the revolution through news and current affairs. 'We are theatre', hippies declared, as both yippies and hippies became media celebrities using Situationist tactics to get their Dada-esque protests into millions of homes. The revolution, in one sense, actually was theatre: Artaud's 'theatre of cruelty' and John Latham's Skoob Towers mixed willy-nilly with love-ins, sit-ins, happenings and be-ins.

Marshall McLuhan believed he saw the significance of the electronic media revolution in such phrases as 'the global village' and 'the medium is the massage' (sic). In his focus on the non-linear, acoustic and spontaneous, McLuhan believed electronic culture to be a return to the 'global village' now freed from its hierarchy and ignorance into a mixture of Athenian democracy and village-pump politics. In his idealisation of the pre-literate, McLuhan actually echoed much debate around 'Cambridge English' and especially the ideal of the lost organic community of F. R. Leavis (who had taught him). The global village was little different from Leavis's Shakespearean community. For the Situationist Guy Debord, McLuhan's ideas were the idealisation of parochialism and ignorance, whilst for some contemporary commentators, McLuhan's ideas were subject to blindness to facts, distortion of history and lack of awareness of the role of print culture in its *decisive* influence on electronic culture and its content.

In America, as elsewhere, revolutionary expectations concretised around individual identity. For Tom Hayden and Abbie Hoffman the gagging of Bobby Seale (and Chicago '69) was nothing less than the persecution of those with 'disrespectful identity' seen by the authorities as 'out of control' (Hayden). The revolutionary war was one fought out in the politics of self; the revolution lived 'in the body' as ontological revolt.

Nowhere was this to be more obvious than in the alliance, or attempted alliances, between radical white positions and black slum dwellers. The new proletarians were the black marginal ghetto dwellers – the third world in the first and at its heart. The fight against capitalism was also to be the fight against imperialism. Such alliances would, it was hoped, bring insurrection out from the heart of capitalism, its invisible heart, that of the disenfranchised who were without a stake in democracy or liberal society. Such protest was, however, to be bought at the expense of the traditional (Marxist) proletariat whose alienation would throw them into the arms of reaction. Third world and ghettoised revolt, revolt from the margins, was the activity of the unassimilated, an absolute refusal of conformism which capitalism *could not absorb* for its own benefit.

For many in the sixties there could be no permanent change nor any meaningful political re-alignment without a change in the individual; if you could free subjectivity (ego) it was felt you freed the community (the political realm). Reformists, civil rights assimilationists and liberal well-wishers would now find that from the margins of the marginal came only terrorism (political insurrection) and Dadaism (aesthetic insurrection). The marginal united all the forces of disruption and in so doing it also gave them an identity and offered them as a target. Despite this, such marginal alliances offered new conditions for the self and gave meaning to 'disrespectful identity' in which the self became the embodiment of an absolute refusal of reformism or compromise.

If the fight against co-operation on behalf of a liberated self had gone on until 1968, by that same year it had also been joined to an active social fight against authoritarianism and the state. By 1969, the refusal of the marginalised had become the chorus of the radicals.

From the neglected margin (Lenin saw the marginal as a mere 'reservoir') a 'new type of popular culture' (UNEF Manifesto) would emerge determined by its 'non-marketable' nature (David Gilbert). Student 'specialists in provocation' (Hervé Bourges) would successfully create the 'permanent contestation' of power and culture only if a clear alliance was made between disaffected white culture (hippies, SDS, etc.) and ghettoised black culture (the Panthers). To achieve liberation through 'non-marketable culture' – a product of the disenfranchised and disaffected underclass, whites would have to dispute class exploitation, blacks dispute racism and colonialism and women dispute gender identity. To remove exploitation (of classes) and oppression (of races) it would be necessary to abandon reformism, to avoid the 'clichés' of Marxist dogma and literally become *lumpen*: in Eldrige Cleaver's phrase 'we're all niggers now'.

In finding the concept of ethnicity, radicals also found the missing term in Marxism. For Marx and Engels the marginal were the reactionary pawns of aristocratic authoritarianism, thuggish dupes, and 'social scum . . . a bribed tool of reactionary intrigue'. For the New Left it was precisely from here that the new culture would arise. National liberation movements became the visible corollary of class warfare.

The aim of such intellectual and practical exertion was the creation of free individuals possessing integrated minds in a commonwealth of mutual aid. Opposing the integration of mind, body and community was the integrated *state*. For most intellectuals and artists of the 1960s the state stood for sheer brutalism, its integration designed to contest, enslave and compartmentalise, spreading propaganda and alienation in order to create *disintegrated* individuals bereft of self-possession and therefore bereft of effective oppositional action. Against this, radicals posed the *integrated personality*: enlightened, empowered and liberated. Such integration could come from an inner quest through drugs and psychedelia or through social struggle on behalf of marginal communities.

Inner struggle tended to be mystic, environmental, communalistic and anarchic whilst outer struggle tended to be 'socialist' – anarchist, ethnic and organised (in some loose fashion). The aim was to challenge *state control of consciousness* with self-control of consciousness. If the inner struggle tended also to happen in white 'bourgeois' circles then the outer quest was directed through the poor and ethnically marginalised. In both cases the struggle was given its impetus by a *necessary paranoia*: a search for deep and hidden wells of meaning unavailable to those for whom liberation was most urgent. Educational methods and literary productions were the main targets for those looking to liberate minds. Thus were campuses occupied, 'free' universities created, teach-ins conducted. From John Calders' *Death of the Word* conferences to John Latham's Skoob project through to John Lennon's frustration at 'endless fucking words', logorrhoea was hunted into silence in order to silence the vehicle of state propaganda. The false word of the state was to be challenged, so radicals thought, by the true 'language' of self – a language of *embodiment* and *action*.

In the sixties no one was yet willing to accept the idea (itself defeatist and deeply *conservative*) that, as Michel Foucault pointed out, 'there [was] nothing outside the text'. Foucault's declaration, which for a decade or more seemed to liberate language and rob discourse of its 'myth' function, played into the hands of the state and of capitalism. The free play of signifiers was little less than the corollary of exchange; the lack of a signified the necessary means to avoid ever having the 'buck' stop at your desk!

For most radicals whose optimism hadn't yet turned sour the attack on the state and its cultural origins (especially the complicity between art and state and corporate patronage) would create a 'personal revolution', a 'new sensibility' and a 'transvaluation of values' (Marcuse), enshrined in 'the liberation of language' (Joseph Ferrandino). Hervé Bourges mused, 'if we can avoid revolution we shall not avoid spiritual resurrection'. In the socialisation of production it was hoped would be found the de-segregation of art and life – a life now possible as authentic and aesthetically pleasing. The virtuous life would now integrate art and lived experience.

In order to cure the alienation of totality (the monolithic bourgeois totality of capitalist exploitation and banality) it would be necessary to take alienation to its extreme possibility thereby promoting *shock*. To create shock (the sudden awareness of the possibility of the New) only that art would do which could dislodge and dislocate: Dada happenings; spontaneous Dada theatricals; terroristic and oppositional Dada – anti-co-operative, non-recuperable and evanescent.

This would be samizdat art from the street, the ghetto and the refusnik. In this way oppositional culture would unite with oppositional politics, itself anarchic and driven by the samizdat manifesto and painted slogan. The result of this symbiosis, this cultural embodiment of the political and the aesthetic (*coup du monde* rather than *coup d' état*), would be a new totality of fluid possibilities and of an art merged into life. The dislocation of aesthetic vision (renewed again and again throughout the twentieth century) was to be the necessary prelude to unity – a unity which transcended precisely because it had been achieved *through* alienation.

The goal of these upheavals and disturbances was the new *self*, both liberated and authentic (capable of *direct* experience of reality). Everywhere one finds a belief in the need to defend or reconstruct a version of *totality* or wholeness and a continuum of mind and body which would finally be free of state control, consumption and capitalism. The new self was to exist in *total self-awareness* and self-fulfilment – a quest many saw in spiritual terms but which was essentially humanistic in its means and its intent. If there was a god it was the god of the transcendentalists rather than of any organised religion. The first rule of evolution was 'organise your head', if indeed the necessary changes were to be experienced in the revolutionary body. Hoffman's 'I am the Revolution' was indicative of the process of embodiment which was both a prerequisite and a social condition of actual social *reconstruction*.

The political was to start with the individual and end with the individual, changing the status of both as change was brought about. The multiplicity of liberated 'selves' and *self-determined* opportunities was not mere non-focus or crude cultural non-identity, nor a concept of hazy identity boundaries (even if it often ended as little else), but an attempt to shift away from the tedium and banality of the conformist I. The I of agency, central to the practical politics of New Leftism, was not to be confused with the subject 'I' or the philosophical (i.e., intellectual) ego. It was the triumph of the sixties radicals that this alternative 'self' could be imagined and occasionally lived and experienced; it was the tragedy that revolutionary identity could never resolve romantic subjectivity and socialist agency. Too easily the practical (romantic and socialist) concept of transcendence was mistaken for the sublime (romantic and reactionary) in which to go beyond was to step into the vertiginous free fall of the abyss of silence.

To create the necessary psychic changes the radical gaze turned to its gods: Wilhelm Reich and Carl Jung, Timothy Leary and R. D. Laing. The mind was to be subjected to experimentation as the body became a laboratory for altering consciousness. From Leary and Reich came psychedelia and the orgone. The (aptly named) 'trip' was to be the means of re-seeing the world, of reuniting its parts, and of escaping the banal. In its ethnographic dimension it linked the Western intellectual to the shaman and the native, and in its technological dimension it linked the intellectual body to the subversive end of the chemical industry (LSD). From Laing and Jung came anti-psychiatry, psychic symbolism and the experience of psychosis. Madness, schizophrenia and chemical-induced hallucination were to be the weapons (and diagnostic tools) to fight the actual madness and psychosis of regular society – mad without being aware of it. Only through self-induced disorientation and alienation could actual alienation be defeated.

These experimental activities were all attempts to go beyond in order to locate an *authenticity* lost or mislaid. To experience the true self, the actual self would have to be negated and transcended. The true self was holistic, self-determining, free and rational. This enlightened self was to be contrasted to its benighted, socialised predecessor, whilst its holistic self-awareness was to be contrasted with the fragmented, psychologised self of the state's institutions. The body became a theatre in which, and through which, the self experienced its own presence in space and time.

The origins of organic unification – the holistic approach just outlined – which saw a direct relationship between the individual, the social and the creative, had its origins in nineteenth-century philosophy and aesthetics, and was strongly associated with revolutionary socialist thought and, more problematically, exemplified by Wagner's theory of the *gesamtkunstwerk*. The desire for unity and communalism enthusiastically embraced the alternative lifestyle of the commune or the harmonious urban 'village'. A wide spectrum of alternative communities sprang up or were redefined. There was Timothy Leary's Castalia Federation; Ginger Island; digger co-ops; ashrams and squats. The British realist drama *Coronation Street* (first shown in December 1960 and later to become a soap opera) seemed to exemplify the nature of an authentic Englishness: self-sufficient, self-healing, self-reliant – a Mancunian corollary of Ronnie and Reggie Kray's cockney East End. The Situationists dreamed of building the 'hacienda' and of dwelling in 'cathedrals', whilst the rain fell at Woodstock and Richard Brautigan's bucolic utopians went trout fishing in America.

In Soviet Russia the avant-garde was defeated when Proletcult was suppressed by the Leninist co-option of Western 'bourgeois' culture on behalf of the Bolshevik vanguard (the party apparatus), as it attempted to suppress Russian Asiatic tendencies during the 1920s. In the West, utopian liberation aesthetics and culture were defeated by the power of liberal democratic co-option and the theoretical swerve away from soci-ological analysis towards identity politics (and the dissolution of the subject) – all of which accompanied the Cold War phase, 'evil-empire' phase and collapse of Soviet politics and the death of Soviet Marxist–Leninism.

The defeat of the sociological analysis of everyday life (itself a product of nineteenth-century liberationist theories) led to the aesthetic analyses of identity, gender and subjectivity. The brilliance of these analyses masked their incapacity to reinvent a left-liberationist philosophy. The decline of a vision of a socialised history as a unified narrative (against which other unified histories might be tested) was in inverse proportion to the rise of *unified* theory which *acted as narrative*. The coherence of theory replaced the coherence of history (and its explanation) and sub-versive reading replaced subversion. By 1981 it was common to find critical work which had substituted the politics of the everyday with the subversion of the aesthetic.

> De-mystifying the process of reading . . . will . . . point to the possibil-
> ity of undoing many texts which work, unconsciously, upon us. In
> the end this may lead to real social transformation.
>
> (Rosemary Jackson, *Fantasy*)

The critique of the nature of everyday lived culture and its represen-tations eventually turned into the critique of representation *as* lived culture: the condition of the simulacrum (which the Situationists feared and execrated) finally came to represent the *only* reality rather than the dominant reality, which remained still open to challenge. Moreover, theory itself, seen in (and only as) its rhetorical dimension seemed for-ever trapped in a tautological and continuous undoing, resistant even to itself. The critique of discourse and representational (i.e., linguistic) ideology soon substituted masculinity, imperialism and the spectacle of consumption for Marxist categories of class division. Women, ethnic groups and the popular now acted as the new proletariat on behalf of whom personal identity 'politics' would act in the place of revolutionary socialism.

The central position of language and its capacity to represent the world (the nature of the real) was the first to find itself under radical scrutiny – if the actual state could not be assaulted then perhaps it could have its orders and self-seeking representations undermined instead. Yet, language was precisely *all* that radicalism could use in its representations of actual experience. Without language (and its ability to *speak differently*) opposition was impossible. All statements were now to be taken as *contrary* to themselves, undermining their own validity and therefore useless as analytic tools (hence Jacques Derrida's fascination with the supplementary, silence, lacunae). The subversion of codes turned all concerns over identity into a fight with 'otherness' which was both internalised and psychologised, but it succeeded in making all forms of resistance merely relative, thus confusing the need for priorities, authority and conformity. Such a situation inevitably reinforced 'natural' and political conservatism, mimicking the mores and motives of the market in an often uncanny way.

7
The Role of the Intellectual at the Turn of the Century

The role of the intellectual, and especially the role of the *revolutionary* intellectual, is not a specialisation. Whilst the intellectual may work in a specific field, it is in the nature of his or her work to have implications for the *whole* field of knowledge. It is this *implication* which is revolutionary, as is the specific demand placed on the intellectual's actual chosen field.

The intellectual, however, is constrained by three factors: in as much as he or she is an academic; in as much as he or she is a radical activist; in as much as he or she is constrained by method. The first two are peripheral to the third, but the third is essential to the first two and they proceed from it. If an intellectual is an academic they are, in essence, a servant of the state – a bureaucrat; if an intellectual is a radical activist they are an organisational member under the immediate necessity of social action, but if they are an intellectual *per se* they are only under the necessity of method.

The intellectual must begin, therefore, by a *refusal*. As a bureaucrat, this realm of refusal may be restricted to negotiations over wages and hours, and belong to trade union economic action on a local or national level. As an activist, the intellectual performs political actions which challenge law and civil obedience. As an intellectual, *per se*, he or she *challenges knowledge* and its accepted organisation. Such a *refusal* puts the two previous categories under permanent question and is prior to them. Refusal is, of course, a contentless rebellion, but it does begin from a determination to address something that has been *missed* in consensus. Indeed, it presupposes a superfluity or superabundance of meaning where a paucity seemed to exist. 'The *overabundance* of the signifier, its *supplementary* character, is thus the result of a finitude, . . . the result of a lack which must be *supplemented*' (Jacques Derrida, 'Structure, Sign and Play in the Discourse of the Human Sciences').

What is present, nevertheless, is something extra, marginal and supplementary, but this supplementarity is *capable of articulation* under the special circumstances of the new gaze. This gaze dislocates language and meaning in order to relocate it elsewhere. Thus is it both intellectual and 'terroristic', appearing both arbitrary and logical all at the same time, obeying the law of the absurd and thus refusing the frame of logic preceding its appearance. As such the gaze is both paranoid and excessive, for not only is the question it raises already considered answered (by implication) but the question has hitherto not been considered a question at all. Moreover (and almost as an insult) this gaze finds what should *not* be there: the hidden and excessive. The terror of that which is missing is no less than the terror of history itself. It is precisely in history as well as *of* history that the 'overabundance of the signifier', far from robbing the processes of meaning of their efficaciousness, produces that very efficaciousness in the abysmal depth of a coming-to-consciousness. Yet it is quite unnecessary to conceive of history as a coming to 'fullness', a fruition or coming to authenticity. Theoretical considerations require only a drive towards such a position in order to articulate the fullest possibility of the superfluity of the signifier, that is *the coming to consciousness of the marginal* (the will to action being, of course, a separate issue).

It is absolutely necessary to imagine that the supplement of the plenitude – its excess and therefore its centre – is, in fact, none other than the 'I' of the intellectual generated as conscious agent and metaphysical presence. Such a conception is determined by my need to *intervene* within the structure both as its centre and its periphery. In such a way, from the periphery I generate a theory that takes its place as the centre only if it acts as a *displacement*. This plenitude is disrupted by my *virtual* presence in order for myself, as an actual person (an agent of change) to operate in the historical sphere. Thus, 'the philosophical I is not the man, not the human body or the soul ... but the metaphysical subject, the limit – not part of this world' (Ludwig Wittgenstein, *Tractatus Logico-Philosophicus*).

The agent of change acts only as the 'person' appropriately attached to the subject of change (the philosophical I) which is the *limit* and *therefore the condition* of thought itself under the new dispensation. As such, the subject is not to be thought of as a substitute person but rather the limit to the condition that allows the subject 'I' to appear. If, as Wittgenstein states, 'I am my world', nevertheless, of 'the thinking, presenting subject; there is no such thing'. When Derrida says, therefore, that the 'absence of a centre is here the absence of a subject and the absence of an author', this is not to be taken to mean the absence of coherence or the absence of agency, nor does it mean that the excessive unconscious of the signified (that which displaces it) is necessarily a continuous, relativist drift away from logic, meaning and intervention. Again and again, a simple or vulgar deconstruction is forced to confront its own inadequacy and a sophisticated deconstruction its absolute adequacy to the subject.

Whence, then, does the spur to intervention come? What generates it? The answer is simply that *anything* generates it. It is generated from a necessary, if arbitrary, myth. Hence, for Jacques Lacan, 'before strictly human relations are established, certain relations have already been determined. They are taken from . . . nature . . . in themes of opposition. Nature provides . . . signifiers . . . and these signifiers organise human relations . . . providing them with structures' ('Agency of the Letter in the Unconscious'). For Lacan, *nature* is the abyss of signification. Signification is generated *as* Nature and as human nature. It is presymbolic as it 'predates the formation of the subject'. In his reading of Claude Lévi-Strauss's structural anthropology, it is incest which Derrida locates as the necessary determinant. Both nature and incest act as catalysts to theory.

Conceived thus, the 'origin' for both Lacanian psychoanalysis and Derridian deconstruction is displaced into the realm of the accidental and pre-linguistc. It has therefore an *accidental* and *arbitrary* relationship to what it generates. Such artifice *generates an intervention* whilst denying 'an origin . . . or absolute *archia*'. 'There is no unity or absolute source of the myth' (Derrida, ibid.). What is generated is not a certain way of speaking but a certain way of *seeing*: the leap Marx and Engels take into the realm of the 'Real' in pursuit of man. It is a visualisation *at once* of how things *are* and therefore the absolute myth of how things must have been. History is born.

History's logic, and therefore the logic of subjectivity, is generated from a random space with no claim to priority but from which the discourses of history and subjectivity take on priority and centrality, even if there is no logical nor originating moment to their generation. By the invocation of this logic and, therefore, this structure, both history and subjectivity use the mythic as part of the logic by which they recognise themselves and thus, 'logic *precedes* any experience' (Wittgenstein, op. cit.). They take on a 'truth' function from which the mythic can now be extracted. Thus is born a type of necessity or conceptual drive inherent to the structuration of the appearance of thought itself, as thought constructs the experience of its own functioning. The result is, in all senses, felt, organic, visceral.

It is true only in the most limited sense to argue that all discourse *is*, of necessity, 'bricolage' and that this is, again, of necessity, opposed to the construction of 'totality' created by the unifying vision of the 'engineer' (Derrida, op. cit.). It is quite insufficient as explanation to accuse the engineer's vision of being 'theological' (at the same time as being technocratic) and therefore authoritarian (or indeed merely modernist).

It is the duty of the radical theorist to provide ideas that *scandalise* current thought, thereby dislocating it and 'terrorising' it (in the sense of intellectual disabuse). The ungrounded space that emerges and from which thought now proceeds is not only the scandal of current thought but it must also be driven by its own extreme goals. Thus it scandalises itself as it realises its *extreme possibility*. Once thought scandalises current practice it has no choice but to go to its own limit (to scandalise itself) or it will retreat and fall into reaction. This drive to extremes is in the nature of all new, ungrounded, marginal thought. Its authoritarian nature is only that of logic *in* method, not a prescription for personal action. Praxis is beside the point here, as we are always dealing with both the methodological 'I' and the I as agency and these cannot be confused.

The scandal of modernity is not that there are no grand narratives left but that the *only scandal is grand narrative generated from the position of marginality*. Such is the terrorisation of consensus and of benevolent authoritarianism. It comes, more or less, from the silent space beyond language as a visceral knowledge in the body of the person-as-agency and in the drive to extremity in the logic of the I-subject-of-speculation (the metaphysical subject as limit). Its peculiar force is that it cannot be contained in a language but is the determinant of a language. If successful, it is the elucidation of an 'ethical' choice whose logic leads to action. The necessity or 'rightness' of the position will always be beyond articulation – an appeal to the justice of a particular feeling or world-view. It will not be authoritarian because radicalism is the permanent revolution of opposition. Critique can never be rule. Critique is the necessary disjunction which dislodges the dictatorship of convention and unmasks naked authority. It is not the requirement of theory to participate in activity. The two are only *arbitrarily* related, but theory will always be the justification for action. Yet should action be set to seize authority, then theory must return to critique, return to becoming orthodoxy's opponent even at the moment of its seizure of power. Critique is crisis in the body of knowledge from the place beyond consensual speech, as a voice in and of the margin.

All intellectual life is refusal of past truisms. From refusal comes *elucidation* and elucidation exists only in the realm of the conceptual. Intellectual life is not scholarship. (I do not denigrate scholarship, but believe it a secondary-level activity.) It is not the careful sifting of empirical evidence, nor a quantitative accumulation of that evidence but a *reordering* of that evidence according to the *prior* demand of method in the realm of conceptualisation. One can be an academic and a political activist and not be an intellectual; one can be an intellectual only if one is committed to challenging accepted positions and therefore a teacher *manqué* and an activist *manqué*. These activities are the consequences that follow rather than the other way round.

Intellectual commitment is not an activity, however, like teaching, agitation or even scholarship but a *sedentary* and private struggle to understand a question that has already been (incorrectly) answered. This sedentary aspect should not be confused with mere 'bookwormery', the worst sort of academicism, but rather should be recognised as the *precondition* of practice itself. The 'organic' intellectual, to borrow Antonio Gramsci's phrase, can never know they act in or on behalf of history, only that they act in historical circumstances which call forth a particular mode of operation: a theoretical position. One can only 'know' that position as an intellectual, be *in* the theory as a part of its conceptual make-up. The force of the conceptual position will determine its rightness to history, nothing else, and that force will itself be contained within the structure of the conceptual. The argument here is not that one should act or that one might act but that theory and action belong to two different realms. Which has priority, constantly fluctuates according to the historical moment.

This commitment is motivated by ethical concerns and is evaluative in as much as it refocuses the subject under inquiry. Nevertheless, the performance of the intellectual task must be severely restricted to the rigours of the method chosen. Once a method is chosen it is the logic of that method only that must be obeyed. Such a logic must be taken to its *extreme*. Only in extreme limits is intellectualism tested: 'the worthy ally of all the terrorists plotting to ruin society', as Jacques Lacan declares. The intellectual question is always obsessional and *urgent*. What is the nature of this method and this extremity? What is the nature of this urgency?

The intellectual quest is constrained by the limits surrounding its available and potential language. Thus it is clear that 'there is no language in existence for which there is any question of its inability to cover the whole field of the signified' (Lacan, *Four Fundamental Concepts*).

Language is both the medium and restraint of intellectual activity. It is, in short, always adequate to its own functional and *representational* needs. There is, in effect, no beyond to which to appeal. As such, language precedes the intellectual endeavour and, buoying it up, as it were, always drags it back into *the past* whence it has been inherited. At the simplest level, in order to communicate to others the ideas fermenting in the mind of an intellectual, his or her language must be couched in a language *already* understood. This immediately creates a hostage to fortune.

Intellectual method cannot, therefore, conform to the rules of common communication for this implies an *already known*. It must rather conform only to its methodological necessity: its rightness to itself. Only in this way can it defeat the pull of history (the idea's own archaeology) and place itself on the side of the future. The future is, however, the present moment, its exact condition and circumstances exquisitely elucidated. In a real sense, until this happens, the accepted positions that have preceded it all belong to *a past* now rendered defunct but still lived as *real*! The new theorist renders all previous and contemporary colleagues redundant – a species of living dead.

The language used in relation to colleagues will in some sense be a performance or enactment of the method used as well as an endorsement of it. As there is no language except the language that is, and that is always, already, adequate to its needs, the truly new can only emerge as a disconnecting force, an undoing of the grammar of the connective plausibility embedded in language – an operation to explore (to enact) its *unconscious deep structure*:

> This is a characteristic phenomenon of the *transition-breaks* that constitute the advent of a new problematic. At certain moments in the history of ideas we see these *practical concepts* emerge, and typically they are *internally unbalanced* concepts. In one aspect they belong to the old ideological universe which serves as their 'theoretical' reference (humanism); but in the other they concern a new domain.
>
> (Louis Althusser, *For Marx*)

Theoretically, if not practically, method and language are not to be confused as one and the same. Method belongs to an ideal space, as a precondition of knowledge and knowledge communication. The unavoidable intention of communicative language (therefore the 'past') is the tautological trap that is every moment negotiated by method. This dilemma was uppermost in Wittgenstein's mind when he opens the

Tractatus Logico-Philosophicus aware that 'this book will perhaps only be understood by those who have themselves already thought [these] thoughts – or similar thoughts'.

Method, while it belongs to a conceptual, and therefore ideal realm, is also prone to its own internal disintegrative forces. Wittgenstein's work was intended to

> [D]raw a limit to thinking, or rather – not to thinking, but to the expression of thoughts; for, in order to draw a limit to thinking we should have to be able to think both sides of this limit (we should therefore have to be able to think what cannot be thought). . . .
>
> The limit can, therefore, only be drawn in language and what lies on the other side of the limit will be . . . nonsense.

What is this 'nonsense', this non-sense on the other side of the limit? And what is it that is experienced when we approach this limit? Method (as language too) is always trapped by its inability to transcend itself (its procedures and rules). As it reaches the limit it retreats back from its own destiny, the implications of its own extreme logic. As such it falls back upon its own past, becoming a type of revisionism. This must be avoided, and can only be avoided by bringing method itself into crisis, not against the pulp of empirical facts but against the vacuum of the *unthinkable*. The *visceral* realisation of the unthinkable is the entry into the tragic and daemonic – it takes the form of an absolute possessive necessity in the field of *vision*. This vision is the crisis of language *beyond* itself, the undoing of method by method. At such a moment a new grammar, which is both structure and critique, appears. It is realised precisely outside the demand of personal needs or desire. This not merely is the ideal 'I' of philosophy transmogrified but also it is the personal 'I' of self-identity. 'It is not a question of knowing whether I speak of myself in a way that conforms to what I am,' as Lacan says, 'but rather of knowing whether I am the same as that of which I speak'.

Enacted upon the 'I' of selfhood, this crisis is the tragedy of old identity and the appearance of new, the freeing of the historical self from its restraints and therefore the dawn of the 'present'. Method 'speaks' the self into appearance – it is the new grammar of *perception*, of seeing differently. 'I' come to know what I am by the journey of the logic I have employed, but this logic is beyond and outside my personal and selfish demands for conformity. I find myself *in* it as it tells me who I am and who I am to be in the ruins of my prehistory. This condition is neither mystical nor humanistic precisely because I recognise myself in the new roles I find myself occupying, in the dimensions I now perform within, and in the perceptual framework from which my values are now generated. The will of the intellectual is the will to let go as a refusal of given identity and a going beyond the will itself into *ungrounded* selfhood.[1]

The disestablishment of the conceptual 'self' is not, of course, the disestablishment of the active *individual* as an agent of change (in whatever realm). Indeed, the emptier the concept of self the easier it is to act *in* the world as an individual no longer weighed down with the cloying debris of self-identity. This has nothing to do with psychological models. The self here is not psychological and can quite easily perform its tasks without the paraphernalia of psychological labelling. The 'empty' self is the self *beyond* psychology – the self as an active *social* and *political* agent, not the solipsistic split self of psychological description. It is simply the *fully conscious* self.

The radical 'self' is always 'mystic', driven to see the very nature of things as embodied in its vision and its alone. The self is the culmination and origin of this embodiment – a focus for history and structure, now realised in thought and action. Such a self is evidently prone to hubris, to reactionary activity and to authoritarian ideology. When the intellectual self sees liberation only in terms of a monolithic version of millennial history (the thousand-year Reich) then it ceases to be intellectual and becomes demonic. A free radical subjectivity requires consistent and continuous *non-alliance* and refusal. As such, the free radical subject is a floating entity capable of multiple possibilities but choosing any *one* possibility in any particular circumstances with a willingness to give that position up as self-knowledge demands.

Between the philosophical I of metaphysics and the agency of the social I, the self becomes merely a *necessary* myth of cohesion and authority. Cohesion and authority are the necessary precondition of an explanatory framework but they must be experienced as 'lived' conditions from which the cohesion and authority of self-awareness flow.

The fragmented self of relativism can only understand lived experience as a series of random shocks from which no lessons can be drawn and no history can be found (such a self always lives in the mere present). The integrated intellectual self, however, 'knows' that the future has already come about (in the already, as yet unacknowledged, paradigm shift lived in the experience of the intellectual body) and that therefore the present is already history and that the past (the paradigmatic *vision* as *already experienced*) is about to be as *the* realised future amongst the innumerable and possible futures that might have been.

The intellectual self is, therefore, constantly struggling in order not to surrender the visionary and unitary to the fragmentary; not to surrender the creative awareness of free association and totality to the merely fragmentary experience of the everyday and banal; not to surrender method to mere empiricism; nor history to the present. The intellectual is, therefore, a figure in struggle, without complacency, curiously only aware of who he or she is when they recognise when and where they stand; confirming their presence as intellectuals (and their *actual presence* as agents of change) only in their coming to awareness. And this awareness tells them that what they thought they knew is the very opposite of where their method leads and what it shows. Thus is experienced the uncertainty of knowing in the certainty of knowledge. Only in abandonment of older positions and refusal of current dogma, and the embrace of the new self-alienated position, does the intellectual free expression from consensus, banality and cliché.

From a deep and corrosive scepticism which 'alienates' the self from its own lived experience can the new 'ungrounded' self appear: a product of its own method of self-seeking. It cannot be denied that at first sight such a formulation seems to smack of that egotism and mystification Marx and Engels castigated in Max Stirner's self-absorption. For his solipsism Stirner was made a 'saint' in *The German Ideology*. Yet the question of the subject status of the intellectual in his or her relationship with both reality and the revolutionary 'condition' is a curious blank in an otherwise astringent critique.

Both Engels and Marx were insistent that *their* mode of revolutionary socialism was grounded in 'real premises', the first of which was 'the existence of living human *individuals*' (emphasis added) upon which 'all human history' rested. This tautological formulation that all human history is predicated upon individuals interacting is the first and necessary step in combating historical abstraction and subjective metaphysics and is strictly verifiable 'in a purely empirical way'. Thus, in full, we find Marx introducing his ideas with the following proposition:

> The premises from which we begin are not arbitrary ones, . . . but real premises from which abstraction can only be made in the imagination. They are the real individuals, their activity and the material conditions under which they live, both those which they find already existing and those produced by their activity. These premises can be verified in a purely empirical way.
>
> (Karl Marx and Friedrich Engels, *The German Ideology*)

Moreover,

> The social structure and the State are continually evolving out of the life-process of definite individuals, but of individuals, not as they may appear in their own or other people's imagination, but as they *really* are; i.e., as they operate, produce materially and hence as they work under definite material limits, presuppositions and conditions independent of their will.
>
> (Marx and Engels, ibid.)

Yet what is it that robs people of the control of their 'imagination' and acts 'independent of their will'? It is *reality* itself – as things *'really'* are, as Marx and Engels emphasise. What constitutes the nature of the reality of human life? It is the *production* of the materiality of subsistence which itself, by circuitous routes, produces 'actual material life.'

> Men can be distinguished from animals by consciousness, by religion or anything else you like. They themselves begin to distinguish themselves from animals as soon as they begin to *produce* their means of subsistence. ... By producing their means of subsistence men are indirectly producing their actual material life.
>
> (Ibid.)

Production and material existence are thus inexorably linked through the 'human'; 'consciousness' is the *result of* this process and not its precondition.

> This mode of production must not be considered simply as being the reproduction of the physical existence of these individuals. Rather it is a definite form of activity of these individuals, a definite form of expressing their life, a definite *mode of life.* ... As individuals express their life, so they are. What they are, therefore, coincides with their production. ... The nature of individuals thus depends on the material conditions determining their production.
>
> (Ibid.)

To repeat, 'as individuals express their life, so they are.' Marx is quite clear that 'what they are ... *coincides* [emphasis added] with their production' and that 'life is not determined by consciousness, but consciousness by life' (i.e. the material conditions of 'actual' people in lived 'reality').

(Ibid.)

Consciousness finds itself only in social relations and these are determined by the reality of the production of materiality and the *exploitation* and *alienation* of production (and therefore of the materiality of the 'self'). History (and its driving force, revolution) are determined precisely by the revolutionary class coming to a consciousness of its potential to overthrow the current exploitative system and its 'total activity' (i.e. its material totality in the completeness of its system and its reproduction *in* consciousness).

> These conditions of life, which different generations find in existence, decide also whether or not the periodically recurring revolutionary convulsion will be strong enough to overthrow the basis of the entire existing system. And if these material elements of a complete revolution are not present (namely, on the one hand the existing productive forces, on the other the formation of a revolutionary mass, which revolts not only against separate conditions of society up till then, but against the very 'production of life' till then, the 'total activity' on which it is based), then, as far as practical development is concerned, it is absolutely immaterial whether the *idea* of this revolution has been expressed a hundred times already, as the history of communism proves.
>
> (Ibid.)

The crux of the matter is the discovery of *the determinant conditions of 'real history'*. This and this alone produces revolutionary ideas and these are themselves predicated on the material existence of a 'revolutionary class'. Thus, 'the existence of revolutionary ideas in a particular period presupposes the existence of a revolutionary class'.

Those discoveries, from the nature of production to the nature of exploited labour, through to the conditions which govern history, are themselves determined by and determined *through reality*; they are all of the nature of this reality. The real is nothing less than the precondition of its own constituents and the result of its components. Yet this *real* is nothing less than the secret historical condition that governs social activity and human consciousness and it is this fact and this alone that Marx and Engels started from. Thus the real is nothing other than an overriding precondition for the success of the *theoretical reconstruction* of that socialism (and 'communism') Marx and Engels wished to promote. In short, the real is a product of a theory of totality and that theory is conditioned by the context and vision of its makers: its coming to awareness through them as they recognise their position in it and as now *conscious* agents of it – an alienation of alienation.

The material presence of insurrectionary agents as social individuals is not the same as the theoretical logic that produces 'revolutionary ideas' and a 'revolutionary class'.[2] The intellectual self is always the subject of metaphysics as well as a social agent. The necessary link between insurrectionary agents and revolutionary class begins with the specific theoretical logic applied to production in Marxist thought. Production is the cornerstone of the totality of the real and of con-sciousness of the real. Yet the real (actual history) is nothing other than an effect of production, itself conceived as the cornerstone of a concep-tual framework. This is not to reduce Marxism to mere tautology or rhetorical flourish, nor is it to reduce it to an easy target for deconstruc-tive technique. Rather, it emphasises the necessary *doubling* that occurs in the radical intellectual self conceived as a product not of its own hubris but as a product of what it has discovered of itself (in its double mode of existence as metaphysical 'I' and agent of change). *The coming to consciousness* of the intellectual self is the freeing of the agent self *from* history. The first prerequisite of the intellectual is to 'free the mind' and in so doing *see* reality *as it is*. The totality of the real and the material existence of actual individuals are expressions of this movement.

The *real* and the *actual* are precisely realisations about the world as its *preconditions*, verifiable *after the event* by empirical investigation. The imposition of these terms makes the world as it is and can thus be tested *as if* they exist in the world. Marx and Engels discover the laws of their own existence both as the *actual* experience of the world and as the *reality* that others have failed to notice. The laws they discover are those laws that as social agents they recognise as determining *their con-sciousness*. This consciousness is liberated from its determinants (as their mere pawn) exactly in proportion to the possibility of *self-awareness* (i.e. as expressed as a general knowledge of reality). None of this need pre-suppose a transcendent principle either of self or world, nor need it convert history into a 'person'. Rather, the self realises its *situation* as consciousness and as agency within the materiality of the world.

The perceptive reader may by now have noticed that the vocabulary employed in these pages bears a more than passing resemblance to that of neo-conservatism, hence Digby Anderson, Director of the right-wing Social Affairs Unit and contributor to the *National Review*, can state,

Words that some had thought and others hoped to see the back of forever are creeping back into social analysis: fidelity, duty, fortitude, toleration, honesty, self-reliance, manliness. And even those who are not ready to stomach the full range of the moral vocabulary are alluding to it collectively and indirectly when they talk of the need to promote 'community'.

(Anderson, *This Will Hurt*)

We cannot invent a new vocabulary, but that does not stop what exists as being a site for struggle in meaning. Such struggle is directly related to attempts to represent, describe, analyse and intervene in reality (the 'real'). Thus, this struggle becomes one with a moral purpose.

For neo-conservatism, the new moralism opposed to Thatcherism and Reaganism, is itself a type of aesthetic classicism, a whole range of social restraints, including public punishments, ostracism, military discipline, formality, repression and restraint, (including enforced responsibility for the working class – [this is not satire]) – ridicule, shame and disgrace are the only means to restore the health of society amidst the chaos and complexity of 'Babylon'.[3] This gut reaction nonsense, argued by passionate yet *woefully* ill-informed people, is itself a reaction to the new authoritarianism (to them, neo-liberalism) of the *extreme* centre.[4] The 'democratic deficit' has thrown the traditional right into confusion and thereby marginalised it. The vocabulary thus employed cannot be reclaimed but it can be widened and used differently, with different meanings attached (meanings always *aware* of these other and more deadly possibilities). The radical thinker must, at one and *the same time*, be aware that a term like 'community' has a meaning for the left, the centre and the right and that the deployment of such terms is always open to the distortion of any two other positions other than that intended.

The belief in the need to expunge certain meanings from language is deeply rooted in radical thought and is especially prevalent amongst writers combating fascism. For Walter Benjamin, the project was equivalent to clearing the way for the 'good' society – a moral quest as much as an aesthetic demand.

The concepts which are introduced into the theory of art in what follows differ from the more familiar terms in that they are completely useless for the purposes of Fascism. They are, on the other hand, useful for the formulation of revolutionary demands in the politics of art.

(Walter Benjamin, 'The Work of Art')

Radical thinkers are only too aware of the 'dislocational' function of language during periods of ideological conflict. Salman Rushdie has noted the effect of the Nazi period on Günter Grass's work and post-war German language and,

> of the need for the language to be rebuilt, pebble by pebble, from the wreckage; because a language in which evil finds so expressive voice is a dangerous tongue. The practitioners of 'rubble literature' – Grass himself being one of the most prominent of these – took upon themselves the Herculean task of re-inventing the German language, of tearing it apart, ripping out the poisoned parts, and putting it back together.
>
> (Salman Rushdie, introduction to Günter Grass, *Writing and Politics*)

Yet such 'utopian' restrictions, however well motivated, simply create authoritarian 'Newspeak', vocabularies whose restrictions liberate nothing other than different forms of oppression. It is simply the case that language is not subject to the power of such censorious control for however good a purpose, and that its meanings are always *appropriable* by anyone. Restriction of meaning by radical thinkers is not, nor can ever be, the same as mere censorship. There is no such thing as the *unthinkably* bad action, nor any means of restricting its articulation except by the insistence of its opponents that they gain access to that same articulation bereft of its original impetus and sense, used now as an antidote to its original meaning.

The tactics employed by post-modern radicals opened up language to multiple meanings and were therefore seen as a way of disarming consensual or conservative meaning. Yet the celebration of slippage also robbed the left of the opportunity to *claim their own meaning*. The need to be precise and to *insist* on one meaning amongst a host of choices robbed the left of the necessary insistence on the authority of their own pronouncements. Instead, multiplicity allowed the rhetoric of power to play all meanings off against each other in order to reduce language (but not action) to absurdity. Nothing is more odious in this regard than the abject grovelling of liberal apologists in the face of political correctness – in this case entirely *self-induced*, so that the Newspeak position can be ritually intoned for an imagined readership of the newly enlightened. Here is a particularly foolish example of genuflection produced during the 1990s in the pages of *The Times Higher Education Supplement*. I leave the writer to anonimity:

> Feminism has taught us many things, though men keep ignoring or forgetting most of them. One is that gender relations are not 'just

natural', but social and historical; accordingly, we may best think about the future through the past and the present, not through some idealist, romanticised or biological conception of how women and men are 'naturally' meant to be. Changing future gender relations involves changing men; changing men involves deconstructing men and men's power; deconstructing men and men's power may involve the abolition of the category of men. Is the new millennium the time (at last) for men to change?

According to the author of this little squib (dressed as learned prose), the *only* defining characteristic of men is brute force, which the magic of 'deconstruction' (he uses the active verb twice, no less) will tame. Deconstruction apparently is a mode of action which undermines 'power'. There is therefore no power (at least for this author) which is not malignant in origin (men) and in fact (hurting women). That feminism uses deconstruction suggests the possibility of the abolition of the category of men (he means 'man') and therefore a new framework of power, which point escapes this guileless and *decent* male professor. Deconstruction is a form of power – that which *negates*. It is, of course, anti-theology but it provides its own orthodoxy and inquisition when its 'originator' is away. The power that negates is still power.

The loss of a 'centre' does not stop the radical intellectual choosing words in order to insist on one meaning and to claim an authority for that meaning. The exposure of the *mechanisms* of meaning does not deny meaning *tout court*, nor meaning's place in logic and symbolic representation. The necessity of rhetoric to language (*pace* DeMan) may be a destabilising factor but it is also a *mobilising* factor whose organisational dynamic allows for the emergence of a pattern of meaning and a structure for representation; not any meaning emerges but *a* meaning. It is not a matter of fixing a meaning forever but of fixing a meaning *now*, in this particular set of circumstances and for this reason. Such a meaning is an intervention and such a meaning is political through and through.

This fixing of meaning is also, of *necessity*, a *restriction* and nowhere is this more so than in the area of the aesthetic or, to be more precise, a restriction in the area of representation and thus the arena of representational analysis: a diminution of the symbolic and an absolute (if not permanent) curb on the signifier. Analyses which foreground the rhetoric of discourse are brought to heal under the impulse of a political reading, if and only if, the field of the signifier is constantly narrowed and its free play confined. The diminution of the sphere of the aesthetic, that is, a diminution of the belief that everything is 'textualised' or is 'discourse', allows for the de-aestheticising of everyday life (its 'spectacular' appearance) and allows for the re-entry of authentication and subjectivity as terms of restriction (*at this moment*) which themselves *liberate* specific meanings.

The belief that every symbolic activity can be treated as a 'signifying practice' is not a political intervention at all. By levelling all symbolic activities to the condition of *mere equivalence* such analyses reproduce the substitutive nature of the society they attempt to critique. Without symbolic hierarchy there can be no politics nor any aesthetic. All political and aesthetic readings come properly from a sense of what is significant: an order and hierarchy based on choice. Without such choices there can be neither a realm of political decision nor a realm of aesthetic taste. To expose the 'irrational' nature of such choices (if indeed they are) is neither to explain them nor rectify them. Meta-discourses based upon rhetorical analysis, whilst they 'reduce' authority by exposing its mechanisms, are quite unable to dismantle the mechanisms of authority nor suggest a means of escape. The overly panoptic explanation, which subsequently arises, suggests that an escape from language is impossible. There is therefore no actual escape and the difference between oppression and liberation becomes merely a degree of rhetorical shading.

As the analysis of language is inevitably tautological, the escape from discourse is an escape back into it. Such thinking is a disavowal of a political reading (rather than a 'subversive' reading). In a political reading it is essential to restrict and diminish in order to strengthen and make significant separate and different discursive practices which cannot be dealt with as mere discourse nor as mere signifying practice. *For a political reading to be significant, a cultural reading must be diminished as a result.*

Readings determined by signifying practice (that is, rhetorical readings) flatten out history, social conditions, production, etc. and treat them as *internal* to the rhetoric of the aesthetic. By so doing not only are these separate, but vital, spheres ignored in as much as what they represent, but the aesthetic is also dismissed as an epiphenomenon of rhetorical structure. By creating an all-in-all, such an analysis can do little in any specific area and can do nothing to challenge such systems (which rest on linear substitution: chain of signifiers and mere differentiation). The diminution of the rhetorical is the reawakening of the historical sense and therefore of the social or political sense.

8
The Abyss of History and the Nature of the Fantastic

When we write the history of discrete literary events we are led to a certain complexity in relation both to the field of literary study and to the processes of history – its objects and its discipline. In its widest sense this brings us to the heart of how literature recognises its historical dimension and its relation to history through the peculiar operations of criticism, itself bound to rules originating *outside* the literary arena but peculiarly attached to it. By a circuitous route we are forcibly returned to the nagging problems of history and language, event and signification, politics and ethics. To speculate about literature and 'the literary' is no less than a speculation about the entire field of critique.

Serious professional literary criticism (practised in universities, declared scientific and objective) which is neither merely partisan nor actually propaganda is determined by a special and peculiar attention, but this attention is not (contrary to expectation) exclusively directed at the book in hand. Rather, the critical gaze is engaged in reading only when it fulfils the criteria of the various (often opposed) schools of thought within criticism itself. Reading is therefore never outside the domain of criticism and criticism is always locked into an approach (or 'objective' reading) which produces effects within the discourses of specific schools.

Whatever oppositions different readings bring to criticism, the schools of thought most prevalent in literary analysis mainly use two models for their approach. One considers works as determined by universal principles to which they adhere. These universals are quite often formal and linguistic and they are exemplified by debates over genre and particularised in work in which is highlighted questions of language and construction. The other considers works in their individuality and contingency, and as such gives technique, nuance, morality and ethics significant roles. The first approach deals in general conditions where the work is always secondary to those general conditions; the second approach deals in specific conditions where the principles of universality are secondary and take on the provisional nature that the studied text had for the first approach. The provisional and contingent cannot be reconciled with the tendency towards universality except by the creation of stability. To this all critics turn their attention.

To create stability, the critic determines a 'field' to which the discipline of literary criticism can be attached and which validates any variety of approaches (even when they disagree). The field (which is not quite the same as a limited canon) is a spatial and structural ideal into which the provisional nature of critical works is fitted. The critic who is interested in general rules will be tied to the field but so will the critic interested in the provisional and contingent. The first critic will make of this field a *formal* space whilst the latter will make it into an ethical dimension. In the first place the field is a structure, in the second it is a tradition.

These two arenas constitute the dynamics of the 'field' and cannot properly be reconciled: the formal approach presupposes a priori questions that the ethical takes as given and the ethical presupposes a moral a priori out of which all else comes. Formalism gives priority to structure and language, whilst ethical criticism puts the moral and 'human' first. In each case the field is made possible by their attention and that attention is validated by the field. Actual works are then validated in canonic blocks determined by attention within the field itself: traditional Marxism and humanism preferring realist texts; post-structuralism preferring fantasy, surreal and detective texts; feminism preferring women's autobiography and science fiction; post-colonialist reading preferring non-European texts; cultural studies preferring popular texts.

It may be objected that the dualistic schema is too narrow, too little cognisant of a third position that negates the prior two. To this we must now turn. On the face of it, the third position is highly attractive. Acting as a rigorous critique of the formal linguistic position, it also apparently demolishes the ethical position through a ruthless interrogation of agency in its relationship to the 'human', 'true' and 'universal'. This attack negates the two other positions and apparently rescues or recuperates a beyond or supplementary 'time', 'space' and 'history' other to both the ideal and to the particular.

In its considerable attention to rhetoric, the third position discovers a hitherto unconsidered *complicity* between the first two positions that it *reveals*. In so doing it finds its own legitimacy. In finding complicity, the third position conflates the first two and thereby becomes the second position *out of which* they each speak, acting as their unconscious. This itself is a politico-ethical turn and it presupposes *agency* of a critical nature capable of both discrimination and judgement. This presupposes an ideal realm *against* which it ponders its own diminishing image.

If the third position is actually the second position all along it must contain the excess of the first (two) positions that accounts for the literary (and therefore critical) field in the first place. The marginal, other, peripheral, supplementary, and 'trace' become the literary as the unspoken impossibility of itself, of its field (into which the canon is slotted). But this position cannot be recovered by the slotting of a canon of alternative (ethnic, gender) texts. This would be to fall back on the ethical-political which has been breached in the first place. Alternative, or more open, canons do not fix the problem, are not more democratic nor equable. Indeed the use of the third position by ethnic, feminist and gender critics resurrects the ideal as an oppositional condition for text itself: a negative sublime located in ethical positions exemplified by particular texts in which a tradition (or community of linked types) is recognised. There is then a subject for the third position only if it relinquishes its own demands on the previous universalities. In almost all cases the ethical-political position prevails as moral rightness.

Here is a field in which objectivity recognises the objects of its quest in order to construct agents for its gaze. This is a tautological fix, no doubt, but it allows those 'unrepresented' a view of themselves gathered around the constellation of appropriate terms which constitute 'black', 'woman' or 'gay' and which enters into their own sense of the provisional via the debates held under those markers of universal relevance each group takes for its own position within their field.

That which escapes the law, in turn, becomes its own law, and more, an article of *faith* with consequent litany and ritual. This new litany invokes the right, the good, and even the beautiful although they may be in reverse or parodied form. In place of conservatism, universalism, idealism, traditionalism, homogeneity, masculinism and imperialism are oppositional terms culled from non-European, non-masculinist, non-imperialist, non-universalist and non-rationalist experience. Here is now placed what is good, right and beautiful (in manner, lifestyle, sexual preference and looks, cultural artefacts, etc.).

For some critics of the 'third' position, an attachment to the linguistic and psychoanalytic registers grants them insight into the workings of the 'floating signifier'. Such a strategy reveals the register of the universal and determinate as they become untenable in the face of indeterminacy. The floating signifier *liquifies* the processes of solidification especially in relationship to the stabilisation of the field. The universal and its specific instances are now uncoupled and an abyss opened between them such that the universal is reduced to its own mere instance.

The negation of all positions of exactitude paradoxically makes the 'signifiers' of dissolution peculiarly positive markers. Hence the 'between' of discourse becomes its own hybrid discourse (in the field of post-colonial studies), the feminine (in the field of gender) or schizo-analysis (in the field of psychoanalytic linguistics).

To accept the polemical rightness of these reverse/positive signifiers (read as signifieds) is to elevate the *fantastic* to an ethical and political level. In other words, it makes a *genre* into a form of critique. If each position equals an infinite hesitancy – an irresolvable bifurcation and indeterminable state – then the formal requirements of the fantastic genre are met. The fantastic now becomes *the* exemplary genre: *the* literary canonic marker (and the structuring principle of the field), backed by a destabilising and *disestablishing* rhetoric which professes to see no field (let alone canon) at all.

It is clear, nevertheless, that in this liquification of boundaries, in transgression and transgressive literature, is to be found *the revolution* in representation that has superseded the political revolution and reconfigured ethico-political action as a whole.

> The value of fantasy reside[s] in ... resistance to definition. ... In this way fantastic literature points to ... the basis upon which cultural order rests, for it opens up ... on to disorder, on to illegality, on to that which lies outside the law. [It] traces the unsaid and the unseen of culture: that which has been silenced.
>
> (Rosemary Jackson, *Fantasy*)

In this most extreme form, the descriptive terminology of genre takes the form of the active becoming of the very field itself. The actual literary fantastic becomes the exemplar, moreover, of 'the fantastic' as mode of being and becoming: a conflation ironically avoided by earlier criticism which wished to make a distinction between the exemplary *specific* instance and the universal whilst still retaining a strong (but flawed) concept of *agency* which this particular position disavows. The subject, as well as the work of literature, may always be 'about to occur', in 'process of becoming', but both must act as if they are already selfpossessed. They can only become agents by so doing. Indeterminacy is a rhetorical position, for its lived dimension is category confusion and psychosis.

Agency does not need total self-recognition but it must have some. Agency requires will, limited recognition, expectation, and a sense of the task in relation to the real which anchors it firmly in the realm of the rational. Subversion must recognise that which it subverts. In other words, it must be aware enough and competent enough to recognise the forces that call to it in both the universal and its exemplary instances. Subversion requires rational agency even if the theoretical position seems to prove antithetical to the possibility of the subversive act itself. The fantastic is, in effect, a willed entry into indeterminacy for the purpose of clearing a space for agency itself. It becomes the origination of a certain history which is also a certain trajectory in meaning. The fantastic is a genre not an undoing – it cannot itself act as an agent, although critics mistake it for a mode of agency and act accordingly.

At this point criticism recognises itself in its abysmal silences. It falls into self-regard and becomes the object of its own gaze. It is now all too easy to invoke the technical terms of the fantastic (as field): logocentrism, phallocentrism, abjection, otherness, etc., and then find their exemplary instances in one (disliked) canon against which an antithetical or subversive canon (the fantastic) is conveniently juxtaposed. Or to find these terms 'acted' out as literature's silenced signifying process: literature's denied reality and hence its determining field. Too many modern critical texts simply call up the litany and proceed as if that proved the positions from which the arguments arose in the first place.

More problematically, if the fantastic is subversive discourse then it must be subversive because it subverts something it perceives to be bad, wrong, ugly, stupid, immoral, authoritarian, etc., (a bad monolithic discourse opposed by a good heterogeneous one). Inherent in the fantastic, just as in its exemplary literary instance of the gothic horror tale, we find the known under surveillance and manipulated by the sinister forces of the unknown and masked. The fantastic is therefore an inherently paranoiac experiential mode. 'In this sense, there is a schizophrenic cogito . . . my . . . discourse . . . coming from other planets', as Gilles Deleuze and Félix Guattari suggest in *A Thousand Plateaus*.

The fantasy wished into existence by the particular and exemplary instance returns the question to necessary but not sufficient models which link causality and particularity to universalised and generalised states. This position exposes the falsity also of the exemplary instance which, in order to recognise itself *as exemplary* must fantasise a universal continuum into which it slots, from which it gains its power and towards which it points.

The exemplary instance thus plays the role of a miraculous event showing, as if by magic, the workings of the universal and eternal (the law) *as process* in the historical and contemporary (the moment of reading). Yet in so doing, the exemplary steps outside history as process of revelation (which only scholarship and exegesis can pronounce upon): an always eternal moment beyond the explanatory and only open to the explicatory or descriptive mode. This returns us to the 'before' of professional literary criticism and the miraculous supplementary space of meaning itself. For W. B. Yeats in 'Symbolism and Poetry',

> All sounds, all colours, all forms, either because of their pre-ordained energies or because of long association, evoke indefinable and yet precise emotions, . . . call down upon us certain disembodied powers. . . . Poets and painters and musicians . . . are continually making and unmaking mankind.

One could be forgiven in seeing here a type of prehistoric cul-de-sac – a prior moment to criticism and a refusal of it. At best the position appears to be a mere reaction or at worst a type of mysticism. Caught between naturalism and modernism, this type of late romantic idealism skips out of sight as professional criticism takes over. And yet this message from 'before' refocuses criticism around the question of agency and literature and its inscription in history. Here, the eccentric, particularised instance, which is also the unique occasion without precedent or parallel, links into the universal transcendent – the sublime. Sublimity is connoted by an excess of affect and therefore an excessive agency which links the literary into the beatific and into history.

For Yeats, language's inherent link with reality (with its hidden 'essences') was greater than its use as a tool in the creation of mere poetic composition, for it was able to go beyond itself into the purely spiritual and connect human consciousness and time with the realm of the ideal. Yet, Yeats was aware that the transcendent can never be greater than the rational which gives the poem sense as well as sound and rhythm. Poetry was poetry only if it did not become merely magical incantation. It was not a conjuring trick but a way of linking event to causation through a paranoid strategy of invisible connection and symbolism. Human history was prefigured by aesthetic configuration and symbolist correspondence.

Yet if all that is so, if there is an ultimate spiritual dimension where rules are dimly and momentarily glimpsed in the exemplary composition, then this is also all undone in the contingent nature of the exemplum. All agency, the exemplum is text as *enactment*, its linguistic supplement the mysterious 'organic community of words and things' beyond sense and beyond language. As neither word nor thing but *relation* this supplement is an effect of the power of its singular instance, the non-repeatable nature of poetry as it 'directs' history. This even as it points elsewhere to a beyond in universal time where things exist in juxtaposition not in sequence.

The poem is, then, a type of miraculous occurrence, produced in a discontinuous 'history' in which the sequence of the field is nowhere predictable and everywhere considered impossible. The poem is that which cannot be: the singular instance of its own rule, disconnected to those other poems, which nevertheless perform similar functions. This miracle makes the poem pure agent but puts it finally beyond or outside history (although enacted within history), connected rather to realms of transcendent experience momentarily available only as the lived experience of the poem. This lived experience is the sublime as experiential fragment, as 'event' and as a condition gathered to itself as the sublimation of the historical conditions of its creation.

The universal can only be experienced discontinuously (in the production of extremely rare true poems) and this discontinuity makes a history impossible – the event becomes a sport, a freak, an anomaly, or a miracle irreducible to anything but itself, but from which all else comes and to which all else points. It becomes the equivalent of a silence surrounded by noise: the noise of literature and history born out of the abyss of linearity.

The mystical always posits the actual moment of fulfilment as outside and beyond – a hole in actual history. The poet/mystic produces pauses in linear time whose *singularity* is ironically the link to continuity out of time in the eternal moment of cosmic space. As singular moment, the exemplary instance is therefore totally full (of symbol, essence) and utterly empty (it is not itself but an invocation of the cosmic-universal). History melts away in the folds of oblivion and the mists of the lyrical – the sublime event of poetry becomes evanescent, ephemeral and intangible. Only an empty space is left, devoid of history but filled with the agency of the sublime; intelligible certainly but not explainable.

Inside time (as literature) and outside time (as invocation) the poem exists as the dimension in which the tension between the particular and the universal is played out. Thus the poem suggests agency without agent, subjectivity beyond the subject and all conditioned by both going beyond and being inside both subjectivity and history. History becomes a quest to find the place beyond history and agency, the annulment of the agent in the space of communion. Romantic sublimity is the product of agency transcending itself in its annulment in union with the cosmic. Beyond history and outside itself, the romantic agent is haunted by death and sex; the sublime as the ultimate event: oblivion, *Liebestod*, Armageddon. This is an aesthetics of tragedy.

In Romanticism there is neither tradition nor canons because the field is always, forever, only one; the singular instance, the one true poem, the *Gesamtkunstwerk* (the totality of totalities, unity conditioned by the exemplar's necessary transcendence and sublimation of all that went before and all that might follow). For the one true work is always the unity of all work, and therefore *the* singularity that transcends its own individuality. It becomes both its own universal and instance of the universal even as its anomalous status lifts it both beyond art and beyond history: its own law, god and moral imperative. No longer merely miraculous, it stands outside temporality as that which creates the miraculous. No longer a link to the eternal-universal, it is rather the condition of the miraculous intervention which can only ever point back to itself as primal cause beyond causation.

Can it be any coincidence that the singular instance of romantic art is conditioned by perversity raised to a universal condition?

> In the consideration ... of the *prima mobile* of the human soul [there is] a propensity which, although existing as a radical, primitive, irreducible sentiment, has been ... overlooked. ... The Spirit of the Imp of the Perverse.
>
> (Edgar Allan Poe, 'The Imp of the Perverse')

The operations of romanticism were answered with modernism's antidote. Here the ruling metaphysics were not magical but technological and subject to the rigid laws of structure. Professional academic criticism began in the self-imposed rigour of law and discipline. Yet these speculations were themselves subject to the peculiar (and necessary) contingency of modernist artistic practice. Here, the ruling discipline was editing (and the peculiar attention paid to *juxtaposition*). Thus collage, montage, Dada, surrealism and accidental placement replaced the necessary determinism of mystical order. The haphazard nature of accidental juxtaposition was given meaning by its relationship to the overall hidden structure of the field as a whole. This field, from which modernism takes its images, was then reconfigured *in time* as tradition. The laws governing art's structure were, however, always there in the first work in the tradition and subsequently 'realised' within other works only later. Later works then gain efficacy by their connection to the first work which is both prime mover and a mere exemplum. The first work is always the anticipation of later works (history and agency) and the exemplification of the first instance of the determining laws.

Even as avant-garde representation was designed to shock the bourgeoisie, it was also designed as the description that heralds the revolution and the new future order: the metaphoric transcendence of all previous positions. The seemingly pointless and the contingent were, in this respect, the methodological necessity which prefigured universal order and idealism. This new order provided a possible scenario for a left-wing aesthetic which moved towards the political, as well as a right-wing aesthetic which moved the political towards the aesthetic. The interpretive anxiety which resulted from Dada and surrealism opened a space for the necessary hesitation which gave the space for the questioning of the old order. This 'blind' and destructive disjunction provided the impetus to those agencies whose task it was to move on and to determine the future.

Such anxiety as the bourgeois reader suffered was the direct corollary of the intended terror in the exemplary instance of the avant-garde art work. Here agency was returned in its entirety as the pointless, illogical, irrational, disruptive, discontinuous, ridiculous, erotic, violent and subversive. But all this had to be irreducible to current art practice, current moral consensus, current social expectation (especially in manners), not to mention universal sense. Pure agency was, therefore, both terroristic and yet passive, blindly caught in the indecision of the repetition compulsion.

> And the incorruptible Professor walked too, averting his eyes from the odious multitude of mankind. He had no future. He disdained it. He was a force. His thoughts caressed the images of ruin and destruction. He walked frail, insignificant, shabby, miserable – and terrible in the simplicity of his idea called madness and despair to the regeneration of the world. Nobody looked at him. He passed on unsuspected and deadly, like a pest in the street of men.
>
> (Joseph Conrad, *The Secret Agent*)

In the avant-garde paradigm, logic, grammar, reference and transcendence through correspondence was replaced by mere sequence, metaphor and metonym and a transcendence achieved through a self-annulling *disjunction*. Revolutionary avant-garde practice, if it was truly to shock, could have no connection with coherence nor regulation, its purity as agency preserved only in its distance from and hatred of current regulation and current conformism.

Opposed to each other, mysticism and revolution seemed to appeal to different and antagonistic constituencies. Nevertheless, in one aspect, that of their avant-gardism, they shared and still share, a curious bond. The revelatory mystico-animistic formulation of correspondence in symbolism can clearly be tied to the primitivism of techno-avant-gardism (futurism's speed was a type of ultimate primitive state of pure sensation, i.e. mystical correspondence). Both determined their aesthetic as a prior moment, a 'just before' of a future time in which the universal is about to be revealed as a new social dispensation.

Thus opposed to rational, logical and progressive consensus both forms of aesthetic experience became 'prior' as either pre-modern (mystical) or primitive (revolutionary), existing as moments between historical epochs and on the cusp of concrete formalisations and universal formations. If there can be no history of the avant-garde it is precisely because in the avant-garde time is annulled in the eternal mystical present of the now which is a coming to consciousness and therefore the preparation for the beginning of history. Hence, Jean-François Lyotard's paradox of the post-modern, as summarised by Fredric Jameson, that, '[Lyotard] has characterized postmodernism, not as that which follows modernism ... but rather as a cyclical moment that returns before the emergence of ever *new* modernisms'.

This is nothing other than theology without God, romanticism mistaken for modernism. The post-modern condition may be the moment which precedes history (as decadent preparation) or it may, however, be an arrested moment, a moment determined by the dynamics of the sublime: outside the rational, the linear and the realm of ethical consensus. For Lyotard such a moment occurs in 1956 in Budapest, in Paris in 1968 and accumulates around the symbol of Auschwitz. Each of these moments acts as an annulment, 'an abyss', as he tells us, of the determinants of – genre!

> These proper names have the following remarkable property: they place modern historical or political commentary in abeyance. Adorno pointed out that Auschwitz is an abyss in which the philosophical genre of Hegelian speculative discourse seems to disappear, because the name 'Auschwitz' invalidates ... that genre, namely that all that is real is rational, and that all that is rational is real. Budapest '56 is another abyss in which the genre of (Marxist) historical materialist discourse seems to disappear ... invalidat[ing] the presupposition of

that genre ... that all that is proletarian is communist. ... Nineteen sixty-eight is an abyss in which the genre of democratic liberal discourse ... seems to disappear, because this name invalidates the presupposition of that genre, ... that all that concerns the political community can be said within the rules of the game of parliamentary representation.

('The Sign of History')

The annulling of the sign of history is undertaken under the sign of an aesthetic effect, the sign of the sublime produced 'without criterion' and leading to '[an] *infinity of heterogeneous finalities*' (Lyotard, ibid.). Only available 'in their specificity', 'abysmal' events such as those of 1956 or 1968 remain trapped in indeterminate space as floating signifiers: 'great historical upheavals ... are the formless and figureless in historical human nature'. Bereft of their moral or political significance, such events, seem as the canonic exemplars of the field of the fantastic, are ironically elevated to the status of the literary and aesthetic – fantastic tales of a fantasy genre: the sign of history.

9
Children of Albion:
Dr Leavis amongst the Dongas Tribe

Our question is simple in one sense: in what way does the study of popular culture generate radical critique? But the question generates many others. From where does such a critique come and on whose behalf? What is the place of literature in the revolution? Can literature and revolution coincide? What position does the literary take in relation to the masses and popular culture? Can the avant-garde align itself with popular culture – on behalf of the insurrection of the popular?

   One could at least get a template for the emotional landscape of rebellion from European and American fiction in the 1960s, read, as often as not, in the lurid, cheap and popular paperback editions available from presses in the United States. Lautréamont, Herman Hesse, Knut Hamsun, Sadegh Hedayat and Alain Robbe Grillet offered a sophisticated and complementary literary diet to more conventional tales of rebellion such as those by Joseph Heller and Ken Kesey, or even British authors such as John Fowles, J. R. R. Tolkien and D. H. Lawrence. All offered an alternative landscape capable of being infused with the philosophy of a whole gamut of gurus from Aleister Crowley to R. D. Laing, from Timothy Leary to Carlos Castenada and from Carl Jung to Marshal McLuhan. The books were always hard to get; counter-cultural, revolutionary, contemporary, marginal, on the edge and neurotic. They were always, somehow, illicit, extravagant, esoterically obscure, surreal, strange. They were violent, sexy, sick, assertive, kinky, deviant, psychotic, thrilling, anarchic, funky, infantile, nasty; satiric, extravaganzas of hip, groove, kharma, love and cool; anti-old, anti-establishment, anti-bourgeois; professing erotic instant enlightenment, political defection, moral health, drug overload, hallucinatory reality, individual integration; holistic, humanistic, ecological, gestural and theatrical, self-consciously arty and appropriately scandalous.

They were the sensibility of an age's minority and so various moral guardians – magistrates, mothers' groups, chief inspectors and righteous excise men – attempted to get them banned, burned, persecuted and prosecuted in order that what was said could be dismissed or suppressed by establishment squares, daddies, the uncool, people in denial and the readers of the *Daily Mail*.

The very form of this new emotional landscape was subversive – inexpensive American paperbacks 'secretly' bought at a fractional price of hardback editions in 'revolutionary' bookshops in London and Edinburgh or through market stalls and travelling book sales. Such a landscape was informed by the strange, complex and sophisticated 'metaphysical' debates of Europe, the young, vigorous, anti-establishment action and culture of American and the sociological, communal and class politics of the United Kingdom. Information filtered in piecemeal, haphazardly informing or confusing by turns. Without pattern or clear process, this new landscape was revealed bit by bit and inconsistently, shown to us as much by T. S. Eliot (an edition of whose collected poems appeared in 1963) and by newer writers such as Marshal McLuhan (whose work filtered through the 1960s). The talismanic names were rarely read but acted as *locations* where one wished to be: Sartre, McLuhan, Blake, Yeats, Hesse, Lawrence – all mixed up and equally fabulous. As for Jacques Derrida, Jacques Lacan, Roland Barthes, and all the other new wave French thinkers – they would have to await their transatlantic journey and translated return to British shores. Such exotic fruit were the delayed effect of the sixties landscape, their impact would be later and elsewhere.

The message from this landscape was one of suspicion, neurosis, anxiety *and* possibility. For Ayn Rand in 1960, it was already a foregone conclusion that 'America [was] culturally bankrupt' (Rand, *For the New Intellectual*), as it was for Norman Mailer in 1957, when he announced that Americans were suffering 'from a collective failure of nerve' (Mailer, 'The White Negro'). As early as 1963, Clive Irving could note that Britain had become 'a nation harbouring a latent neurosis', for Nathalie Sarraute the time was 'an era of suspicions' fed by a 'literature of exhaustion' and for Allen Ginsberg, looking back from the 1970s, it seemed as if '[Americans] were in the middle of an identity crisis prefiguring nervous breakdown for the whole United States' (Preface to *Collected Poems*). Hardly surprisingly, by 1968 Maurice Girondias could note that 'the pixies were moving in, pretty fast' (Preface to Valerie Solanas, *SCUM Manifesto*).

Too soon the rebellion of literature was mistaken for the literature of rebellion, too soon rebelliousness was mistaken for revolution and individual anarchy taken for a collective programme. 'Subversive' reading habits were soon mistaken for actual subversion, or at least as soon as the failure of the revolution led to the success of its illegitimate offspring: textual studies. Utterly defeated on the streets and in the institutions, the revolutionary energy flowed back upon itself to reveal itself as a merely exemplary form of reading habit. By the 1980s the habit (and its subject matter) had been entirely substituted for actual political endeavour (and mistaken for it). The astringent critiques of the Frankfurt School and the Situationists became the armchair dilettant-ism of television sociologists, unmindful of their own rhetoric or the very context, production and consuming conditions of the relatively ephemeral (and *conformist*) subjects of their gaze. Hence, Tony Bennett sincerely believed in 1981 that,

> Whilst an exact categorization of programmes such as *Monty Python's Flying Circus*, *Not the 9 o'clock News* and *Ripping Yarns* may be diffi-cult, it is clear, first, that they are *popular* and they are *fiction*; and, second, that they are not *just* ideology: they disrupt not merely con-ventional narrative forms but are often profoundly, if anarchically, *subversive* [emphasis added] of the dominant ideological discourses of class, nation, sexism and so on.
>
> (Bennett, 'Marxism and Popular Fiction')

From the standpoint of the very late 1990s, one can only wonder what Bennett actually *thought* he saw?[1]

We do however, get a sense of what the author of this exercise thought he was about in comments to be found in a recent primer on British Cultural Studies, edited by Graeme Turner, in which there is an attempt to characterise the significance of such studies and, in reference to Richard Johnson, a former head of the Centre for Contemporary Cultural Studies at Birmingham University, justify them.

> This means that while cultural studies' subject matter may be pop-ular culture, and while this may even be dealt with in ways that involve an element of nostalgia, for instance, the objective of cultural studies is not simply to recover aspects of social experience that were dear to the researchers' own hearts. It is all too easy to characterise work on the media, or on youth cultures, or on the music industry, as a kind of 'slumming' by middle-aged academics who want to legitimate the activities of their youth. Such motiva-tions are at odds with the basic enterprise of British cultural studies.

As Richard Johnson says, it is important to recognise the inadequacy of studies of popular culture that occur for 'purely academic purposes or when ... divorced from the analysis of power and of social responsibilities'. Popular culture is a site where the construction of everyday life may be examined; the point of doing this is not only academic ... it is also political, to examine the power relations that constitute this form of everyday life and thus to reveal the configuration of interests its construction serves.

(Turner, *British Cultural Studies*)

The rebuke is expected (although we know that everybody writes about what they *enjoy* and that the attraction of one's past does not preclude a commitment to mature reflection). Richard Johnson's denigration of studying popular culture *for pleasure*, of divorcing it from all values except those of a *political expediency* connected to power and contention (as critique), makes it quite clear that studying popular culture is a discipline for Puritans, not a recreation for aesthetes. If Johnson sees the 'popular' as a site upon (or through) which the ideological battle for *democracy* is to be fought, it is also a site of *correction* (of misperceptions) and of a reprimand (to overly nostalgic pleasure seekers and single-minded historical analysis). All this is so much corrective designed to save popular culture *from itself*; to reduce it to a demand put upon it to lose its erotic, sentimental, violent, dysfunctional side along with its conformism and consensus. It makes it safe and at once robs it of its *dangerous potency* – its vitality lived for itself alone. This smacks less of Marx and Engels, than Lenin force-feeding his intellectuals *Oblomov* until they recanted their past wrongs. Johnson's position is recommended to us, as one that exemplifies radical engagement: struggling to liberate meanings and lifestyles considered illegitimate or repressed by the ruling media/political élite.

Who, then, are the élite? They are, or course, the traitors from our own party ranks of whom a parcel can be made up from the likes of T. S. Eliot, Denys Thompson, L. C. Knights and, of course, the formidable Leavises (Dr and Mrs). Without any due care or attention to what any of these long dead critics thought (did not F. R. Leavis deeply distrust Eliot's conservative and reactionary views, did not *Scrutiny* oppose all that *The Criterion* stood for?), we are rashly told that 'these approaches were unashamedly élitist'. Here élitism is reduced to mere reverse snobbery.

If it is true that Eliot was an élitist (and unashamedly so) it is absolutely not so that the same can be said of F. R. Leavis.[2] Whatever faults

Leavis had, snobbery was not particularly one (except perhaps that diffident lower middle-class snobbery of self-righteousness). Leavis's project was to restore, by the invocation of a 'lost' community, the utopian possibility of a *present* liberal democracy. Opposed to the mass culture, consumerism and production-line techniques of America, the totalitarian politics of the USSR, Germany, Spain and Japan, growing authoritarianism on both sides of the Atlantic and apathy and paro-chialism at home, Leavis and others attempted to think through (using literature) the value system of a liberal democracy. As with thinkers of the right (Eliot, Wyndham Lewis, Pound, etc.) and thinkers of the left (Christopher Caudwell, George Orwell) the necessity of this task was central to their aesthetic (as was the memory of the First World War – their Great War), and the fear of its repetition. If one is looking for élite attitudes, one should, at least, look to the class from which they might emerge, that is, the class that gave us *Monty Python* in the first place.

   Licensed televised carnival is not the same as spontaneous insurrec-tion. (How was that to occur on the BBC?) Lenin, a conservative reader at best, spent a lifetime reading fiction and poetry to find signs of the revolution (to know he was right, all along). The exercise was an utter failure. Disgusted by Dostoevsky whom he called 'that rubbish' full of 'two-pence worth of horrors', Lenin had no understanding of actual revolutionary literature or art. His dislike of Futurism and all forms of modernism, led him into hopeless debates with Lunacharsky and dis-missive diatribes against modernist form, which was 'all disconnected (and) difficult to read!' as well as against Mayakovsky, against whom he raved: 'The revolution does not need buffoons playing at revolution' (in Leonard Schapiro and Peter Reddaway, *Lenin*). René Fueloep-Miller observed in 1926 that,

> The bolshevik poets, painters, sculptors and architects, who have been trying to crown Lenin's mighty work . . . complain despairingly about the complete blindness and deafness of the Master, who was unable to grasp the supreme and ultimate manifestations of his own system.
>
> (quoted in Schapiro and Reddaway, ibid.)

   It is true that, 'Lenin did not . . . oppose new forms of art, unless they took on a political tinge . . . but he showed no desire to appreciate them'. Speaking frankly to Klara Zetkin: 'it is not for us to chase after the new art, we'll limp along behind' (ibid.). Importantly, Lenin had no real theory of proletarian culture and believed that on the basis of a well-fed population and a good education, 'there must grow up a really new, great communist art which will create a form corresponding to its content'.

Lenin's political and cultural agenda dismissed art that was non-'educative' and that could not serve the propaganda machine and the party.[3] Lenin's choice of laureate was the propagandist Dem'yan Bedny, to whom he gave the order of the Red Banner. Lenin distrusted intellectuals and dismissed artists who did not serve the party. With the triumph of Stalin the state abrogated to itself the representational function: the rebellion of literature (its oppositional force) had been usurped by the literature of the rebellion, that which conformed to the state's view of itself and its history. As a consequence, the language of 'refusal' became more and more nationalistic, mystical and fascistic, mistaken by the West for a language of democracy and freedom of thought.

For British critics (to a greater extent that in America or even Europe) Marxian Labourism is the equivalent of Marxist–Leninism. The dominance of Marxist-influenced approaches in cultural studies has blinded it to other forms of analysis which take their language from anarchistic or libertarian origins. The focus on the 'popular' has blinded it to the necessary re-examination of 'the élite'; the focus on dominance has ignored many ingredients of escape; the focus on the media has ignored the state; the focus on class has said nothing about the individual; the focus on the body has forgotten the mind (except when repressed); the focus on mass consumption has (until recently) ignored choice and enjoyment; the focus on language as a *site of struggle* has ignored language as a *symptom* of struggle and history; the emphasis on representational structure has finally vanquished history.

These emphases and lacunae in British cultural studies are precisely what undermines their Marxism and allows it to float free into bourgeois or social democratic delight. Thus, we are told that only, 'stereotyped representations of Marxist thought conventionalise it as a monolithic and revolutionary body of theory'. In other words, it is conventional to see Marxism as a *coherent* and *revolutionary* theory and that indeed, in the realm of culture: 'Marxist approaches . . . have insisted on the relative autonomy of culture' (Tony Bennett, quoted in Turner, *British Cultural Studies*).

It is clear that British Marxist cultural studies uses Marx *contra* Marx. Marxism cannot be a body of theory without *insisting* on its *coherence* as a theory, its *revolutionary* nature and its belief that culture and art are *not* semi or relatively autonomous. Marx and Engels's holistic approach may be problematic, but it is clear on these points.[4] One critic has made this quite clear. Ben Watson points out: 'totality proposes seeing things in their connectedness: it is a prerequisite for dialectical thought' and is determined, in the first instance, by a revolutionary gaze – one already detectable in the 'imagination' of the Romantic poets.

> The idea of the connectedness of things was what the romantics wished to save from . . . bourgeois commonsense: they were preserving a revolutionary tradition, the key to a critique of class society.
>
> (Ben Watson, *Art, Class and Cleavage*)

Coleridge's 'imagination' was a pivot for class struggle, the key term for the social orientation of his literary endeavour. In the immediate aftermath of the French Revolution, it stood for an attempt to conceive the interconnectedness of the real things in the world – something with revolutionary consequences.

In what sense is culture 'relatively autonomous'? In an illuminating comparison of Stalin and Marx, Watson provides one answer,

> Stalin wrote: 'Whatever is the mode of production of society, such in the main is the society itself, its ideas and theories, its political views and institutions.' This paraphrases Marx who wrote: 'The mode of production of material life determines the social, political and intellectual life process in general'. . . . Stalin asserts that the mode of production *is* the society, a blunt statement of identity. Marx, however, says that the mode of production *determines* the social process. Saying the mode of production 'determines the social, political and intellectual life process' gives openings to politically-informed intervention denied to those who say the mode of production 'is the society itself'. Structuralism, with its fantasy of synoptic structures detailed with geometric precision, is peculiarly ill-equipped to tell the difference between Stalin and Marx.
>
> (Watson, ibid.)

Watson is surely correct when he tells us that Marxism is 'the science of bringing consciousness to bear on social conflict' but here the nub of the aesthetic question is to be found. In what sense is Marxism a science if not one that in its 'totality' can account for the *random* as a possibility of the innate nature of the structure (i.e. society as a whole in historical process). If totality can account for the random it cannot answer for the appearance of particular constituents – their specific and *individual* nature. The random is therefore both absolutely itself and conditioned as itself – it comes not from nowhere but from a past (it is produced). This semi-autonomy of cultural objects (and attitudes) is therefore not sufficiently explained either by reference to attached terms (social class, economic base, ideology) nor by the notion of totality. Cultural products which appear to be 'unique' (works of art) cannot be predicted in their specific nature – the mode of production only *determines* social process (which is itself dynamic) and cannot account for its particular products of which (in the cultural realm) art is the most problematic.

Marxism is a science only in as much as it 'brings consciousness to bear on social conflict', understood as a historical process which has revolutionary and liberationist tendencies in relation to a future. Art products, because they are unpredictable, non-sequential and random epiphenomena of history, cannot clearly be accounted for in a theory of history and, as such, cannot be put into the framework of a future. Art only serves a perpetual present between the *advent* of history and the culmination of 'history' as it is vanquished in a utopian future.

Art is useless to revolutionary practice precisely because it exists outside predictive space (within totality, part of it, but erratically produced). Lenin's dislike of modernism stemmed precisely from his innate theoretical conservatism. If art works are part of the totality but produced erratically (randomly) and unpredictively, they are capable of being revolutionary without exemplifying the revolutionary programme. Art's ambiguous relationship to the whole puts it at the service of revolution but *not* at the service of a revolutionary programme. Lenin realised that art could not be predicted nor simply ordered up on the revolutionary menu – it was part of the 'dark side of totality': what could not be predicted could not be used by the party and therefore could not serve the state's immediate economic and *political* (i.e. intellectual) needs. Instead, revolutionary art, avant-garde art, proceeded on behalf of the proletariat as their cultural embodiment and as the revolution's exemplification (its commitment to a future). It therefore always appeared anarcho-libertarian: exactly what Lenin wished to suppress.

It is said that Lenin read literature to find the signs of revolution; it is also said that he failed. Revolutionary art is itself revolutionary because it embodies disruption and dislocation – it cannot *conform* to disruption and dislocation. They do not have a logic attached nor a timetable, nor an agenda.

Avant-garde intellectual thought is always constituted by its antagonism to the present regimes of thought and exploits their incapacity to recuperate its message. The aim of this new intellectual method is to bring into being the regime of the future, but the *raison d'etre* of avant-gardism is to oppose the present on behalf of the future. Thus the regime of the future (realised *now* in thought) is itself *opposed* to avant-gardism as avant-gardism encapsulates the irrevocable: that which opposes *per se*. The aim of avant-garde thinking is therefore utopian and corrective and can never be fully realised in its programmatical totality. The double activity of avant-garde thought (to perfect and critique) is the necessary and contradictory mode of its procedures and activity. To advance in though one must hold to a necessary naïvety on these points, realising their incompatibility. To act within this contradiction is not to fall into bourgeois error or to be a dupe of capital and its agents; it is, instead, to realise the full potential of oppositional thought.

The avant-garde is therefore only possible in the space between the past and future, a space that however does not constitute the present or is even constituted in the present precisely because it recognises itself *as the past* lived *now*. Intellectual avant-gardism represents breakage, and 'rupture', disruption, the non-co-operative, the anarchic and illicit. It represents these, at its core. There can be no history of avant-gardism because 'the possible linear chronology of the avant-garde disguises the impossible sequence presented by the set of gaps opened in and by avant gardism' (Hegarty, unpublished article). In what sense is the avant-garde to be reunited to the question of culture – its 'relative auto-nomy' and its constitution in the notion of the popular?

Cultural studies is specifically the study of the 'popular'. It is connected to the popular by theories (mostly Marxian in origin) and operates on behalf of the popular (as its 'politics'). In these senses, cultural studies is determined by the same concerns as the avant-garde artist in relation to proletarian culture at the beginning of the twentieth century.

At the end of the nineteenth century the word 'cheap' ceased to mean only inexpensive and took on its modern meaning of 'nasty'; in the same way, by the end of the twentieth century the word 'élite' has been confused with mere snobbery. It is true, of course, that the change in the meaning of cheap coincided with the triumph of mass produc-tion; coincided, that is, with *mass produced pleasure* for the lower classes. Cheapness became synonymous with mass culture, a term firmly *opposed* to popular culture. Now, it is quite true that almost all British critics of culture are contemptuous, indeed *snobs*, regarding mass culture which they saw (and still see) as immature, impersonal and authoritar-ian. Leavis was certainly a snob as far as mass culture goes. The mission of cultural critics in Britain, from Arnold to Eagleton, has been to *liberate* popular culture from mass culture, in other words, liberate the masses from their burdensome leisure; hence so much talk of 'subversive reading', slippage and 'struggle'.

Criticism too brings its snobbery to bear, for it is clear that no one wants to be liberated from their collection of old blues records, but desperate measures must be taken to rescue those under the thrall of the latest craze in soft toy collecting; popular culture is *authentic* (and in this case black); mass culture is infantile and inauthentic (and in this case feminine).

Distaste for popular culture is often the more vehement from those who set about creating it *on behalf* of the 'masses'. After the start of commercial television in 1955, Norman Collins (Deputy Chairman of Associated Television) reported:

> that the overwhelming mass of viewers' letters which Associated Television received were illiterate. 'They are ungrammatical and execrably written,' he said. 'And what is more distressing, they evidence an attitude of mind that I do not think can be regarded as very admirable.' All the writers wanted, he said, were pictures of film stars, television stars, or reasons why there were not more jazz programmes, or why there could not be more programmes of a musical kind. 'I hold teachers very largely responsible if that is the attitude of people in their teens and early twenties,' he said. 'If we provided simply that it would be deplorable.'
>
> (quoted in John Montgomery, *The Fifties*)

Luckily, this was an attitude *not* shared by all his colleagues in commercial television. Sidney Bernstein, founder and chairman of Granada Television (from whose studios the social realist drama of *Coronation Street* emerged in December 1960) found that

> The public has supported good programmes even on subjects like homosexuality and venereal disease. I am not satisfied with our efforts, but they are improving every day and we are training people who we think will produce better television in the future.
>
> (Ibid.)

Giving the public what they wanted was not merely a matter of offering 'bread and circuses' but of offering programmes which challenged consensual thought, made to the highest standards. What was absolutely clear was that the public did not want sermons but they did demand entertainment – relaxation and education in a variety of presentational forms.

It is precisely here, in this division between authentic and inauthentic culture, between mass and popular taste, that the critical gaze is most blurred, that the faculties of discrimination both political and aesthetic become most confused. It is, in a sense, (despite 'audience' studies and fan analysis), impossible to bring the analytic faculty fully to bear on lumpen mass culture, the culture almost exclusively generated from below, and from *popular* forms of consumption unburdened by questions of good taste or propriety. How exactly is one to account *clearly*, in terms of the idea of historical struggle, for those kitsch pleasures *we all* enjoy – from saucy seaside postcards to collecting Beanie Baby toys? Mass taste and popular taste cross and recross, emblazoned with the illuminated 'K' of tastelessness and lack of decorum. Kitsch is unruly and sentimental. It is not to be applauded any more than deplored (one *can* just avoid it) but it speaks directly of an aesthetic pleasure and a *lived experience* of culture which cultural critics find hard to square with the moral burden of liberating the popular from the mass.

José Ortega y Gasset thought that kitschman was man in the present, in his own solipsism. In other words kitschman was relativist man, one prey to authoritarian tendencies and to the romanticisation of the self, swayed by history because a prey to his own selfish tendencies, feeling that, in some way, the now is all there is, a point of absolute superiority to all other eras and places and selves.

The intellectual is under no compunction to support kitsch culture nor is he or she under any compunction to liberate the masses (who was Ortega y Gasset's 'average' person?) from their burden of pleasure. The intellectual is required to notice the *aesthetic* of mass cultural products and *in this* to notice their emotional dynamic. There is no more reason for intellectuals to abandon a commitment to everything that is excellent, individual, qualified and select, as Ortega y Gasset suggests, than there is to abandon the pleasures of what should be considered *illicit*. The intellectual has to understand those contradictions 'in the body' as it were. There can be no truer spur to insurrectionary sense than guilty pleasures taken in secret!

The pop-studies consensus that decries any critique of mass culture as 'élitist' could only arrive from such a top–down perspective. Down here in the cheap seats, we never stop scrapping. Central to Marxist doctrine has always been its attachment to the social conditions governing the mass of the population. As a corollary to this, Marxist critics interested in culture have long since struggled with the conditions from which mass culture arises, its attachment to political

commitment and the perceptual framework within which an analysis of such culture can be validated, given traditional Marxism's
silence on the matter. At the heart of such interest is the attempt to
align a sophisticated avant-garde methodology with the concept of
the 'popular'.[5]

(Watson, *Art, Class and Cleavage*)

By the late 1980s, the alignment of Marxist analysis with concepts of
the popular was under acute pressure from both political and cultural
challenges; on the one hand Thatcherite Conservatism seemed to
threaten an endless Conservative 'revolution' to which the left had no
solution, on the other hand cultural criticism, especially deconstruction,
post-structuralism and linguistic feminism, seemed to highlight the
inadequacies of Marx's original formulations and produce more radical,
'politicised' readings. By 1988, Stuart Hall was berating colleagues:

Political analysis on the left seems pitifully thin....This is...
because the left...tends to hold a very reductionist conception of
politics and ideology where, 'in the last instance' (whenever that is),
both are determined by, and so can be 'read off' against, some (often
ill defined) notion of 'economic' or 'class' determination.

(Hall, quoted in Roger Eatwell and Noel O'Sullivan,
The Nature of Right)

Marxist doctrine, if it was to survive, would have to become more
sophisticated towards determining factors ('automatic linkages') in an
age of fragmentary class relationships (how else could one account for a
Conservative working class?). Thus,

The underlying social, economic and cultural forces which are bringing the era of 'organised capitalism' to a close...have decomposed
and fragmented class as a unified political force, fracturing any
so-called automatic linkages between economics and politics.

(Ibid.)

Infected by a cultural virus they believed was a more powerful engine of
analysis, Marxist critics were exhorted to embrace an analysis of culture
which saw it as a semi-autonomous region, its class base uncertain and
its economic impulses secondary. The sociology of society was to
become the sociology of culture, an investigation of the realm of political
power produced by the unconscious (because 'naturalised') habituation

of the masses to the ideology of power fed incessantly through the mass (Tory) media.

The effective disengagement of culture from social formation and therefore disengagement from a final determining base in the mode of production meant that Marxist critics would have no choice but to embrace other analytic approaches in order to be Marxist at all! In the face of a seemingly endless Conservatism based upon the vote of a misguided Conservative working class, new left-wing answers would have to be sought, it was believed, outside classic Marxist doctrine. Throughout the 1980s Marxism was hyphenated: feminist-Marxism; deconstructive-Marxism; post-structuralist Marxism.

The call for a 'return' to a political reading of culture must be seen against this background. For left-wing cultural writers who had, since the late 1960s and early 1970s, been educated within the cultural materialism of British Marxism, a return to politics would at once have to endorse the autonomy of the realm of culture and post-structural multiplicity whilst avoiding falling into the trap of either a revisionist humanism (represented by Leavis) or a revisionist (economistic) Marxism.

> The Marxism which informs the cultural studies approach is a *critical* Marxism in the sense that it has contested the reductionist implications of earlier Marxist approaches to the study of culture. These . . . often tend to view culture . . . as being totally determined by economic relationships. The Marxist approaches that have informed the development of the cultural studies perspective, . . . have insisted on the 'relative autonomy' of culture – on the fact that it is not simply dependant on economic relationships and cannot, . . . be reduced to . . . a mere reflection of these.
>
> (Tony Bennett, 'Marxism and Popular Fiction')

Even more to the point, the conjunction of literature, history and politics seemed central to the definition of *British* culture (and to a lesser extent European culture) – this conjunction, and this alone, from which the most powerful analytic voices spoke when attempting to make sense of all three terms and the modes by which they express social consciousness and its radical potential. Catherine Belsey, for instance, rightly claimed that

> To bring these three terms together is hardly to do anything new. *Literature and History* has been doing it since its inception; the Essex Conference volumes do it; Raymond Williams . . . spent his life

doing it; historians like E. P. Thompson and Christopher Hill . . . have frequently done it. . . . T. S. Eliot, F. R. Leavis and E. M. W. Tillyard did it when they constructed . . . a lost Elizabethan utopia . . . an organic community.

(Catherine Belsey, 'Literature, History, Politics')

Despite this tradition of radical alignment, nevertheless, for Belsey, to bring the terms together *'explicitly'* was to 'scandalise' literary criticism and attack the essentialist ideology of community. Using the obligatory insights of Saussurian linguistics and Foucaultian method, Belsey is quick to seize on the inadequacy of traditional *empirical* history using her own textual insights:

But documents do not merely transcribe experience: to the extent that they inevitably come from a context where power is at stake, they are worth analysis . . . as locations of power and resistance to power. . . . This is the history not of an irrecoverable experience, but of meanings, of the signified in its plurality, not the referent in its singular but imaginary presence. It is, therefore, a history of struggle and, in consequence, a political history.

(Ibid.)

To relativise a set of texts is, for Belsey, to re-politicise them, rob them of an essentialist residue. No longer 'evidence of how it felt', historical texts and literary texts are to be 'read' in their plurality. At her most radically left position, Belsey has already slipped beyond Marxism, she has already conflated history and literature, documentary evidence and fictions. It is an important slippage, rhetorically powerful (and therefore in some sense political) but also revisionist, for it immediately leads to the dismissal of the very place from which and only from which a radical reading (and therefore a radical politics) could emerge – the popular. Thus she reiterates Tony Bennett in her desire to

Call into question both the category – the autonomy of literary studies – and the value – Literature as distinct from its residue, popular fiction. We need to replace the quest for value by an 'analysis of the social contestation of value'.

(Ibid.)

What are we to make of 'popular fiction' as a mere 'residue' of 'literature'? The very *site* of struggle is dismissed as an effect of a previous precious substance. Demanding a challenge to the category literature, Belsey dismisses the very position from which to launch such a challenge and from which such a challenge could lead to a political and radical *refusal* of consensus. In attempting to challenge literature as a 'category' and therefore demolish category boundaries whilst exposing the pedagogical and historical contexts of literature's construction, Belsey simply falls back into a 'post' Marxist consensus: a fight between consenting adults. Because she will not 'privilege literature' (because to do so is *value laden*). Belsey is unwilling to privilege *any* discourse, (the 'signified in its plurality'). Nevertheless, she still claims 'that ... a formal indeterminancy does not mean that we can never speak of form, any more than the polyphony of "freedom" prevents us from condemning police states' (Belsey, ibid.). Without the ability to privilege a specific value-laden, coherent language of opposition that challenges authoritarian power, Belsey is only able to come up with a weak version of challenge based on polyphonic reading:

> The reading practice implied by this enterprise – the production of a political history from the raw material of literary texts – is a result of all that post structuralism has urged about meaning: its often marginal location, its disunity and discontinuity, as well as its plurality. In this way the text reappears, but not as it 'really is', or 'really was'. On the contrary, this is the text as it never was, though it was never anything else – dispersed, fragmented, produced, politicised.
>
> (Ibid.)

Polyphonic reading robs the challenger of an authoritative position as well as those he or she challenges (who already have the power that is being contested). Such an approach produces the very relativism that Belsey and others sought to avoid in the 1980s: producing not a political reading but a consensual one, amenable to those whose power remained not only unchallenged but reassured by such analysis. Throughout the 1980s and early 1990s this line of argument could be found amongst the 'official' opposition at its centres at Essex University, Cardiff and the polytechnics; nevertheless, the argument found itself severely critiqued from at least two directions and open to refutation from a third.

From the more orthodox of Marxists, ideas of fragmentation and relative autonomy were excuses for an idealist revisionism that ignored Marx's insistence on a 'holistic' approach. Dismemberment of the system not only reduced the power of the critic trying to analyse the totality but also robbed the critic of a concept of totality. Marx's recognition of fragmentation was not the same as post-structuralist-Marxism's and therefore,

> Because cultural materialism, through the significance it attributes to the evident materiality of cultural practice, threatens to prise loose determinate relationships between modes of production and cultural production, cultural materialism is itself on the way to such incorporation.
>
> (R. S. Neale, *Writing Marxist History*)

Cultural materialism constantly faced the problem, therefore, of dealing with the epiphenomena of power, unable to trace power to its origination and its brokers.

A further critique came from those who wished to work with concepts of production and consumption within the popular itself and who recognised the ironic narrowing of focus that was then occurring. Target of their concerns was statements such as this from those who controlled academic access to popular studies:

> Statements to the effect that Joyce opened up the possibilities of language in a way that Conan Doyle ... did not seem to me to be quite unproblematic.
>
> (Bennett, 'Marxism and Popular Fiction')

Such statements, which reperipheralised popular fiction and which left it as a mere 'residue' did nothing except show up the bankruptcy of those who chose to study popular fiction without having any feeling for it. That such blatantly biased and ill-informed comments could remain 'unproblematic' led to my own publication of *Cult Fiction* in which I commented, with a certain amount of outrage,

> My admiration for [cultural materialism's] exploratory abilities is offset by my inability to accept such general statements as make simplistic equations without either theoretical or carefully tested empirical evidence. While these are still important books one cannot help but think that the writers were trying hard to understand low brow writing but could not rid themselves of the belief that there is a *conspiracy* behind mass culture which must be *resisted*.
>
> (Clive Bloom, *Cult Fiction*)

The most surprising challenge to Belsey's position came not from those already mentioned, but from the area she and her colleagues most disliked and feared, Leavisism – or more properly one of its central tenets: the lost organic community. Such was the ferocity of the attack that,

> The proposal was to reverse the Leavisian enterprise of constructing (inventing) a lost organic world of unfallen orality, undissociated sensibility and uncontested order.
>
> (Belsey, op. cit.)

Whilst Leavis's 'narrowness, humanism, a-political position', élitism and smugness may or may not have been legitimate targets for critical ire, what hostile critics failed to notice was that the concept of the organic community could be recuperated as a radical and practical term within mass (popular) society and on its behalf in ways both specifically political and traditional – a very British revolution going on at the *same time* as the academic assault reached a crescendo. Wilful misreading and dismissal of Leavisite 'concepts' led otherwise skilful critics to overlook their own *radical* position and to misconstrue the *potential* of an idea of organic community which seemed historically inaccurate, suspiciously revisionist and the obsession of a personal fantasy.

By the 1970s a number of radicals, anarchists and libertarians had started to embrace Leavisian positions towards community even if they personally had never heard of Leavis (who would have wholeheartedly disapproved of them!). Nevertheless, with the failure of mainstream radical protest, the 'remnant' had survived in sufficient numbers to create *secret* protest movements based around festivals and travelling. These new, if disparate, movements, based upon Avalonian, druidic, hippy-punk and rave cultures took an alternative view of the organic community (ecological and folkloristic) which they put into *practical* effect *within* mass culture. This was popular culture (and revolt), within mass culture (and consensus), lived simultaneously. Faced with such challenges of a lived and pragmatic nature (these lifestyles are not theorised), critics retreat into NIMBY-dom![6]

Throughout the 1970s and 1980s, fairs, free festivals and gatherings began to proliferate throughout southern and eastern England, some peaceful, some confrontational; some hippy, some punk; some legal, some illegal. For many organisers, the inspiration was as much California as 'merry old England', extending and adapting Monterey, Altamont or New York State's Woodstock cultures. 'The use of "Albion" [moreover] illustrate[d] a desire for a truly alternative society, even an alternative history, a dub version of Britain', as George McKay put it.

At one such fair, for instance,

> Nostalgia begins to multiply: the historical references of the Barsham Faires are several: an initial medievalism, a pre-Industrial Revolution agricultural ideal, the 'dream' of the (first) Summer of Love. Versions of Olde England are comfortably mixed with the 1960s, producing energy and humour, even some politics, maybe. Albion as constructed is an earthy, mystical, mythical Blakean alternate world of British history, all mists and Merlin, using a language whose words are spelled with extra *es* on the end to signal the link with a contructed past: Follye Fayre, Faerie Fair.... Whatever politics functions here in the early 1970s is a political rejection of technology, a contribution to a hippy organic ideal through a parody of history.
>
> (George McKay, *Senseless Acts of Beauty*)

Such constructions of history, myth and self were, however, *self-aware*. These were conscious attempts to remake a social environment *of choice* based on a third, though 'organic' communal sense: nostalgic and contemporary.

> Fair organisers, then, foregrounded the *situatedness* of their events: the sense of locality, of landscape, of rural tradition and history was central to the East Anglian fairs. The social and cultural hegemomy of urban space, the idea of the city as hero and site of modernity (and post modernity, in spite of its claims to focus on the margins), is challenged a bit by things like the fairs. The British countryside ignored by the Romantics, since Hardy and the Edwardians, was claiming back some territory, was interrogating the limits of enclosure.
>
> (McKay, ibid.)

By the late 1980s, such groups as made up the 'Albion Free State' had allied themselves with more conformist groups and individuals protesting against the poll tax, veal exports and unnecessary road developments. Dongas (road protesters), travellers and Tree People became the new 'enemy within', vilified in the popular media but ironically turned into eco-icons by many ordinary readers. The margin was now centre; had, finally, come home for a few brief radical moments when the critics weren't looking, put up its banners and maypole in Parliament Square, created a 'guerrilla garden' and had itself a riot.[7]

Notes

Notes to Chapter 1: Introduction

1. The Bootleg Beatles, a tribute Beatles band of look- and soundalikes, enjoyed a twenty-fifth anniversary concert at the Albert Hall in 1999.
2. In fact, the book enjoyed a huge rise in sales after its promotion by Waterstone's and Channel 4 during 1997. *The Hobbit* was voted nineteenth in the list. In 1999 the BBC launched a new television comedy show called 'Hippies', whilst the National Westminster Bank featured psychedelic leaflets for its personal loans scheme.
3. The 1999 Award went to J. M. Coetze's *Disgrace* without any controversy but in a competition devoid of interest and excitement.
4. Leo Baxendale's use of public school symbols such as a mortar board and gown was measured against the context of Bash Street School so that ' "Bash Street" ' would appeal to the everyday life of the greater number of children in the country' as ' "ordinary" secondary school children'. The school was neither secondary modern nor grammar. He firmly rejects 'the Bash Street Kids as "rebels" ' as this would have 'diminish[ed] their force' and 'constrain[ed] their being', creating a 'vertical structure of comedy' in which there was a straight contest between authority and childhood (the people). Baxendale 'held a horizontal structure in [his] mind' with characters and situations 'colliding with each other'. This allowed for anarchy akin to 'the Warner Bros. animated cartoon' (see Leo Baxendale, *On Comedy*).
5. 'The success of the NHS lies in its achievement, since its inception in 1948, in reconciling the principles of equal access and state provision with the reality of entrenched class divisions [nevertheless] . . . the NHS has emphatically not succeeded in equalising the health of the nation. . . . the NHS is lauded as the single greatest triumph for socialisation in British history'. See Anthony Howard in Andrew Adonis and Stephen Pollard, *A Class Act: The Myth of Britain's Classless Society* (Harmondsworth: Penguin, 1997).
6. The incumbent at the end of the century was Chris Smith. The Department was renamed the Ministry of Culture, Media and Sport.
7. The reaction to this vision of the future did not take long to set in. E. F. Schumacher in his 1973 book *Small is Beautiful* offered this rebuke to the age: 'man assuredly needs to rise above this humdrum "world"; wisdom shows him the way to do it; without wisdom, he is driven to build up a monster economy, which destroys the world, and to seek fantastic satisfactions, like landing a man on the moon'.

   By the 1990s the retreat from the 'future' had become a veritable stampede, nowhere more so than in medicine. In the face of seemingly invincible and infinitely mutating viruses, world health authorities were openly stating the uselessness of modern antibiotics and the possible need to return to older methods of surgical treatment which had become redundant. The unexpected and terrible appearance of HIV, confusion over the transferable nature of so-called 'mad cow disease' and the newer strains of viruses emanating from *within* hospitals lent medical discussion an apocalyptic air. This itself 'infected' other areas such as, for instance, the philosophy of history, lending an unreal and hysterical voice. Thus, Jean-François Lyotard could pronounce the end of days without a hint of self irony or self reflection.

> While we talk, the sun is getting older. It will explode in 4.5 billion years. . . . That in my view, is the sole serious question to face humanity today. In comparison, everything else seems insignificant. Wars, conflicts, political tension, shifts in opinion, philosophical debates, even passions – everything's dead already if this infinite reserve from which you now draw energy to defer answers, if, in short, thought as quest, dies out with the sun.
>
> (Lyotard, *The Inhuman*)

The end of the future is the moment when, in a blinding revelation, we see that 'everything's dead already'.

8. The concept that Britain is a country of immigrants holds true only in a very limited sense; newly arrived immigrants and second-and third-generation children of immigrants still know the different there is between themselves and the wider population, a feeling that rarely quite goes away. The tradition and continuity of British life *may* have immigrant roots but these are ancient, rooted in habit, tradition and domestic arrangement, lived in the deep structures of British class affiliation, geographic location and urban or rural sensibility. From almost all of these things recent arrivals and their children are often at one remove. Hybridity in these circumstances is a *desire* not a fact. The Commission for Racial Equality's declaration that 'most people in Britain today are either immigrants or the descendants of immigrants' is a statement directed at legitimising the work of the Commission rather than a clear statement of fact. Indeed, by suggesting that we are all children of immigrants (and should therefore be more tolerant of differences in others) the more absurd the statement tested against hard cases and hard facts becomes. The indigenous white population of England is not *merely* one group amongst a group of aliens, but the vast majority against whom the *minority* expects to be protected by the Commission and its policies.

9. Readers of the last third of this work may rightly suggest that there appears a contradiction between the anarchist–liberatarian slant of the argument there and my support of the welfare state here. It is clear to me that the welfare state (adapted by all European countries after the Second World War) remains the best solution to social reform within the current system. I do not propose disbanding it nor cutting its relation to state control when its privatisation by Conservative governments did not democratise it but put it into the hands of corporate monopolies acting as government agencies.

Until a clear solution to the problem of the social fabric is articulated, welfare state capitalism still remains the greatest national unifier. This does not make it immune to the need for a ruthless critical scrutiny but it does mean that it must be defended against *laissez-faire* short-termism and chic neo-liberalism.

10. The use of hyphenation when designating national identity may itself be considered a form of racism because in Britain, unlike the United States, we tend to subordinate ethnicity to the legal status of the (political) subject. We are all simply British. This subordination to a singular term requires strong commitment to willingly assimilate in public whilst keeping one's private life strictly separate. This consensual and unspoken social contract is the backbone of the idea that Britain is a tolerant country but it fails in periods of racial uncertainty when the use of hyphenated national identity allows us to expose inherent tensions. I have therefore retained its use.

11. Even small immigrant groups can be subjected to violent harassment. In South Shields in August 1930 the tiny population of Arab seamen who had settled in the town between journeys was attacked by a mob.

12. '[Francis] Maude, supported by David [Heathcoat-Amory] said [Nigel] Lawson couldn't be Foreign Sec as Jew' (Alan Clark diary entry, 19 December 1987). Both denied the statement.

13. Debates in the educational press have focused on the possibility that parental choice would result in segregation by 'default' at secondary level. The Commission for Racial Equality also feared this possibility but found its own legislation took second place when the question arose in Parliament.

Notes to Chapter 2: Just the Way it is

1. My view of class is socialist-Marxist in essence and it therefore should not be confused with either a market researcher's analysis nor the Goldthorpe seven-class schema. I contend that class is essentially a matter of *power relations*. As such, whilst economic mobility may be greater amongst classes, the essential power relationships – those of ownership and management – really haven't changed. If, as some commentators have suggested, 'The old labels "working" and "middle" class make less and less sense', yet they still remain overridingly pertinent in ordinary people's minds (MORI survey 1991) even if pollsters break such distinctions down into still more discrete units (the English obsession with even more complex hierarchies under pressure from market researchers). The idea that a new super-class based on city finance has created another layer is unlikely given the concept of power relationships (relationships of ownership and control rooted in family education, social inclinations, etc.). The *nouveau* super-rich still fall into older class categories.

2. John Major's decency was his ultimate undoing, expecting his party (and Mrs Thatcher) to 'play the game', which they refused to do. After he resigned he went to a cricket match.

3. Later, after losing office, Major made quite clear his distaste for Margaret Thatcher and his astonishment at her disloyalty.

4. In the late 1990s he formed an independent Labour Party.

5. In March 1999, Ingham, now Sir Bernard, was bound over to keep the peace by Croydon Magistrates Court for attacking his neighbour's car during a domestic dispute.

6. Margaret Thatcher was essentially a 'non-aligned' Tory; she thus acted and continues to act through 'conviction', supporting, for instance, James Goldsmith's Referendum Party in the 1997 elections.

7. Some recent extreme commentators have suggested that the autonomous, participating and interventionist citizen is now defunct, but there is no need to accept a model predicated upon an essentialistic and absolute version of a totally 'free' citizen versus a totally trapped consumer. The concept of 'active citizenship' propagated by the right (both Conservative and Labour) denies the very nature of citizenship by leaving no role for common effort and democratic process (both expressed through support of elected governments and the role of law) – it essentially turns everyone into an entrepreneurial vigilante and is no better than an appeal to authoritarian, anti-liberal, populism.

Notes to Chapter 4: Eyes on the Prize

1. In Italy there are the Bagutta Prize (1927), the Bancarella Prize (1952) and the Campiella Prize (1963) amongst others.
2. The Whitbread Prize (1985) and the Orange Prize (1996) also carry corporate associations. A Russian version of the Booker Prize was established in 1992.
3. During the 1990s.
4. The judges in 1999 were Gerald Kaufman, MP (chair); Shena Mackay (author); Professor John Sutherland; Boyd Tonkin (literary editor of *The Independent*); Natasha Walter (author).
5. In an article about her experience as a judge for the Mind Book of the Year/ Allen Lane Award, Fay Weldon commented that,

   The Booker Prize is vague to the point of agony about what its judges are meant to be doing, and the Whitbread refers enigmatically to 'best'. Choosing winners of those prizes is rather like trying to select the 'best' from a bag of liquorice allsorts.... Happily for the judges of the Mind award... its terms are at least specific. The award goes to the title which makes 'the most significant contribution to public awareness of mental health problems'.

   Weldon's relief that the judges were given a distinct set of criteria is evident even though none were experts in mental health.
6. The television series ran between 1981 and 1989.

Notes to Chapter 5: The University at the Present Time

1. He became Secretary of State for Northern Ireland.
2. Secretary of State for Education.
3. Such genres are left as pastiche or nostalgia and are read for those reasons.

Notes to Chapter 6: The Sixties in your Head

1. 'Anyone with the slightest knowledge of ideological history could recognise the spirit of Bakunin or even Nechaev in the student radicals of 1968' (Eric Hobsbawn, *Age of Extremes: The Short Twentieth Century, 1914–1991*, London: Abacus, 1995).

2. The American New Left was formed around real and pressing issues (civil rights; the Vietnam War; state repression) uniting a broad spectrum of beliefs into a loosely knit but effective *mass* movement. In contrast, the British New Left was an *onlooker* to those issues, was narrow in political focus (Marxist) and recruited from a narrow band of enthusiasts. The most successful elements of the British counter-culture were those *outside* the New Left, through their embracing anarchistic-individualist critiques which were both personal and social. The New Left's cultural critique was therefore far more successful than its political critique, which in a period of high employment, rising wages and a successful Western state was utterly lacking in those *domestic* targets available in the United States. The British New Left would have remained the British *Old* Left if these American pressures had not existed. See Lin Chun, *The British New Left* (Edinburgh University Press, 1993).

    The troubles which began at the London School of Economics in the autumn of 1966 and which escalated in the spring of 1967 were initiated by a South African student union president and American students and lecturers. The initial cause of the demands for greater student democracy was the appointment of a Rhodesian to the post of Director. Indeed, the major policy adoptions of the National Union of Students in early 1967 were centrally concerned with Vietnam and Rhodesia *not* internal British political problems. LSE had a significant level of foreign students, including many from the United States who considered issues in the light of American experience (at Berkeley, etc.) and 'civil rights' – something many British students felt totally alien to their experience. The 'Radical Student Alliance' stood for more than its British context and the problems that year at LSE could not really bear the might of questions of international importance. The specific question of student democracy was a translation into parochial terms of a wider *international* debate in which the American émigré New Left *led* the indigenous socialist New Left. See Harry Kidd, *The Trouble at LSE, 1966–1967* (Oxford: Oxford University Press, 1969).

Notes to Chapter 7: The Intellectual at the Turn of the Century

1. 'If God, if mankind, as you affirm, have substance enough in themselves to be all in all to themselves, then I feel that I shall still less lack that, and that I shall have no complaint to make of my 'emptiness'. I am not nothing in the sense of emptiness, but I am the creative nothing, the nothing out of which I myself as creator create everything' (Max Stirner, *The Ego and his Own*).
2. Marx does not 'see' the proletariat as one sees a chair or a table, nor can he see class consciousness. The proletariat does not see its role in and on behalf of history; rather, Marx projects the 'real' into the mundane in order to bring to consciousness, to realise the actual conditions of history. The revolutionary class is that class discovered by the procedure of a method, not by the scrutiny of empiricism. The 'human' is the goal of this process; the free self and the determining agent of history. Yet this human dimension (that of the individual in actuality) has to be posited as prior to all further facts. Method discovers what is prior to it only as a product of itself – the human individual.

It is upon this discovery, that of the human (individual) in its actuality, that Marx's early work rests and his later work expands.

3. See, for example, *Civitas: Newsletter of the Classical Architecture League* (no. 4, Spring 1999):

    > The city used to be a place where people were born into families that were supported by neighborhoods, that were in turn supported by the city or town. Children grew up with a political awareness about their existence and were able to contribute and participate in the social life of their homes, streets, neighborhoods and towns. In the city, they learned about balancing their private and public lives. They relied on their elders, shop-keepers, friends and relatives in a continuous unbroken web. The physical fabric of the city facilitated this existence. In this world, the dialectic of rights and duties was understood. In this place, a commitment to its future came easily.

4. This term should not be confused with its use by political commentators to designate forms of non-parliamentary fascist government. What is suggested is that in radicalising its own base, New Labour learnt the lesson of 'revolutionary' Conservative populism and in so doing became more authoritarian and less tolerant of dissent. Thatcherism effectively cleared the path for Blair's 'third way', by taking the offensive against socialist and left-wing opponents ('the enemy within') whilst Neil Kinnock and John Smith 'modernised' Labour.

Notes to Chapter 9: Children of Albion

1. The fact that the Monty Python team were always political and social conformists does not detract from their extraordinary comic genius.
2. Leavis was an exclusionist but he did not want to exclude popular sentiment nor feeling, only their debased expression in mass culture which he saw as manufactured.
3. The Bolshoi was to Lenin revoltingly decadent. The theatre was only useful to help relax workers after a day at the factory.
4. The problem occurs in the manner and order of reading Marx's work and in the changes in his thought from the early to the later writings and not least in his total disregard for art!
5. Leon Trotsky was quite clear that there was no such thing as proletarian culture – no such thing as popular culture – only a bourgeois culture that had to be assimilated by the proletariat on its own revolutionary terms and then be superseded by communist culture. The period of the dictatorship of the proletariat would be too short to create its own culture, which would be undesirable anyway as it would delay or even postpone full communist culture. Neither Trotsky nor Lenin saw the need to ignore bourgeois culture.

    > The main task of the proletarian intelligentsia is not the abstract formation of a new culture regardless of the absence of a basis for it, but definite culture bearing, that is, a systematic, planful and, of course, critical importing

> to *the backward* masses of the essential elements of the culture *that already exists.*
>
> (Leon Trotsky, *Literature and Revolution*; emphasis added)

6. 'Not In My Back Yard'.
7. I refer to the 'guerrilla gardening' action of 1 May 2000.

Following a well-attended and orderly conference, the main occupation of Parliament Square was both good humoured and had a carnival atmosphere. The event was *not* intended as a demonstration but a gathering and 'celebration' of an alliance between various groups whose agendas are politico-ethical. The subsequent march on Trafalgar Square was largely orchestrated by militant Kurdish elements (one group Maoist and one Trotskyist) whose graffiti can clearly be seen on photo and film footage of the defacement of various statues. The subsequent *limited* violence cannot be separated from their actions which represented a detachment of an earlier 1960s/70s politics into a 1990s setting where (in this case) it was not appropriate.

The event illustrated the danger of loose networks and spontaneity whose core contains a complex and unclear *melange* of issues open to appropriation by violent, neo-fascist or uncontrollable elements who do little except divert attention from the issues at hand. Equally of concern are those anarchist-communitarian developments (so-called non-hierarchical determinants) that can easily lead not to liberation but to cantonment, retrogression, neo-feudalism, aimless nomadism and accumulative primitivism.

For a full account of the nature of anarchist activity that day see Clive Bloom, *Violent London* (forthcoming); for an interesting account of recent non-mainstream liberal politics see Tim Jordan and Adam Lent (eds), *Storming the Millennium*; for an account of the theoretical diversity of both the left and right in a post-modern age see Andreas Schedler (ed.), *The End of Politics*, and Roger Eatwell and Noel O'Sullivan (eds), *The Nature of the Right*.

Works Cited

Adair, Gilbert, *The Postmodernist Always Rings Twice* (London: Fourth Estate, 1993).

Allen, Walter, *The English Novel* (Harmondsworth: Penguin, [1954] 1975).

Althusser, Louis, *For Marx*, trans. Ben Brewster (London: Verso, [1965] 1977).

Anderson, Digby (ed.), *This Will Hurt: The Restoration of Virtue and Civic Order* (Washington, DC: Social Affairs Unit, 1995).

Anonymous, *Guide to Literary Prizes, Grants and Awards in Britain and Ireland* (London Book Trust in Association with the Society of Authors, 1992).

Anonymous, *Sunday Times*, 24 May 1992.

Anonymous review, *Tripwire*, September 1997.

Appleyard, Bryan, in *Sunday Times*, 29 September 1991.

Baudrillard, Jean, *Revenge of the Crystal*, trans. Paul Foss and Julian Pefanis (London: Pluto, 1990).

Baxendale, Leo, *On Comedy: 'The Beano' and Ideology* (Eastcombe, Stroud: Reaper Books, 1989).

Belsey, Catherine, 'Literature, History, Politics', quoted in David Lodge (ed.), *Modern Criticism and Theory: A Reader* (Harlow, Essex: Longman, 1988).

Benjamin, Walter, 'The Work of Art in the Age of Mechanical Reproduction', in *Illuminations*, trans. Harry Zahn (London: Fontana, 1973).

Bennett, Tony, 'Marxism and Popular Fiction', in *Literature and History*, Autumn (1981).

Bhabha, Homi, *The Location of Culture* (London: Routledge and Kegan Paul, 1994).

Birkerts, Sven, *The Gutenberg Elegies: The Fate of Reading in an Electronic Age* (London: Faber and Faber, 1994).

Bloom, Clive, *Cult Fiction: Popular Reading and Pulp Theory* (London: Macmillan, 1996).

Blond, Anthony, *The Book Book* (London: Jonathan Cape, 1985).

Bly, Robert, *Iron John: A Book about Men* (Dorset: Element, 1991).

The Bookseller, 24 July 1992; 22 May 1992; 27 March 1992.

Botton, Alain de, *The Sunday Telegraph*, 17 February 1999.

Bradbury, Malcolm (ed.), *The Novel Today* (London: Fontana, 1972).

Burgess, Anthony, *Observer*, 30 August 1992.

Campbell, Beatrix, *Wigan Pier Revisited: Poverty and Politics in the 80s* (London: Virago, 1984).

Carey, John, *The 1982 Booker McConnell Prize Speech* (London: Faber and Faber, 1982).

Castles F. G., D. J. Murray, C. J. Pollitt and D. C. Porter (eds), *Decisions, Organisations and Society* (Harmondsworth: Penguin, [1967] 1976).

Chun, Lin, *The British New Left* (Edinburgh University Press, 1993).

Civitas: Newsletter of the Classical Architecture League, no.4, Spring 1999.

Clark, Alan, *The Alan Clark Diaries* (London: Phoenix, 1994).

Clarke, Arthur C., *Profiles of the Future: An Enquiry into the Limits of the Possible* (London: Gollancz, 1981).

Cleaver, Eldridge, 'Three Notes from Exile' in William Slate (ed.), *Power to the People: New Left Writings* (New York: Tower, 1970).

Cohn-Bendit, Danny, Alain Geismer, J. Sauvageot, in Hervé Bourges, *The Student Revolt: The Activists Speak*, trans. B. R. Brewster (London: Panther, 1968).

Collins, Norman and Sidney Bernstein, quoted in John Montgomery, *The Fifties* (London: George Allen and Unwin, 1965).

Conrad, Joseph, *The Secret Agent* (London: Methuen, [1907] 1946).

Courtroom Television, October 1994.

Crewe, Ivor, 'Electoral Behaviour', in D. Kavanagh and A. Seldon (eds), *The Major Effect* (London: Macmillan, 1994).

——, 'Has the Electorate become Thatcherite?', in Robert Skidelsky (ed.), *Thatcherism* (London: Macmillan, 1988).

Cunningham, Valentine, *Times Higher Education Supplement*, 6 November 1998.

Curtis, Anthony, in *Financial Times*, 28 September 1991.

Daly, Mary, *Gyn/Ecology: The Metaethics of Radical Feminism* (London: The Women's Press, [1979] 1991).

Deeb, Elyse, unpublished research paper (1997).

Deleuze, Gilles and Felix Guattari, *A Thousand Plateaus: Capitalism and Schizophrenia*, trans. Brian Massumi (London: Athlone, 1997).

Derrida, Jacques, *Writing and Difference*, trans. Alan Bass (London: Routledge and Kegan Paul, 1978).

Downs, A., 'Decision Making in Bureaucracy' in F. G. Castles et al. (eds), *Decision, Organisations, and Society* (Harmondsworth: Penguin, 1976).

Drucker, Peter, *The New Realities* (London: Heinemann, 1986).

——, *The Practice of Management* (London: Heinemann, [1955] 1989).

Eagleton, Terry, *Criticism and Ideology: A Study in Marxist Literary Theory* (London: Verso, 1975).

——, *The Function of Criticism: From the Spectator to Post Structuralism* (London: Verso, 1984).

——, *The Times Higher Education Supplement*, 25 October 1997.

Eco, Umberto, *Travels in Hyper-reality*, trans. William Weaver (London: Pinder, 1987).

Eisenstein, Zillah, *Hatreds: Racialized and Sexualized Conflicts in the 21st Century* (London: Routledge and Kegan Paul, 1996).

Eliot, T. S., 'Tradition and the Individual Talent', in David Lodge (ed.), *Twentieth-Century Criticism* (Harlow: Longman, [1919] 1992).

Ellmann, Maud, quoted in Terry Eagleton, 25 October 1997.

Ferrandino, Joseph, quoted in Jack Newfield, *The American Left* (London: Anthony Blond, 1967).

Fitzgerald, Penelope, *The Times*, 23 October 1991.

Ford, Boris (ed.), *The Pelican Guide to English Literature: The Modern Age* (Harmondsworth: Penguin, [1961] 1975).

Foucault, Michel, Preface to Gilles Deleuze and Felix Guattari, *Anti-Oedipus: Capitalism and Schizophrenia*, trans. Helen R. Lane, Robert Hurley and Mark Seem (New York: Viking, 1977).

Gates, Bill (with Nathan Myhrvold and Peter Rinearson), *The Road Ahead* (Harmondsworth: Penguin, [1995] 1996).

Ginsburg, Allen, *Collected Poems* (London: Faber and Faber, 1976).

Girondias, Maurice, Publisher's Preface to Valerie Solanas, *SCUM Manifesto* (New York: Olympia Press, 1969).

Goff, Martyn, *Prize Writing* (London: Hodder and Stoughton, 1989).

——, *Viva*, August 1991.

Goldman, Emma and Alexander Berkman, in Kenneth C. Wenzer (ed.), *Anarchists Adrift* (New York State: Brandywine Press, 1996).

Gowrie, Lord, in *Sunday Telegraph*, 29 September 1991.

Greer, Germaine, *The Whole Woman* (London: Doubleday, 1999).

Guide to Literary Prizes, Grants and Awards (London: Book Trust and Society of Authors, 1992).

Hain, Peter, *Ayes to the Left* (London: Lawrence and Wishart, 1995).

Halcrow, Morrison, *Keith Joseph: A Single Mind* (London: Macmillan, 1989).

Hall, Peter, *Independent*, 22 February 1999.

——, *Independent*, 8 February 1999.

Hall, Stuart, broadcast, BBC Radio 4, quoted in John Solomos and Les Black, *Racism and Society* (London: Macmillan, 1986).

——, in Roger Eatwell and Noel O'Sullivan (eds), *The Nature of the Right: America and European Politics and Political Thought since 1789* (London: Pinter, 1989).

——, 'New Ethnicities', in K. Mercer (ed.), *Black Film/Black Cinema* (London: ICA, 1988).

——, *New Left Review*, 56, July/August 1969.

Harris, Robert, *Good and Faithful Servant: The Unauthorised Biography of Bernard Ingham* (London: Faber, 1990).

Harrison, Paul, *Inside the Inner City: Life under the Cutting Edge* (Harmondsworth: Penguin, 1983).

Hayden, Tom, *Trial* (London: Jonathan Cape, 1971).

Hearn, Jeff, in *Times Higher Education Supplement*, 13 February 1998.

Hegarty, Paul, 'The Time of the Avant Garde: the Space of Performance' (unpublished research paper).

Held, David, *Models of Democracy* (Cambridge: Polity Press, 1996).

Hewison, Robert, *Culture and Consensus, England, Art and Politics since 1940* (London: Methuen, 1975).

——, 'The Arts', in D. Kavanagh and A. Seldon (eds), *The Major Effect* (London: Macmillan, 1994).

Hiro, Dilip, *Black British/White British: A History of Race Relations in Britain* (London: Grafton, 1991).

Hobsbawm, Eric, *Age of Extremes: The Short Twentieth Century, 1914–1991* (London: Abacus, 1995).

Hoffman, Abbie ('Free'), *Revolution for the Hell of It* (New York: Dial Press, 1968).

Hoggart, Richard, *The Way We Live Now* (London: Michael Joseph, 1995).

Holmes, Colin, *John Bull's Island: Immigration and British Society, 1871–1971* (London: Macmillan, 1988).

Hudson, Ray and Allan M. Williams, *Divided Britain* (Chichester: John Wiley, 1995).

Hutton, Will, *The State We're In* (London: Verso, 1996).

The Independent, 27 September 1991.

Irving, Clive, Ron Hall and Jeremy Wallington, *Scandal 63: A Study of the Profumo Affair* (London: Heinemann, 1963).

Jackson, Rosemary, *Fantasy* (London: Methuen, 1981).

James, William, in Bertrand Russell, *Philosophical Essays* (London: George Allen and Unwin, [1910], 1988).

Jameson, Fredric, in Jean-François Lyotard, *The Postmodern Condition: A Report of Knowledge*, trans. Geoff Bennington and Brian Massumi (Manchester: Manchester University Press, 1989).

Jordan, Tim and Lent Adam (eds), *Storming the Millennium: The New Politics of Change* (London: Lawrence and Wishart, 1999).

Jowell, Roger, Sharon Witherspoon and Lindsay Brook, *British Social Attitudes: The Fifth Report* (Aldershot: Gower, 1988).

Kavanagh, Dennis, 'A Major Agenda', in Kavanagh and Seldon (eds) (1994).

Kavanagh, Dennis and Anthony Seldon (eds), *The Major Effect* (London: Macmillan, 1994).

Keates, Jonathan in *The Observer*, 27 October 1991.

——, in *Independent*, 26 October 1991.

Keneally, Thomas, *Schindler's Ark* (London: Hodder and Stoughton, 1982).

Kidd, Harry, *The Trouble at LSE, 1966–1967* (Oxford: Oxford University Press, 1969).

King, A., 'Overload: Problems of Governing in the 1970s' [1975] in F. G. Castles *et al.* (eds), *Decisions, Organisations and Society* (Harmondsworth: Penguin [1969] 1976).

Lacan, Jacques, *The Four Fundamental Concepts of Psycho-analysis*, trans. Alan Sheridan (Harmondsworth: Penguin, 1977).

——, *Écrits: A Selection*, trans. Alan Sheridan (London: Tavistock, 1980).

Lasch, Christopher, *The True and Only Heaven: Progress and its Critics* (New York: Knopf, 1991).

Layton-Henry, Zig, *The Politics of Race in Britain* (London: George Allen and Unwin, 1984).

Leavis, F. R., 'Under which King, Bezonian?', in *Scrutiny*, vol. 1 (1932).

Leavis, Q. D., 'The Case of Miss Dorothy L. Sayers', in F. R. Leavis (ed.), *A Selection from Scrutiny* (Cambridge: Cambridge University Press [1937] 1968).

Lennon, John, quoted in Ian MacDonald, *Revolution in the Head: The Beatles' Records and the Sixties* (London: Pimlico, 1995).

Lessing, Doris, Preface to *The Golden Notebook* (London: Michael Joseph, [1971] 1972).

Lewis, Philip, *Islamic Britain: Religion, Politics and Identity among British Moslems: Bradford in the 1990s* (London: I. B. Tauris, 1994).

Lifton, Robert J. and Eric Markusen, *The Genocidal Mentality: Nazi Holocaust and Nuclear Threat* (London: Macmillan, 1990).

Lord, Graham, in *Sunday Express*, 29 September 1991.

Lyotard, Jean-François, 'The Sign of History', trans. Geoff Bennington, in Derek Attridge, Geoff Bennington and Robert Young (eds), *Post-Structuralism and the Question of History* (Cambridge: Cambridge University Press, 1987).

Jean-François Lyotard, *The Inhuman: Reflections on Time*, trans. Geoffrey Bennington and Rachel Bowlby (London: Polity, 1991).

MacDonald, Ian, *Revolution in the Head* (London: Pimlico, 1995).

Mailer, Norman, 'The White Negro: Superficial Reflections on the Hipster', in *Dissent* (1957).

Mandel, Ernest, in *Black Dwarf*, July, 1969.

Marcus, Greil, *In the Fascist Bathroom* (Harmondsworth: Penguin, 1984).

Marcuse, Herbert, *One-Dimensional Man* (London: Routledge and Kegan Paul [1964] 1991).

——, *An Essay on Liberation* (Harmondsworth: Penguin, 1969).

Marquand, David, *The Unprincipled Society: New Demands and Old Politics* (London: Jonathan Cape, 1988).

Marx, Karl and Fredrich Engels, *The German Ideology* (London: Routledge and Kegan Paul [1922] 1968).

Mason, Richard (ed.), *Cambridge Minds* (Cambridge: Cambridge University Press, 1994).

McKay, George, *Senseless Acts of Beauty: Cultures of Resistance since the Sixties* (London: Verso, 1996).

McLoughlin, Jane, *The Demographic Revolution* (London: Pandora, 1991).

Modern Review, vol. 1, no. 1 (1991).

Mosely, Nicholas, in *The Times*, 26 September 1991.

——, in *Daily Telegraph*, 26 September 1991.

Murdoch, Iris, 'Against Dryness' in Malcolm Bradbury (ed.), *The Novel Today* (London: Fontana, [1977] 1972).

Murry, J. Middleton, *The Problem of Style* (Oxford: Oxford University Press [1922] 1976).

Myers, Norman, *The Gaia Atlas of Future Worlds* (London: Robertson McCarta, 1990).

Neale, R. S., *Writing Marxist History: British Society, Economy and Culture since 1700* (Oxford: Basil Blackwell, 1985).

Neil, Andrew in *Sunday Times*, 12 April 1992.

Neville, Peter, in *The Raven*, no. 33.

Oglesby, Carl, 'Notes on a Decade Ready for the Dustbin', in William Slate (ed.), *Power to the People* (New York: Tower Public Affairs Book, [1969] 1970).

Ohmae, Kenichi, *The Borderless World: Power and Strategy in the International Economy* (London: Collins, 1990).

Onslow, James Hughes, in *The Evening Standard*, October 1991.

Ortega, José y Gasset, *The Revolt of the Masses* (New York: Mentor, [1932] 1950).

Pacione, John, *A History of the Booker Prize* (unpublished manuscript, 1991).

Palmer, Richard, in *Sunday Times*, 17 May 1992.

Parsons, Tony, 'The Tattooed Jungle' in *Arena*, Sept/Oct, 1989.

Peck, M. Scott, *A World Waiting to be Born: The Search for Civility* (London: Rider, 1993).

Phelps, Gilbert, *The Penguin Guide to English Literature* (Harmondsworth: Penguin [1961] 1973).

Poe, Edgar Allan, 'The Imp of the Perverse', *Graham's Magazine*, July 1845.

Porritt, Jonathon, *Seeing Green: The Politics of Ecology Explained* (London: Routledge and Kegan Paul, 1984).

Poster, Mark, introductory remarks in Jean Baudrillard, *Selected Writings*, trans. Mark Poster (Oxford: Basil Blackwell, 1989).

Quiller-Couch, Sir Arthur, *On the Art of Reading* (Cambridge: Guild Books, [1920] 1947).

——, *The Poet as Citizen* (Cambridge: Cambridge University Press, 1934).

Raleigh, Sir Walter, quoted in John Simons, unpublished research paper (1997).

Rand, Ayn, *For the New Intellectual: The Philosophy of Ayn Rand* (New York: Knopf, [1960] 1961).

Reich, Charles A., *The Greening of America* (New York: Knopf, 1970).
Richards, I. A., *Principles of Literary Criticism* (London: Routledge and Kegan Paul, 1924).
Robertson, James, *Future Work* (Aldershot: Gower, 1985).
Robutham, Michael, in *Mail on Sunday*, 27 October 1991.
Rushdie, Salman, introduction to Günter Grass, *Writing and Politics, 1967–1983*, trans. Ralph Mannheim (Harmondsworth: Penguin, 1984).
Sampson, George, *The Concise Cambridge History of English Literature* (Cambridge: Cambridge University Press, [1941] 1945).
Sarraute, Nathalie, in Hervé Bourges, *The Student Revolt: The Activists Speak*, trans. B. R. Brewster (London, Panther, 1968).
Schapiro, Leonard and Peter Reddaway, *Lenin: The Man, the Theorist, the Leader* (London: Pall Mall Press, 1967).
Schedler, Andreas, *The End of Politics: Explorations in Modern Anti-Politics* (London: Macmillan, 1997).
Schumacher, E. F., *Small is Beautiful* (London: Abacus, 1973).
Seale, Bobby, quoted in Anon, *Contempt: Transcript of the Contempt Citations, Sentences, and the Responses of the Chicago Conspiracy 10* (Chicago: Swallow, 1970).
Secrest, Meryl, *Being Bernard Berenson* (Harmondsworth: Penguin, 1975).
Shields, Carol, *Happenstance* (London: Fourth Estate, 1991).
Slate, William (ed.), *Power to the People: New Left Writings* (New York: Tower, 1970).
Snow, C. P., *The Two Cultures: A Second Look* (Cambridge: Cambridge University Press, [1959] 1965).
Solomos, John and Les Black, *Racism and Society* (London: Macmillan, 1996).
Steiner, George, 'Critical Reader', in Philip Davis (ed.), *Real Voices on Reading* (London: Macmillan, 1997).
Stirner, Max, *The Ego and His Own: The Case of the Individual against Authority*, trans. Steven T. Byington (New York: Dover, 1973).
Sutherland, John, *Independent*, 22 February 1999.
——, *Independent*, 8 February 1999.
Taylor, D. J., *After the War: The Novel and England since 1945* (London: Flamingo, 1994).
——, *Independent*, 26 October 1990.
The Times, 4 October 1968; 26 September 1991.
Times Higher Education Supplement, 13 November 1998; 27 September 1998.
Todd, Richard, *Consuming Fictions: The Booker Prize and Fiction in Britain Today* (London: Bloomsbury, 1996).
Toffler, Alvin, *Power Shift: Knowledge, Wealth and Violence at the end of the 21st Century* (New York: Bantam, 1990).
——, *Future Shock* (London: Bodley Head, 1970).
——, *The Third Wave* (London: Collins, 1990).
Treglown, Jeremy, in *The Times*, 28 September 1991.
——, in *Daily Telegraph*, 28 September 1991.
Trevor, William, *Two Lives* (London: Viking, 1991).
Trotsky, Leon, *Literature and Revolution* (Michigan: University of Michigan Press, 1975).
Turner, Graeme, *British Cultural Studies: An Introduction* (London: Routledge and Kegan Paul, 1996).

Walford, A. J., *Reviews and Reviewing: A Guide* (London: Mansell Publishing, 1986).

Ward, A. C., *Twentieth-Century Literature* (London: Methuen, 1928).

Watson, Ben, *Art, Class and Cleavage: Quantulumcunque Concerning Materialist Esthetix* (London: Quartet, 1998).

Weldon, Fay, in *Independent on Sunday*, 16 May 1993.

Wenzer, Kenneth C., *Anarchists Adrift: Emma Goldman and Alexander Berkman* (St James, New York: Brandywine Press, 1996).

Wilden, Anthony, *System and Structure: Essays in Communication and Exchange* (London: Tavistock, [1972] 1980).

Williams, Raymond, *Towards 2000* (London: Methuen, 1983).

Williams, Sir William Emrys, *The Penguin Story* (Harmondsworth: Penguin, 1956).

Wilson, A. N., *Evening Standard*, 23 October 1991.

Wittgenstein, Ludwig, *Tractatus Logico-Philosophicus*, trans. C. K. Ogdon (London: Routledge and Kegan Paul, [1922] 1988).

Wood, James, *The Guardian*, 27 November 1992.

Woolf, Virginia, 'Mr Bennett and Mrs Brown', in *A Woman's Essays* (Harmondsworth: Penguin [1924] 1992).

Wright, Patrick, *A Journey through Ruins: A Keyhole Portrait of British Postwar Life and Culture* (London: Flamingo, 1993).

Yeats, W. B., 'Symbolism and Poetry', in David Lodge (ed.), *Twentieth-Century Literary Criticism* (Harlow: Longman [1900] 1972).

Young, Hugo, 'The Prime Minister', in D. Kavanagh and A. Seldon (eds), *The Major Effect* (London: Macmillan, 1994).

Index

Adam Smith Institute, 44
Albert Hall, 210n
Albion, 208
Albion Free State, 209
Aldiss, Brian, 99
Allen, Walter, 85
Althusser, Louis, 170
America, 6
Americanisation, 6, 67
Americans, 133
Amin, Idi, 111
Amis, Kingsley, 102
Amis, Martin, 105, 115
anarchism, 152, 208, 211
Anderson, Digby, 35, 176, 177
Angry Brigade, 148
Animal Farm, 86
Anstey, F., 84
anti-Semitism, 39, 64
Appleyard, Bryan, 104
Arena, 57
Arnold, Matthew, 6, 10, 28,
    91, 113, 200
Arts Council of Great Britain, 17
Associated Television, 201
Athenaeum Club, 14
Austen, Jane, 27, 52
Avalon, 208
avant-garde, The, 147, 200

'Back to Basics', 48
Back to the Future (film), 52
Bagehot, Walter, 41
Bagutta Prize, 213n
Bainbridge, Beryl, 28, 111
Bakewell, Joan, 99
Bakunin, Michael, 147, 155, 213n
Bancarella Prize, 213n
Bank of England, 69
Barsham Fairs, 209
Barthes, Roland, 193
Bash Street Kids, 13
Baudrillard, Jean, 141, 149, 150

Baxendale, Leo, 210n
Bayley, John, 111
Beanie Baby toys, 202
Beatles, 3
Bedny, Dem'yan, 197
Bellow, Saul, 100
Belsey, Catherine, 204–6, 208
Benjamin, Walter, 177
Benn, Tony, 63, 65
Bennett, Arnold, 74, 82–3, 85, 87
Bennett, Tony, 194, 197, 204–5, 207
Berenson, Bernard, 77
Beresford, J. D., 82–3
Berkeley (State University of
    California), 157
Berkman, Alexander, 154–6
Bernstein, Sidney, 201
Bhabha, Homi, 32
Birkerts, Sven, 8
Black Dwarf, 156
Blair, Tony, 40
Blake, William, 193
Blond, Anthony, 114
Bloom, Allan, 6
Bloom, Clive, 207, 216n
Blunkett, David, 138
Bly, Robert, 6, 46, 47, 49
body (and representation), 29–30
Bolschevik, 163
Bolshoi Ballet, 215n
Bolton, Michael, 4
Booker McConnell Ltd, 95
Booker plc, 95
Booker Prize, 4, 91, 94–5
Bookseller, The, 73
Bootleg Beatles, 210n
Bowen, Elizabeth, 85
Boyce, Leah, 119
Bradbury, Malcolm, 8
Bragg, Melvyn, 100
British Social Attitudes,
    (5th Report), 56
Brookner, Anita, 111

Bubbosh, Lola, 115
Burchill, Julie, 66, 115–16
Burgess, Anthony, 96, 114, 116–17
Burrows, Ken, 119

Caine, Michael, Sir, 95–6, 98
Calder, John, 8
California, 208
Callagy, Robert, 119–20
Callil, Carmen, 4
Campbell, Beatrix, 64
Campiella Prize, 213n
Canada, 46
Cape Kennedy Space Centre, 31
capitalism ('stakeholders'), 69
Cardiff, University College, 206
Carey, John, 99, 105, 113
Carey, Peter, 105
Carry on films, 13
Cary, Joyce, 85
Castenada, Carlos, 192
Castle, Barbara, 65
Castles, F. G., 134
Caudwell, Christopher, 196
Centre for Contemporary Cultural
    Studies (Birmingham University),
    194
Centre for Policy Studies, 64–5
Channel Four, 210n
Cheetham, Rosemary, 119
Chernyshevsky, N. G., 155
Chicago, 154, 158
Chippendales, 50
Christian Socialism, 66
Christie, Agatha, 95
Chun, Lin, 214n
Citizen's Charter, 48, 60
citizenship, 123
City Limits, 103
Clapp, Susannah, 100
Clarke, Arthur C., 42
Cleaver, Eldridge, 154
Coetze, J. M., 210n
Cohn-Bendit, Danny, 156
Coleridge, Samuel Taylor, 198
Collins, Jackie, 118
Collins, Joan, 118–20
Collins, Norman, 201
Commission for Racial Equality, 211n

Communication Studies, 25
community
    black and Asian, 36–7, 42
    Chinese, 37
    Muslim, 38–9
Community Charge, 53
computerisation, 49
Condon, Paul, Sir, 36
Conrad, Joseph, 82–5, 189
Conservatism, 16, 35,
    51, 57, 63
Conservative Central Office, 58
Conservatives, 57, 59, 61, 64–5,
    203–4, 213n, 215n
    'Wets', 64
Coronation Street, 201
Crewe, Ivor, 58–9
Crowley, Aleister, 192
Crystal Palace, 36, 74
Cultural Studies, 25–7, 197
Culture, Media and Sport,
    Ministry of, 17
Curtis, Anthony, 109
Cyber-Culture, 10
Cyber-English, 10

Dada, 158, 161
Daily Express, 61
Daily Mail, 103, 193
Daily Star, 61
Daily Telegraph, 105, 111
Dalston (London), 14
Daly, Mary, 45
Darwin, Charles, 147
Deeb, Elyse, 73
Defence of the Realm Act,
    (DORA), 75
Deleuze, Gilles, 150, 185
Dell, Ethel M., 83
DeMan, Paul, 179
Department of National Heritage,
    17, 210n
deregulation, 43
Derrida, Jacques, 165–6, 168, 193
devolution (Welsh and
    Scottish), 34, 39
Diamond, John, 111
Disraeli, Benjamin, 125
Dongas, 209

Downs, A., 134–5
Drucker, Peter, 127–31, 137
Dynasty, 118

Eagleton, Terry, 20–3, 63, 200
Eco, Umberto, 115, 141
Edward VII, 73
Eisenstein, Zillah, 29
Eliot, T. S., 74–5, 77–8, 81,
    126, 193, 195–6, 205
'Elizabeth', 84
Elizabethan Age, 85
Ellmann, Maud, 21, 23
Emerson, Ralph Waldo, 155
Enfield, Harry, 56
Engels, Friedrich, 147, 173–5, 197
English Patient, The, 52, 91
ERM (Exchange Rate Mechanism), 60
Essex University, 206
Essex University Conferences, 204
Europe, 37, 39

Farrer, David, 100
Fascism, 39, 153
    in Italy, 82
federalisation, 69
feminism, 45, 63, 139, 152
Festival of Britain (1951), 36
Financial Times, 109
Fitzgerald, Penelope, 100,
    102, 104, 109
Fleming, Ian, 95
Foden, Giles, 111
Forman, Denis, 100
Forster, E. M., 74, 83
Forsythe, Frederick, 117
Foucault, Michel, 150
Four Weddings and a Funeral, 52
Fowles, John, 192
Frankfurt School, 6, 194
Freud, Sigmund, 147
Freudianism, 139, 150
Fukuyama, Francis, 33
Fussell, Paul, 6

Gaia philosophy, 45
Galsworthy, John, 74, 82, 83, 85, 87
Gammerman, Ira, Judge, 120
Gasset, José Ortega y, 202

Gates, Bill, 11, 12
Geismer, Alain, 156
Germany, 38, 196
Gesamtkunstwerk, 188
Ginsburg, Allen, 193
Girondias, Maurice, 193
Goethe Prize, 90
Goff, Martyn, 94–8, 100–2
Goldberg, Lucianne, 120
Golding, William, 96
Goldman, Emma, 154–6
Goldsmith, James, 212n
Goldwyn, Sam, 42
Gordimer, Nadine, 97, 111
Gould, Nat, 74, 82
Gowrie, Lord, 104
Grahame, Kenneth, 84
Gramsci, Antonio, 169
Grant, Hugh, 52
Grass, Gunter, 3, 178
Great Expectations, 107
Green, Benny, 102
Green, Henry, 85
Green activist, 47
Green politics, 44–5, 47–8, 55
Greene, Graham, 85, 95
Greenham Common, 46
Greer, Germaine, 4
Grierson, John, 81
Grillet, Alain Robbe, 192
Guardian, 61
Guattari, Félix, 150, 185
Guerrilla Gardening Riot, 209, 216n

Haggard, H. Rider, 82
Hague, Douglas, Sir, 137
Hain, Peter, 67–8
Haines, Anthony, 98
Halcrow, Morrison, 65
Hall, Stuart, 31–2, 63, 203
Hamsun, Knut, 192
Hanley, James, 85
Hardinge of Penshurst, Lord, 95
Harman, Harriet, 40
Harris, Robert, 65
Hartley, L. P., 85
Hayden, Tom, 152
Heathcoat-Amory, David, 212n
Hebden Bridge (Yorkshire), 65

Hedayat, Sadegh, 192
Heine, Heinrich, 76
Heller, Joseph, 192
Herzen, Alexander, 155
Hesse, Hermann, 192–2
Hewison, Robert, 6, 16
Hill, Christopher, 205
Hindley, Myra, 4
Hirst, Damien, 4
Hitler, Adolf, 151
HIV, 210n
Hoffman, Abbie, 151–2
Hoggart, Richard, 6–7, 14, 100
Holroyd, Michael, 100
Howard, Anthony, 16
Howard, Philip, 114
Hughes, Roberts, 6
Hull, E. M., 83
Hutton, Will, 68, 70
Huxley, Aldous, 36, 40
hybridity, 32
Hynes, Samuel, 99

Independent, The, 61, 104, 106, 109
Ingham, Bernard, 64–6, 212n
Internet, 10–13, 54
Ireland, 42
Irving, Clive, 193

Jackson, Rosemary, 163, 184
James, Henry, 83
James, P. D., 98
James, William, 132
Jameson, Fredric, 141
Japan, 196
Jardine, Lisa, 111
Jenkins, Alan, 115–17
Jenkins, Roy, 37
Jerome, Jerome K., 84
John, Elton, Sir, 4
Johnson, Richard, 194–5
Joint University Club, 14
Jonathan Cape Ltd, 95
Joseph, Keith, Sir, 56, 64
Joyce, James, 26, 74, 75, 82–3, 85, 87
Jung, Carl, 192

Katharine Briggs Folklore Award, 95
Kaufman, Gerald, 213n

Kavanagh, Dennis, 60
Kay-Smith, Sheila, 82
Keates, Jonathan, 100, 104, 107–8
Keneally, Thomas, 91, 99
Kent, University of, 15
Kermode, Frank, 100
Kershaw, Ian, 111
Kesey, Ken, 3, 30, 192
King, A., 136
Kinnock, Neil, 62
Kipling, Rudyard, 83
Knights, L. C., 195
Kropotkin, Peter, 147, 155
Kundera, Milan, 115

Labour Party, 16, 34, 40–2, 57–63,
        66–7, 70, 138, 212n, 215n
Lacan, Jacques, 167, 171, 193
Laing, R. D., 192
Landesman, Cosmo, 66
Lane, Allen, 7
Lasch, Christopher, 44
Latham, Jane, 8
Lautreamont, 192
Lawrence, D. H., 10, 52, 74, 82–3, 86
Lawrence, Stephen, 36
Lawson, Nigel, 212n
le Carré, John, 116
Leary, Timothy, 192
Leavis, F. R., 5–7, 10–11, 26, 87, 91,
        113, 192–3, 195, 200, 204–5, 208
Leavis, Queenie, 91, 124–6, 130, 132
Lee, Hermione, 99
Lenin, V. I., 196–7, 199, 215n
Lennon, John, 3, 160
Lessing, Doris, 9
Levin, Bernard, 113
Lévi-Strauss, Claude, 167
Lewis, Wyndham, 196
Liberal Democracy, 81
Lifton, Robert J., 44
Lilley, Peter, 37
Literature and History, 204
Litz, A. Walton, 100
London, 132
London School of Economics, 214n
Lumley, Joanna, 102
Lyotard, Jean-François, 10, 141,
        149, 211n

Macaulay, Rose, 82–3
MacDonald, Ian, 151
MacDonald, Trevor, 102
MacKay, Sheena, 213n
MacKenzie, Compton, 82–3
Mailer, Norman, 153, 193
Major, John, 16, 48, 51, 58–60, 212n
management, 127–30
Mandel, Ernest, 156
Mandelson, Peter, 138
Mandelson, Francis, 212n
Mansfield, Katherine, 84
Manson family, 148
Mantel, Hilary, 100
Maoism, 216n
Marcuse, Herbert, 150–7
Markusen, Eric, 44
Marquand, David, 69
Marx, Groucho, 151
Marx, Karl, 33, 147, 154, 167, 173–5,
    197, 207, 214n
Marxism, 9, 150–2, 156, 176, 197
Marxist, 6, 22, 52–3, 66, 87, 139,
    150, 157, 203–4, 206
Marxist–Leninist, 67, 152, 154–6
Maschler, Tom, 95
mascularity, 46–7
Massie, Allan, 104–5
Maughan, Somerset, 83
Maxwell, Robert, 55
Mayakovsky, Vladimir V., 196
McEwan, Ian, 4, 111
McKay, George, 209–10
McLoughlin, Jane, 49–51
McLuhan, Marshal, 10, 158,
    192, 193
Mellor, David, 17
Merlin, 3, 208
Metropolitan Police, 36
Mill on the Floss, 107
Millennium Dome (and project),
    35–6
Miller, Karl, 100
Mills, Magnus, 111
Mind Award, 213n
Minghella, Anthony, 91
miniaturisation, 49
Ministry of Information, 76
Mirror, The, 61

Mitsubishi Pencil Company, 110
Mo, Timothy, 106
Modern Review, 66
Moi, Toril, 63
Molotov Cocktail Party, 148
Monty Python's Flying Circus, 194,
    196, 215n
Moore, George, 83
Morgan, William de, 86
Morrison, Allan, 85
Mosley, Nicholas, 100, 102–7
Motherfuckers, 148
MTV, 14
Murdoch, Iris, 9–10, 16
Murdoch, Rupert, 55, 61
Murphy, John, 95
Murry, John Middleton, 77–9, 81
Myers, Norman, 45–6

Narodnik Movement, 155
National Health Service, 57, 210n
National Lottery, 17
National Union of Students, 214n
National Westminster Bank, 210n
Neale, R. S., 207
Nechaev, Sergei G., 213n
Neil, Andrew, 58
New Age travellers, 47, 54
New Critics, the, 6, 79
New Left (Great Britain), 152, 159,
    214n
New Left (United States), 151, 153,
    156, 159
New York, 132, 154
Newby, P. H., 85
Newfield, Jack, 154
Newman, Cardinal, 15
Newspeak, 89, 178
Nobel Prize, 90
Norrie, Ian, 96
Nostradamus, 42
Not the 9 O'clock News, 194

Observer, 69, 107, 117
Ofili, Chris, 4–5
Oglesby, Carl, 154
Ohmae, Kenichi, 43, 133
Ondaatje, Michael, 91
Orange Prize, 95, 110, 213n

Organic Community, 11, 205, 209
Orwell, George, 6–7, 28, 36, 64, 77, 86, 196

Pain, Barry, 85
Paradise Lost, 20
Parsons, Tony, 3, 6, 56
Penguin, 6
Perrick, Penny, 115
Peterhouse Group (Cambridge), 66
Pettridge, W., 85
Phelps, Gilbert, 86
Phillips, Oppenheim, E., 74, 82
Poe, Edgar Allan, 188
Porritt, Jonathan, 47–8
Post-Impressionist Exhibition, 73
Poster, Mark, 141
Pound, Ezra, 196
Powell, Anthony, 85
Powell, Enoch, 37
Preston (Lancashire), 56
Pritchard, Matthew, 98
Prix Goncourt, 90
Proudhon, Pierre-Joseph, 155, 157
Pugh, Edwin, 85
Pulitzer Prize, 90

Quiller-Couch, Arthur, Sir ('Q'), 20, 24, 79–82

Radical Student Alliance, 214n
Raleigh, Walter, Sir, 75–7
Random House, 118–20
Rand, Ayn, 153, 193
Ray, Robin, 102
Reagan, Roland, 67
Reaganism, 177
Reaganomics, 43
Red Army Faction, the, 148
Referendum Party, 212n
Reich, Charles, A., 44
Reich, Wilhelm, 162
Republicanisation, 69
Richard, Cliff, 4
Richards, I. A., 19, 26, 80
Richardson, Dorothy, 82–3, 85
Riet, Richard van der, 42
Ripping Yarns, 194
Robertson, James, 43, 49

Robins, Elizabeth, 82
Rocker, Rudolf, 154
Roy, Arundhati, 4
Royal Academy, 4
Rushdie, Salman, 38, 177–8
Russell, Bertram, 132
Russia, 38

'Saki' (H. H. Munro), 84
Salisbury Review, 66
Sampson, George, 83–4, 87
Sarraute, Nathalie, 193
Sartre, Jean Paul, 193
Saunders, Kate, 100
Saussure, Ferdinand de, 141
Sayers, Dorothy L., 124
Scargill, Arthur, 63
Schindler's Ark, 91
Schlee, Ann, 100, 102
Schumacher, E. F., 210n
Scrutiny, 5, 195
Scruton, Roger, 66
Seale, Bobby, 152
Second World War, 53
Secrest, Meryle, 77
Self, Will, 4
Shaftesbury Theatre, 3
Shakespeare, William, 27
Shakespeare in Love, 52
Shaw, Christine, 98
Sherman, Alfred, 65
Shields, Carol, 99
Showalter, Elaine, 111
Shute, Alison, 98
Sigma 2, 156
Simbionese Liberation Army, 148
Simons, John, 76
Sinclair, Mary, 82
Skidelsky, Robert, 58
Skylon (Festival of Britain), 36
Smith, Adam, 11, 44
Smith, Christine, 210n
Snow, C. P., 125–6, 130
Snyder, Gary, 156
Social and Community Planning, Research Group, the (SCPR), 57
Social Democrat Party, 62, 69
Solanas, Valerie, 193
Sons and Lovers, 107

South Bank Show, 100
Soviet Union, 196
Spain, 196
Spender, Stephen, 100
Spice Girls, 4
Spielberg, Stephen, 91
St John-Stevas, Norman, 100
Stalin, Josef, 151, 197–9
Stalinism, 82
Steiner, George, 28, 100
Stevens, Dave, 156
Stirner, Max, 147, 155, 173, 214n
Strachey, Lytton, 74
Strauss, Peter, 98
Sunday Express Book of the Year, 95
Sunday Telegraph, 104
Sunday Times, 58–9, 104
Sutherland, John, 213n
Swinnerton, Frank, 82, 83, 85

Tate Gallery, 4–5
Thatcherism, 14–16, 41, 43, 51,
    53–4, 57–8, 60–2, 64–9, 177,
    212n
Thatcher, Margaret, 30, 33, 52
Thompson, Denys, 195
Thompson, E. P., 205
Thoreau, David, 147, 155
Tillyard, E. M. W., 205
Times Higher Education Supplement,
    20, 178
Times, The, 97, 104–6, 109, 114
Today, 61
Toffler, Alvin, 43, 55, 128,
    130–1, 133
Tokyo, 132
Tolkien, J. R. R., 3, 192
Tolstoy, Leo, 155
Tommy (rock opera), 3
Tonkin, Boyd, 213n
Treglown, Jeremy, 100, 102–6,
    108, 110
Trevor, William, 99
Trewin, Ion, 98
Tripwire, 23
Trocchi, Alexander, 156
Trotsky, Leon, 215n
Trotskyists, 216n
Turner, Graeme, 194–5

Turner, Jenny, 115
Tyrell, Charles, 95

unemployment, 53
United Kingdom, 42
United States of America, 3

Vietnam, 47
Virago, 4
Voter AB and C2, 51, 56

Walford, A. J., 114
Walpole, Hugh, 82–3
Walter, Natasha, 213n
Ward, A. C., 82–3, 85, 87
Warner Brothers, 210n
Waterstone, Tim, 98
Watson, Ben, 198, 202–3
Weatherman Collective,
    (Weather People), 148
Webb, Mary, 83
Webb, W. L., 100
Webber, Andrew Lloyd, 5
Weldon, Fay, 100, 213n
Welfare State, 9, 51
Wells, H. G., 74, 82–3, 85, 87
West, Rebecca, 100
Whitbread Prize, 95, 111
Wilden, Anthony, 45
Williams, Raymond, 7, 45, 51–2,
    54–5, 63, 204
Wilson, A. N., 104
Wilson, Lady Mary, 102
Wittgenstein, Ludwig, 167, 170, 171
Wodehouse, P. G., 84
Wood, Greg, 116
Wood, Sam Taylor, 4
Woolf, Virginia, 74–5, 82–3, 85–7
working class, 54–7
World Book Day, 111
Wright, Patrick, 14, 15

Yeats, W. B., 186, 193
Young, Francis Brett, 82
Young, Lola, 111
Young, Toby, 66

Zangwill, Israel, 85
Zetkin, Klara, 196